THE ENCYCLOPEDIA OF
SEASHELLS

THE ENCYCLOPEDIA OF
SEASHELLS

GARY ROSENBERG

ROBERT HALE • LONDON

A FRIEDMAN GROUP BOOK

Copyright © 1992 by Michael Friedman Publishing Group, Inc.
First published in Great Britain 1993

ISBN 0 7090 5092 5

Robert Hale Limited
Clerkenwell House
45-47 Clerkenwell Green
London EC1R 0HT

THE ENCYCLOPEDIA OF SEASHELLS
was prepared and produced by
Michael Friedman Publishing Group, Inc.
15 West 26th Street
New York, New York 10010

Editor: Elizabeth Viscott Sullivan
Art Director: Jeff Batzli
Designer: Judy Morgan
Photography Editor: Christopher C. Bain

Typeset by Classic Type, Inc.
Colour separations by Excel Graphic Arts Ltd.
Printed and bound in Hong Kong by Leefung-Asco Printers Ltd.

All of the photographs in this book are © Gary Rosenberg 1992, with the following exceptions:

© Chris Mooney/Balfour Walker/FPG International: 2
© Dennis Hallinan/FPG International: 6
© Mathilde Duffy: 10, 26–27, 46b, 57b, 84b, 108a, 110, 123b, 124a, 182–183, 184, 194, 204
© F. Stuart Westmoreland/Tom Stack & Associates: 17
© Larry Tackett/Tom Stack & Associates: 19
© Ann & Myron Sutton/Tom Stack & Associates: 193b
© Dave B. Fleetham/Visuals Unlimited: 202
© Ed Robinson/Tom Stack & Associates: 201
© Joel Arrington/Visuals Unlimited: 203
© Albert J. Copley/Visuals Unlimited: 207a
© Paulette Brunner/Tom Stack & Associates: 209b
© Barbara Von Hoffman/Tom Stack & Associates: 16
© Doug Wechsler: 14, 193a, 206, 208
© James McFalls: 191b, 191c
© Geological Society of America: 13a
Scala/Art Resource: 199a, 199b
Sassonian/Art Resource: 190, 197
Illustration on page 21 was adapted from "The Shell Makers" (Alan G. Solem, Wiley & Sons, 1974)
Christopher Bain: 8, 12, 18, 25, 27, 188, 189, 192, 200, 210

To my parents,
Bonnie and Elliott Rosenberg

CONTENTS

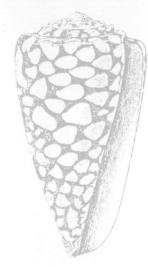

PREFACE

When asked to name their favorite shell, most shell collectors quickly think of half a dozen species, but few can settle on a single favorite. I faced a similar problem in choosing 250 species of seashells to discuss and illustrate. I decided to select members from as many marine families as possible, to show a part of the spectrum of diversity of mollusks and support the title's encyclopedic claim. There are, of course, many families of mollusks that are not covered in this book: those which live exclusively on land or in fresh water, those which lack a shell (slugs and octopuses, for example), and those which live only in the deep sea or are otherwise unlikely to be encountered by collectors. Despite these limitations, members of more than 220 families of mollusks are treated.

A hand-colored plate from J. C. Chenu's *Illustrations Conchyliologiques* showing *Harpa articularis, Harpa costata,* and *Harpa ventricosa.*

Within each family I again faced the question of which species to choose, and the answer varied with the family. Sometimes I illustrate the most characteristic member; other times the prettiest, rarest, largest, most unusual, or most storied. After the discussion of each species, information is presented about its family (or subfamily in some cases). I summarize features that distinguish members of similar families, although sometimes the primary differences are anatomical rather than in the shell, and thus of little immediate value to the shell collector. These anatomical distinctions, however, are of great importance to biologists in establishing the evolutionary relationships among various groups of mollusks and allowing them to be classified and named.

Following the body of the encylopedia are several chapters that illustrate how mollusks have become interwoven with human cultures. My colleague Eric Kjellgren has contributed a chapter on mollusks in religion, folklore, and mythology, adapted from his master's thesis. Another chapter looks at cultural and commercial uses of mollusks, and the concluding chapter discusses how to collect, conserve, and study shells, and how to maintain and computerize a shell collection.

WHAT IS A MOLLUSK?

The phylum Mollusca includes organisms such as clams, snails, slugs, octopuses, squid, and chitons. As the phylum is currently defined, several features are common to all or most mollusks:

- A *mantle* that secretes calcium carbonate in the form of spicules or shell
- A *mantle cavity* where respiration occurs, usually through the *ctenidium* (gill) in aquatic forms, or through the mantle wall in air in terrestrial ones, and where excretory and reproductive organs discharge
- A body divided into three regions: the *head, foot,* and *visceral mass*
- Three *coelomic spaces,* for kidney, heart, and gonad
- A *radula,* a ribbon of teeth used in feeding

The living mollusks are divided into seven classes, Aplacophora, Monoplacophora, Polyplacophora, Gastropoda, Bivalvia, Scaphopoda, and Cephalopoda. Members of the last five groups are treated in this book.

The word "mollusk" derives from the Latin *mollis* meaning "soft," just as the term "malacology," the study of mollusks, comes from the Greek word for soft, *malakos.* Originally Mollusca was used for naked, soft-bodied animals, whereas shelled animals were placed in the Testacea. In the early 1800s, Baron Georges Cuvier realized that gastropods, bivalves, scaphopods, and cephalopods belonged in one group, but he also included barnacles and brachiopods in the Mollusca, which have since been removed. The modern term "shellfish" refers to shelled mollusks and to crustaceans, which are members of

Detail of a drawing by Mathilde Duffy showing scallops and the heart shell, *Corculum cardissa.*

the phylum Arthropoda. The term "conchology" is also used for the study of mollusks, although it is sometimes applied to the study of shells alone.

MOLLUSCAN CLASSES

Aplacophora contains about 250 species of marine, wormlike, bilaterally symmetrical animals. They have no shell, but have calcareous spicules in the body surface. The foot is restricted to an anterior pedal shield or to a narrow groove running the length of the body. Aplacophorans have a radula and a posterior mantle cavity. Some are detritus feeders, others are predators. They range in length from 0.04 to 12 inches (1 to 300 millimeters).

Monoplacophora is represented by about a dozen living species, the first of which was discovered in the 1950s. Previously the group had been known only as fossils dating from 550 to 370 million years ago. Monoplacophorans have a capped-shaped, limpetlike shell, a well-developed foot, and a posterior anus; they are usually bilaterally symmetrical. They were once thought to represent a link to the annelid worms, in having several pairs of foot retractor muscles, gills, and hearts, but unlike annelids, their bodies are not segmented. Monoplacophorans live at depths of 650 to 20,000 feet (200 to 6,000 meters); they graze on algae and microorganisms on hard bottoms. Size ranges from 0.08 to 1.4 inches (2 to 35 millimeters).

Members of the Polyplacophora, known as chitons, have a shell of eight usually overlapping plates, held together by a leathery girdle. The animal is bilaterally symmetrical, with a well-developed foot surrounded by a groove in which there are six to eighty-eight pairs of gills.

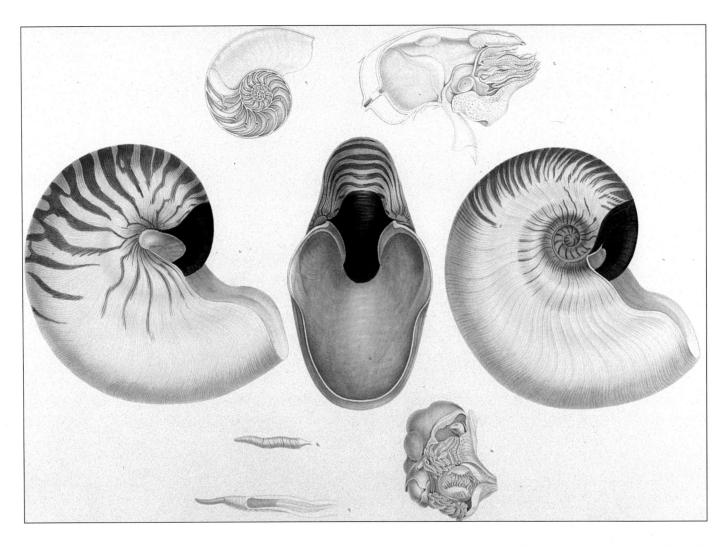

The head lacks eyes and tentacles; some species have light sensing organs (esthetes) in the shell. The radular teeth contain the mineral magnetite, which hardens them. There are about 800 species of chitons worldwide. All are marine and many are grazers on rocks in shallow water, but a few occur in depths beyond 16,000 feet (5,000 meters). They range in length from 0.1 to 16 inches (3 to 400 millimeters). In this book I discuss only one or two members of each polyplacophoran suborder, rather than one member of each family, and so have not treated the chitons as thoroughly as the scaphopods, bivalves, and gastropods.

Scaphopods, also known as tusk shells, are bilaterally symmetrical and have elongate, tubular, tapering shells that are open at both ends. The head is rudimentary, and lacks eyes and tentacles. It has contractile filaments called captacula used in feeding. The ctenidium is absent and the heart is reduced. The conical foot can be protruded for use in burrowing. All 350 or so species are marine;

they live buried in muddy or sandy bottoms. Length ranges from 0.1 to 6 inches (3 to 150 millimeters).

The cephalopods include the octopus, squid, cuttlefish, and nautilus. They are bilaterally symmetrical, and often highly streamlined. The head is surrounded by tentacles and a funnel from the mantle cavity provides jet propulsion. Members of only a few of the several dozens of families produce a calcareous shell. Cephalopods have a concentrated nervous system and include the most intelligent animals among the invertebrates. All 600 to 650 species are marine predators or scavengers and have parrotlike beaks or jaws in addition to the radula. Length ranges from 0.4 inches (10 millimeters) for male argonauts to 65 feet (20 meters) for giant squid.

Nautilus pompilius and *Nautilus scrobiculatus* from J. C. Chenu's *Illustrations Conchyliologiques.*

Gastropods have a single-valved shell which is usually spirally coiled and is reduced or absent in slugs and semi-slugs. They have a prominent head with cephalic tentacles and usually a well-developed foot used in crawling. In the early larval stage of gastropods, the visceral mass and mantle cavity rotate up to 180 degrees counterclockwise in a process called torsion. This brings them from a posterior position to an anterior position behind the head. The animal in most cases is able to retract into the shell. An operculum is present in the larvae of most groups, and is often present in the adults; it serves to seal the aperture of the shell when the animal is retracted. (In the text, when I state that the operculum is absent, I mean that it is lacking in the adult.) Gastropods are one of the few groups of organisms well represented in marine, freshwater, and terrestrial habitats. There are about 60,000 species. Size ranges from 0.02 to 30 inches (0.5 millimeters to 0.75 meters).

Bivalves have two valves connected by a flexible ligament. The mantle cavity is enlarged, enclosing the visceral mass and other internal organs. There is no differentiated head or cephalic region and the radula is absent. Most bivalves are filter feeders, with the gill acting as a food collecting and sorting organ, in addition to filling its respiratory function. The mouth usually has a pair of labial palps on either side, which handle food collected by the gill. There are about 10,000 living species of bivalves in marine and freshwater habitats worldwide.

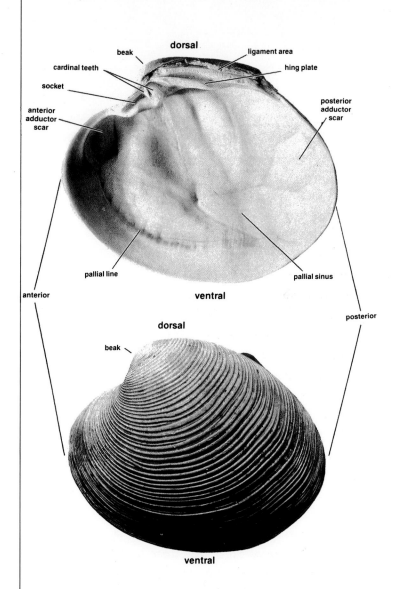

Parts of a gastropod shell. The anterior end is at the bottom. Additional features are defined in the glossary.

Parts of a bivalve shell. The inside of the right valve and the outside of the left valve are shown here.

Pink scallops, *Chlamys hastata,* of the northwest Pacific.

Size ranges from 0.02 to 50 inches (0.5 millimeters to 1.3 meters).

When identifying bivalves, you must be able to distinguish anterior from posterior and left valve from right valve. The left valve in members of one family might look like the right valve in another. In general, if the ligament is restricted to one side of the beak, it is on the posterior side. Also, if the shell has a pallial sinus, it is posterior. If you hold a bivalve with beaks upward, with one valve in each hand and its posterior end toward you, the right valve is in your right hand, the left in your left. Other landmarks are given in the description of each family.

NAMING NAMES

The practice of giving species a two-part name composed of a generic and a specific name started with Carl von Linné in 1758, when he published the tenth edition of *Systema Naturae.* Previously there had been no clearcut distinction between the name of a species and its description. Species names are based on *type specimens.* These are the specimens an author used in describing a particular species. A single specimen, the *holotype,* is chosen by the author to represent the species; his other specimens are *paratypes.* If the original author did not choose a holotype, his specimens are called *syntypes.* A later author can designate what is called a *lectotype* from the syntypes. The lectotype serves the same function as the holotype and the other syntypes become *paralectotypes.* Some of the shells illustrated in this book are type specimens of their species.

Generic names are based on a *type species,* designated by the original author or a later worker. Familial names must be formed from the root word of their *type genus.* There is a hierarchy of names ranging from kingdom to subspecies:

Rank	Example
Kingdom	Animalia
Phylum	Mollusca
Class	Gastropoda
Order	Caenogastropoda
Suborder	Neotaenioglossa
Infraorder	Discopoda
Superfamily	Tonnacea
Family	Ranellidae
Subfamily	Charoniinae
Tribe	Charoniini
Genus	*Charonia*
Subgenus	*(Charonia)*
Species	*tritonis*
Subspecies	*variegata*

Ranks in addition to these are possible, such as subclass, superorder, subtribe, and are used as necessary to specify relationships.

Various rules apply to the formation of some of these names. Superfamily names must end in "-oidea" or "-acea." I prefer -acea endings because they are much more difficult to misspell in a misleading way. (For example, is "Tonnidea" a misspelling of Tonnoidea or of Tonnidae?) Family names end in -idae, subfamily names in -inae, and tribe names in -ini.

If the specific name of a species is an adjective, it must agree with the gender of the genus it is combined with. Specific names that are nouns do not change endings. Most specific names are Latin or are treated as Latin. The two most common kinds of Latin adjectives have the

EVOLUTIONARY TREE

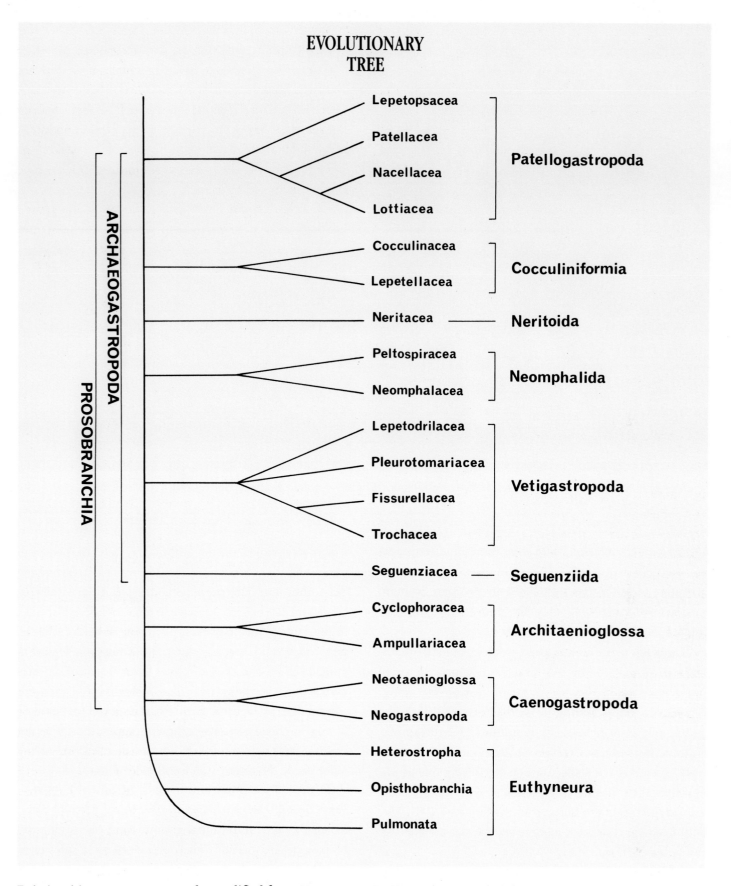

Relationships among gastropods, modified from Haszprunar (1988), to show the classification used herein. Archaeogastropoda and Prosobranchia are used as descriptive terms, not as names of taxa. See discussion on page 20.

Scallops and other shells on the beach in Baja California. The sand dollar at upper right is not a mollusk but an echinoderm.

endings *-us, -a, -um* and *-is, -is, -e* for masculine, feminine, and neuter respectively. The endings *-i, -ae, -orum,* or *-arum* are used for species named after a man, woman, men, or women, respectively. The ending *-ensis* (or *-ense*) is often used for species named for places.

The gender of a genus must be determined from a Latin dictionary, or by the manner in which the original author used it if it is not a Latin (or Greek) word. Beware—a genus ending in *-us* is not necessarily masculine, nor is *-a* necessarily feminine. As an example, *Cyphoma* is neuter, so *Cyphoma gibbosum* (rather than "gibbosa") is correct. If a species is changed from one genus to another, its ending might change. *Cyphoma gibbosum* was originally named *Bulla gibbosa* by Linné in 1758. The ending changed to *-um* when the species was assigned to the genus *Cyphoma*.

The author and date of description are not part of the species name, but are often cited with it: *Bulla gibbosa* Linné, 1758. If the species is no longer placed in the genus that it was named in, the author and date are placed in parentheses: *Cyphoma gibbosum* (Linné, 1758). Specifying the author and date prevents confusion if the same specific name has been used twice to refer to different species in the same genus. For example, *Conus abbreviatus* Reeve, 1843, is a valid species, but *Conus abbreviatus* Dautzenberg, 1937, is a variety of *Conus textile*. Identical species names such as these are called *homonyms* and only the older name can be used. Similarly, if a species (or genus or family) has been given two different names, the names are *synonyms* and only the older one can be used (unless the older one is a homonym of a still older name).

The rules of nomenclature are codified in the *International Code of Zoological Nomenclature* (third edition) published by the International Commission on Zoological Nomenclature in 1985. The purpose of these rules is to ensure that the names given to groups of animals are unique and therefore unambiguous. (Other groups of organisms have their own codes of nomenclature.)

ESTABLISHING RELATIONSHIPS

Three closely related terms—classification, systematics, and taxonomy—are important for understanding how biological groups are recognized and named:

Classification is the distribution of objects into groups. In biology, the objects are organisms (individuals), populations, species, or groups of higher rank.

Systematics is the science of classifying biological diversity. Biologists use various methods for estimating how closely species are related to each other, including comparative anatomy, genetics, and paleontology (the study of fossil organisms). The groups reflect biologists' best estimate of the relationships of the organisms.

Taxonomy is the naming of biological groups. These groups are called "taxa." The singular of "taxa" is "taxon." In the hierarchy of names above, each of the examples is a taxon.

To biologists, it is not similarity per se that allows recognition of groups, because not all similarity indicates relatedness. For example, whales and sharks both have fins, but many other features of their anatomy lead us to believe that they evolved fins independently. Biologists attempt to identify similarities due to descent from a common ancestor.

Organisms can have *primitive* similarity because of distant ancestry, or *derived* similarity because of immediate ancestry. Derived similarities in particular allow identification of biological groups. For example, both humans and chimpanzees have four limbs, hair, and nurse their young, but these features do not tell us that humans and chimps are closely related, because all mammals have these features. They are primitive characteristics that reflect distant ancestry. These same features are derived similarities in relation to other groups. Thus, having four limbs is a derived feature that separates tetrapods (mammals, birds, amphibians, reptiles, and some fish) from all other organisms. Hair is a derived feature that separates mammals from other tetrapods. This means that the immediate common ancestor of all mammals had hair, and no other organism did.

The pattern of derived similarities is used to infer the relationships of the taxa, and is presented in a branching diagram called a cladogram (*clados* is Greek for branch), which is an evolutionary tree. It can be very difficult to determine whether a given similarity is convergent (as in fish and whale fins), primitive, or derived. This means that it can be very difficult to find the correct tree showing the relationships of a group of organisms. Biologists are continually refining their ideas of the relationships of organisms and, as a result, groups are often redefined or undergo name changes as our knowledge increases.

There is always a temptation to take evolutionary trees as representing progress. People often refer to one organism as primitive and another as advanced, but an organism is never entirely primitive—it will have some primitive features and some derived ones. The broadest definition of evolution is simply "change over time." Evolution does not necessarily mean progress. A species that is restricted to caves might become blind—this is change, but it is progress only in a local sense.

The Ringed Top-shell, *Calliostoma annulatum,* ranges from Alaska to southern California.

ORIGINS OF DIVERSITY

There are more than 70,000 living species of mollusks worldwide, classified in thousands of genera and hundreds of families. Mollusks have been evolving for more than 550 million years, an immense amount of time for speciation and divergence. Divergence can occur whenever a population (a group of organisms of one species) is split into two or more parts that have no chance to interbreed. This can happen as a result of chance dispersal to isolated islands or through geological changes, such as the uplift of the Isthmus of Panama, which separated the Western Atlantic and Eastern Pacific.

Speciation can result from isolation. Because of natural selection, separated populations of a species will adapt to different conditions in different regions, per-

haps developing different mating behaviors or breeding seasons, or accumulating enough genetic differences to render egg and sperm incompatible. If they are reunited, they might not be able to interbreed, or hybrid offspring might be at a disadvantage relative to purebred ones. In organisms with two sexes, populations that cannot interbreed are usually regarded as separate species. In practice we usually do not know whether two supposed species can interbreed successfully. Thus, we usually must rely on morphological (and genetic) criteria to define species.

Phylloceras heterophyllus (J. Sowerby, 1820), a 190-million-year-old fossil from the Lower Jurassic of England, is a representative of the ammonites, a group of extinct cephalopods related to the nautiloids.

DIVISIONS OF GEOLOGIC TIME

Era	Period	Millions of Years Before the Present
Cenozoic	Pleistocene	0–1.6
	Pliocene	1.6–5.3
	Miocene	5.3–24
	Oligocene	24–37
	Eocene	37–58
	Paleocene	58–66
Mesozoic	Cretaceous	66–144
	Jurassic	144–208
	Triassic	208–245
Paleozoic	Permian	245–286
	Carboniferous	286–360
	Devonian	360–406
	Silurian	406–438
	Ordovician	438–505
	Cambrian	505–570

SPECIES

For each species treated herein, I have given information about its size, distribution, ecology (if known), and appearance. Each of these subjects requires some explanation. For size I have given a single number, which represents the greatest dimension of a large adult individual of the species as reflected in the collections at the Academy of Natural Sciences of Philadelphia, and as recorded in the literature. In some species, adults continue growing until death, and the largest specimens can be huge compared to typical adults. In other species, growth terminates at maturity, which in gastropods is often signaled by the formation of a thick outer lip. In many species of mollusks, the largest adults are more than twice the size of the smallest ones.

The Venus Comb Murex, *Murex pecten.* The three rows of long spines on this shell have inspired its names. The scientific name derives from the Latin *pecten,* which means "comb."

Species are often patchy in distribution, and may not be found everywhere throughout their ranges, often because of lack of appropriate habitat in a given area. I have listed the known geographical extremes of each species, usually from north to south in the Atlantic and Eastern Pacific, and from east to west in the Indo-Pacific, which extends from South Africa and the Red Sea to Hawaii, the Marquesas, and Easter Island. Many parts of the world are still inadequately sampled for mollusks, and the true ranges of some of the species are probably broader than those stated here.

For a surprising number of species, nothing is known about their habitats other than the depths in which they have been collected. Even depth may not accurately reflect habitat, as depth records are often based on dead-collected shells, which might have been transported into depths different from those in which the animal lived. Observations of living animals by shell collectors can often generate valuable scientific information, as discussed in the concluding chapter of this book.

Some species are so distinctive or constant in coloration and sculpture as to be instantly recognizable. Others vary so greatly that seemingly no two specimens are alike, and many hundreds or thousands must be examined to understand the ranges of variation and features separating them from similar species. In some cases, variation is under direct genetic control, as is the case with the bright, variable color patterns of the coquina (*Donax variabilis*). In other cases, coloration and even sculpture varies with diet. For example, some ovulids incorporate in their shells pigments from the soft corals on which they live and feed. Individuals on yellow coral have yellow shells, but if transferred to a purple coral of the same species start making purple shells. Each species of mollusk varies in a different way, making generalizations about coloration and sculpture difficult to find, but endlessly fascinating to search for.

FAMILIES

The familial classification presented here is synthesized from many sources, but draws heavily on Boss (1982) and Ponder and Warén (1988). Boss is an excellent source for summaries of anatomical data on molluscan families. Information on the earliest known occurrences of families in the fossil record is taken in large part from Moore (1960, 1969); data for neogastropods is mostly from Taylor et al. (1980), which was also the source for much information on neogastropod feeding biology. Estimates on the number of species in families refer to living species only, and reflect the most recent ones in the literature, or in some cases are based on the collections at the Academy of Natural Sciences.

CLASSIFICATION

The next three pages detail the classification used herein, which reflects many changes in ideas of molluscan relationships in the last ten years, particularly among gastropods. The subclass Prosobranchia, which is normally considered to include all the gastropods except the pulmonates and opisthobranchs, is not recognized. Biological groups should include the common ancestor and all of its descendants, but when defined in this way, Prosobranchia becomes a synonym of Gastropoda. Thus, along with an increasing number of biologists, I use prosobranch as a descriptive term, rather than as the name of a taxon. The Archaeogastropoda suffer from the same problem. Some workers restrict the archaeogastropods to the Pleurotomariacea, Fissurellacea, and Trochacea, excluding the Cocculiniformia and Patellogastropoda; but I prefer the name Vetigastropoda for this group, to avoid confusion between a narrowly and a broadly defined Archaeogastropoda.

As shown in the evolutionary tree on page 15, there are many different major lineages of gastropods. If this tree is correct, it would be appropriate to consider each of these lineages a subclass. In the classification herein, they are ranked as orders, because no name of subclass rank has been introduced for some of them. In order to maintain consistency of ranks within the tree, I have called Pulmonata and Opisthobranchia orders, although they are usually considered subclasses. The problem of non-equivalence of ranks results from various groups of workers with disparate traditions working on different groups of gastropods. At present it is impossible to present a classification that simultaneously gives consistent ranks and reflects current usage, so I have compromised between the two.

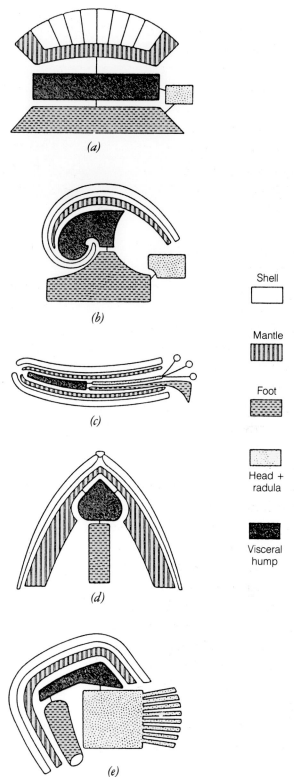

Shell color in some ovulid gastropods depends on their diets. These gastropods match the colors of the soft corals on which they live and feed. *Above: Sandalia triticea* (Lamarck, 1810) from Japan. *Below: Neosimnia aequalis* (Sowerby, 1832) from southern California.

Schematic body plans of some of the molluscan classes. (a) Polyplacophora, (b) Gastropoda, (c) Scaphopoda, (d) Bivalvia, (e) Cephalopoda.

CLASS GASTROPODA
  Order Patellogastropoda
    Superfamily Lottiacea
      Lottiidae
      Acmaeidae
      Lepetidae
    Superfamily Nacellacea
      Nacellidae
    Superfamily Patellacea
      Patellidae
  Order Cocculiniformia
    Superfamily Lepetellacea
      Addisoniidae
  Order Neritoida
    Superfamily Neritacea
      Neritidae
      Neritopsidae
      Phenacolepadidae
  Order Neomphalida
    Superfamily Neomphalacea
      Neomphalidae
  Order Vetigastropoda
    Superfamily Pleurotomariacea
      Pleurotomariidae
      Scissurellidae
      Haliotidae
    Superfamily Fissurellacea
      Fissurellidae
    Superfamily Trochacea
      Trochidae
        Calliostomatinae
        Stomatellinae
        Trochinae
      Turbinidae
        Turbininae
        Angariinae
        Liotiinae
        Phasianellinae
      Skeneidae
  Order Seguenziida
    Superfamily Seguenziacea
      Seguenziidae
  Order Caenogastropoda
  Suborder Neotaenioglossa
  Infraorder Discopoda
    Superfamily Loxonematacea
      Abyssochrysidae
    Superfamily Campanilacea
      Campanilidae
    Superfamily Cerithiacea
      Diastomatidae
      Dialidae
      Litiopidae

Obtortionidae
Scaliolidae
Cerithiidae
Cerithideidae
Potamididae
Batillariidae
Fossaridae
Planaxidae
Modulidae
Turritellidae
Siliquariidae
Superfamily Vermetacea
  Vermetidae
Superfamily Littorinacea
  Littorinidae
  Skeneopsidae
Superfamily Cingulopsacea
  Cingulopsidae
  Eatoniellidae
Superfamily Rissoacea
  Anabathridae
  Barleeidae
  Emblandidae
  Caecidae
  Elachisinidae
  Epigridae
  Falsicingulidae
  Iravadiidae
  Rissoidae
  Assimineidae
  Truncatellidae
  Tornidae
  Vitrinellidae
Superfamily Strombacea
  Aporrhaidae
  Strombidae
  Struthiolariidae
  Seraphidae
Superfamily Xenophoracea
  Xenophoridae
Superfamily Calyptraeacea
  Calyptraeidae
  Capulidae
Superfamily Vanikoracea
  Vanikoridae
  Hipponicidae
Superfamily Cypraeacea
  Cypraeidae
  Ovulidae
    Ovulinae
    Eocypraeinae

Superfamily Velutinacea
  Triviidae
    Triviinae
    Eratoinae
  Velutinidae
Superfamily Naticacea
  Naticidae
Superfamily Tonnacea
  Cassidae
  Bursidae
  Personidae
  Ranellidae
  Ficidae
  Tonnidae
  Laubierinidae
Infraorder Heteropoda
  Superfamily Carinariacea
    Atlantidae
    Carinariidae
Infraorder Ptenoglossa
  Superfamily Triphoracea
    Triphoridae
    Cerithiopsidae
    Triforidae
  Superfamily Epitoniacea
    Epitoniidae
    Aclididae
    Janthinidae
  Superfamily Eulimacea
    Eulimidae
Suborder Neogastropoda
  Superfamily Muricacea
    Muricidae
      Muricinae
      Thaidinae
      Coralliophilinae
    Turbinellidae
      Turbinellinae
      Columbariinae
      Vasinae
    Buccinidae
      Buccininae
      Fasciolariinae
      Melongeninae
      Nassariinae
    Columbellidae
    Harpidae
      Harpinae
      Moruminae
    Marginellidae
    Pleioptygmatidae
    Mitridae

Costellariidae
Olividae
Olivinae
Ancillinae
Volutidae
Volutomitridae
Superfamily Cancellariacea
Cancellariidae
Superfamily Conacea
Conidae
Terebridae
Turridae
Turrinae
Borsoniinae
Cochlespirinae
Crassispirinae
Daphnellinae
Drilliinae
Mangeliinae
Order Heterostropha
Superfamily Valvatacea
Orbitestellidae
Superfamily Rissoellacea
Rissoellidae
Superfamily Omalogyracea
Omalogyridae
Superfamily Architectonicacea
Architectonicidae
Mathildidae
Superfamily Pyramidellacea
Pyramidellidae
Amathinidae
Order Opisthobranchia
Suborder Cephalaspidea
Superfamily Ringiculacea
Ringiculidae
Superfamily Acteonacea
Acteonidae
Bullinidae
Hydatinidae
Superfamily Philinacea
Philinidae
Cylichnidae
Superfamily Retusacea
Retusidae
Superfamily Diaphanacea
Diaphanidae
Superfamily Bullacea
Bullidae
Superfamily Haminoeacea
Haminoeidae

Superfamily Cylindrobullacea
Cylindrobullidae
Suborder Anaspidea
Superfamily Aplysiacea
Aplysiidae
Akeridae
Suborder Sacoglossa
Superfamily Juliacea
Juliidae
Superfamily Oxynoacea
Oxynoidae
Volvatellidae
Suborder Notaspidea
Superfamily Umbraculacea
Umbraculidae
Tylodinidae
Suborder Thecosomata
Infraorder Euthecosomata
Superfamily Limacinacea
Cavoliniidae
Limacinidae
Infraorder Pseudothecosomata
Superfamily Cymbuliacea
Peraclidae
Order Pulmonata
Suborder Archaepulmonata
Superfamily Ellobiacea
Ellobiidae
Suborder Basommatophora
Superfamily Amphibolacea
Amphibolidae
Superfamily Siphonariacea
Siphonariidae
Trimusculidae
CLASS BIVALVIA
Subclass Paleotaxodonta
Order Nuculoida
Superfamily Nuculacea
Nuculidae
Superfamily Nuculanacea
Nuculanidae
Malletiidae
Tindariidae
Subclass Cryptodonta
Order Solemyoida
Superfamily Solemyacea
Solemyidae
Subclass Pteriomorphia
Superorder Isofilibranchia
Order Mytiloida
Superfamily Mytilacea
Mytilidae

Superorder Prionodonta
Order Arcoida
Superfamily Arcacea
Arcidae
Cucullaeidae
Noetiidae
Parallelodontidae
Superfamily Limopsacea
Limopsidae
Glycymerididae
Philobryidae
Superorder Eupteriomorphia
Order Pterioida
Superfamily Pteriacea
Pteriidae
Malleidae
Isognomonidae
Superfamily Pinnacea
Pinnidae
Order Limoida
Superfamily Limacea
Limidae
Order Ostreoida
Suborder Ostreina
Superfamily Ostreacea
Ostreidae
Gryphaeidae
Superfamily Dimyacea
Dimyidae
Superfamily Plicatulacea
Plicatulidae
Suborder Pectinina
Superfamily Anomiacea
Anomiidae
Placunidae
Superfamily Pectinacea
Pectinidae
Propeamussiidae
Spondylidae
Subclass Paleoheterodonta
Order Trigonioida
Superfamily Trigoniacea
Trigoniidae
Subclass Heterodonta
Order Veneroida
Superfamily Lucinacea
Lucinidae
Fimbriidae
Thyasiridae
Ungulinidae
Superfamily Cyamiacea
Cyamiidae

Gaimardiidae
Superfamily Galeommatacea
  Galeommatidae
  Lasaeidae
  Montacutidae
Superfamily Carditacea
  Carditidae
Superfamily Chamacea
  Chamidae
Superfamily Crassatellacea
  Crassatellidae
  Astartidae
Superfamily Cardiacea
  Cardiidae
  Hemidonacidae
  Tridacnidae
Superfamily Mactracea
  Mactridae
  Mesodesmatidae
  Cardiliidae
  Anatinellidae
Superfamily Solenacea
  Solenidae
  Cultellidae
Superfamily Tellinacea
  Tellinidae
  Donacidae
  Psammobiidae
  Semelidae
Superfamily Arcticacea
  Arcticidae
  Trapeziidae
Superfamily Glossacea
  Glossidae

Vesicomyidae
Superfamily Corbiculacea
  Corbiculidae
Superfamily Veneracea
  Veneridae
  Petricolidae
  Cooperellidae
  Glauconomidae
Order Myoida
  Superfamily Myacea
    Myidae
    Corbulidae
  Superfamily Gastrochaenacea
    Gastrochaenidae
  Superfamily Hiatellacea
    Hiatellidae
  Superfamily Pholadacea
    Pholadidae
    Teredinidae
Subclass Anomalodesmata
Order Pholadomyoida
  Superfamily Pholadomyacea
    Pholadomyidae
  Superfamily Pandoracea
    Pandoridae
    Lyonsiidae
    Cleidothaeridae
    Myochamidae
  Superfamily Poromyacea
    Poromyidae
    Cuspidariidae
    Verticordiidae
  Superfamily Thraciacea
    Laternulidae
    Periplomatidae
    Thraciidae
  Superfamily Clavagellacea
    Clavagellidae

CLASS SCAPHOPODA
Order Dentaliida
  Dentaliidae
  Gadilinidae
  Laevidentaliidae
  Omniglyptidae
Order Gadilida
  Gadilidae
  Entalinidae
  Pulsellidae
  Siphonodentaliidae
CLASS CEPHALOPODA
Subclass Nautiloida
Order Nautilida
  Nautilidae
Subclass Coleoida
Order Octopoda
  Argonautidae
Order Sepiida
  Sepiidae
  Spirulidae
CLASS POLYPLACOPHORA
Suborder Lepidopleurina
  Lepidopleuridae
Suborder Ischnochitonina
  Chitonidae
  Ischnochitonidae
Suborder Acanthochitonina
  Acanthochitonidae

HOW TO USE THIS BOOK

In using the entries in this encyclopedia, you should be aware of several features of the book and the conventions that have been followed.

Each entry begins with the classification of the species treated, but ranks are not repeated in each entry. Thus, for example, a superfamily is listed only once and includes all succeeding families until a new superfamily is listed. A summary of the classification is given at the end of the introduction. The introduction also contains a geological time scale that gives the ages, in millions of years, of the geological periods cited for fossil occurrences of the taxa.

The glossary at the back of the book defines many of the terms used in describing the species and their biological characteristics, and many common features of shells are also labeled in diagrams in the introduction.

The references listed at the end of each entry refer to the author and the date of publication of works listed in the bibliography. Once you have determined the family of a particular specimen by reading and comparing the descriptions in the entries, the cited references will serve as a guide to publications that might help to narrow the identification to species level, or that will give additional information about the family.

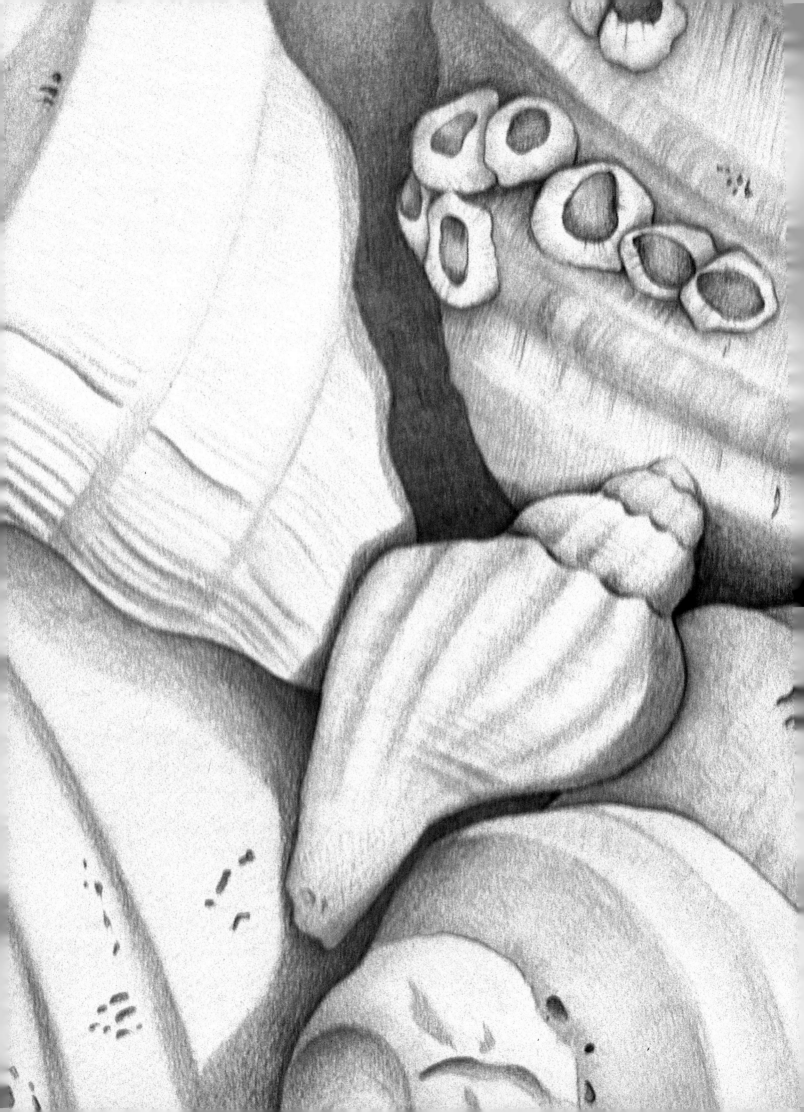

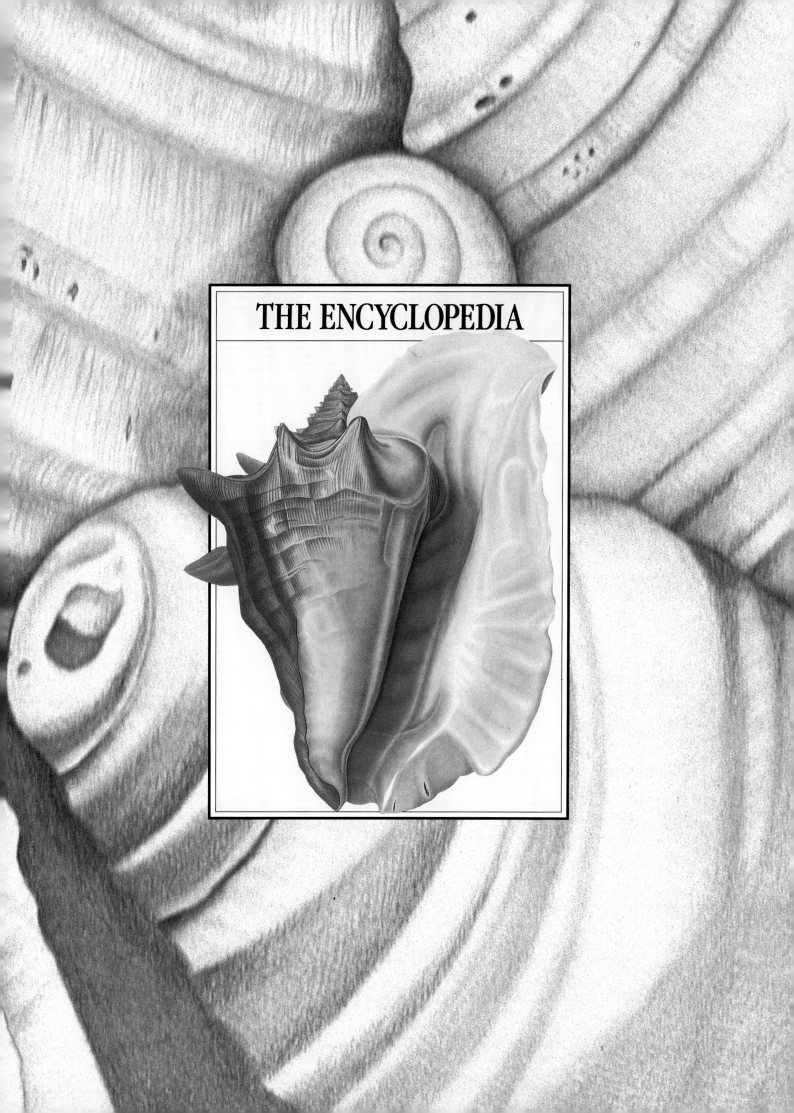

THE ENCYCLOPEDIA

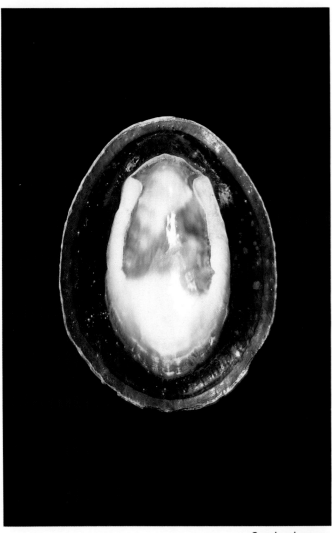

Lottia gigantea

Class: Gastropoda Cuvier, 1797
Order: Patellogastropoda Lindberg, 1986
Superfamily: Lottiacea Gray, 1840
Family: LOTTIIDAE Gray, 1840
Species: *Lottia gigantea* Sowerby, 1834
Common Name: Owl Limpet
Size: 4 inches (100 mm)
Distribution: Washington to Baja California

Lottia gigantea is called the Owl Limpet because the central area of the inner surface, outlined by the muscle scar, is shaped like an owl. The muscle scar is white or bluish white, and contrasts with the brown markings of the central area. The border of the shell is black or dark brown. The shell has slightly raised radial ribs and is often eroded dorsally by fungal infections. Members of the species are sequential hermaphrodites—they start life as males and later change sex, becoming females. The animals live on open coasts, in areas where the intertidal zone is exposed to strong waves.

The family Lottiidae has recently been separated from the Acmaeidae on the basis of differences in anatomy and the crystalline layers that make up the shells. Most species previously called acmaeids are now considered to be lottiids. Lottiid limpets range in shape from flattened to high-profile. The shell is porcelaneous rather than nacreous. Most species have planktonic larvae; the protoconch is broken off soon after the larva has settled to the ocean floor and adult shell growth has begun. The protoconch is saclike rather than spirally coiled. The apex of the shell is nearer the anterior end, which is usually the narrower end. The muscle scar is horseshoe-shaped, opening anteriorly. In addition to the primary gill (the ctenidium), some species have a secondary, external gill in the pallial groove. Most lottiids live intertidally, and feed on vegetation growing on rocks. Some live on the blades of marine grasses; these species often have more compressed shapes as they are limited in size by the width of the blade. There are about 100 species in the family. They range in size from 0.5 to 4 inches (12 to 100 millimeters) at maturity; *Lottia gigantea* is the largest. Species occur worldwide, but the greatest diversity is on the west coast of North America, with more than twenty species.

References: Boss (1982), Lindberg (1981, 1988).

Family: ACMAEIDAE Forbes, 1850
Species: *Acmaea mitra* Rathke, 1833
Common Name: White-cap Limpet
Size: 1.2 inches (30 mm)
Distribution: Aleutian Islands to Baja California

Acmaea mitra has a taller shell than most limpets, with the height being 50 to 80 percent of the length. At a quick glance, the shell appears triangular in profile, but the front slope is slightly convex, whereas the rear slope is straight or slightly concave. The apex is closer to the front of the shell, and the horseshoe-shaped muscle scar opens toward the front as well. Sculpture consists of concentric growth lines, which are usually hidden by an overgrowth of encrusting coralline algae. The shell is entirely white. The animal lives in the low intertidal zone and subtidally to depths of 100 feet (30 meters).

As noted, most species previously placed in Acmaeidae recently have been transferred to Lottiidae. The only remaining members of Acmaeidae are *Acmaea mitra* and the few species of *Pectinodonta,* a genus of deep-sea limpets that are blind and have small, white shells with cancellate sculpture. Thus, fewer than ten species of acmaeids are known. The acmaeids are more closely related to the lepetids, another group of deep-sea limpets, than to the lottiids.

References: Lindberg (1981, 1986).

. . . .

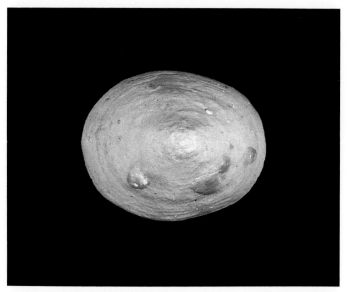

Acmaea mitra

Lepeta concentrica

Family: LEPETIDAE Dall, 1869
Species: *Lepeta concentrica* (Middendorff, 1851)
Common Name: Ringed Blind Limpet
Size: 0.8 inches (20 mm)
Distribution: Northern Pacific and Arctic Oceans

Lepeta concentrica occurs in depths to 165 feet (50 meters) on rocks in muddy areas. It apparently feeds on deposits of sediment rather than grazing on the rock. Lepetid limpets have small, white, symmetric shells with an anterior apex. Members of the family are unusual among marine gastropods because they completely lack gills. Although some limpets lack the primary gill (ctenidium), which is located in a cavity in the neck region behind the head, its function is usually taken over by a secondary gill in the space around the foot. Lepetids also lack an osphradium and eyes. They occur in cold seas in both the northern and southern hemispheres; some in shallow water, but most in the deep sea, in depths as great as 2 miles (3,400 meters). There are seven genera: *Bathylepeta, Iotha, Lepeta, Limalepeta, Propilidium, Punctolepeta,* and *Sagamilepeta.*

References: Lindberg (1988), Yonge (1960).

. . . .

Nacella deaurata

Superfamily: Nacellacea Thiele, 1891
Family: NACELLIDAE Thiele, 1891
Species: *Nacella deaurata* (Gmelin, 1791)
Common Name: Patagonian Copper Limpet
Size: 2.5 inches (60 mm)
Distribution: Falkland Islands, Southern Argentina,
and Chile

Nacella deaurata has thirty-six to forty radial ribs, which are nodular or slightly scaly. The apex is about one-third of the shell length, back from the anterior end. *Nacella magellanica* (Gmelin, 1791) resembles *Nacella deaurata,* but is more broadly ovate and lacks the nodulations on the radial ribs. *Nacella deaurata* was formerly known as *Nacella aenea* (Martyn, 1784). Martyn's name, however, is not accepted as his work did not conform to the Linnaean standard of binomial names. Gmelin's name for the species is the first to be validly proposed.

The twelve species of *Nacella* are all Antarctic or subantarctic in distribution. Many of the species live attached to large seaweed. The other thirty species in the family are members of the genus *Cellana,* which are grazers on intertidal rocks in the tropical Indo-Pacific. The radular ribbon can be five times the length of the shell in *Cellana.* Some nacellids are known to brood their young; they retain the eggs in the nuchal cavity behind the head, where they are fertilized and develop. Upon hatching, the young crawl away. In contrast, patellid limpets release egg and sperm into the sea, where fertilization and larval development occur.

References: Powell (1973), Lindberg (1988).

. . . .

Patella longicosta

Superfamily: Patellacea Rafinesque, 1815
Family: PATELLIDAE Rafinesque, 1815
Species: *Patella longicosta* Lamarck, 1819
Common Name: Long-ribbed Limpet
Size: 3 inches (75 mm)
Distribution: South Africa

Adults of *Patella longicosta* live on rocks in the lower midtidal zone. They are territorial, living in cleared homescars—areas where the rock has been etched to conform to the shape of the shell. Each home-scar is surrounded by a "garden" of *Ralfsia,* an encrusting brown seaweed on which the limpets feed. Juveniles live in small *Ralfsia* gardens on the shells of the adults, where their home-scars are sometimes seen. When a juvenile grows too large to live on the adult, it becomes vagrant, crawling about until it finds an empty *Ralfsia* garden large enough to support it. The shell in this species has seven to eleven strong, projecting ribs; some specimens are almost star-shaped, causing some South African collectors to call the shells "Ducks' Feet." South Africa has the world's most diverse *Patella* fauna with twelve species, as many as ten of which can occur on the same shoreline. These limpets were an important part of the diet of the coastal Hottentots, as shown by the abundance of the shells in old middens, and are still eaten in quantity in the Transkei.

There are about forty-five species of patellid limpets worldwide, mostly in the genus *Patella,* with a few species in the genus *Helcion.* Length ranges from one inch to more than 1 foot (25 to 300 millimeters) in the case of *Patella mexicana* Broderip & Sowerby, 1829, the world's largest species of limpet. Individuals of some species live more than fifteen years. Most patellids feed on algae growing on rocks; some can travel as far away as 5 feet (1.5 meters) while foraging and then return to their home-scar, which exactly fits the margin of the shell. Because the shape of these limpets is influenced by that of the rock and by the average force of the waves, members of a species can vary considerably in appearance. Patellids and nacellids have a horseshoe-shaped muscle scar, like that of the lottiids. The primary gill (ctenidium) is lost and respiration occurs through a secondary gill that entirely circles the animal between the mantle and the foot. Patellids, nacellids, and lottiids are difficult to tell apart by the shell alone, as most differences are anatomical. Lottiids always have a porcelaneous shell, whereas the interiors of some patellid and most nacellid shells have a somewhat glossy, transparent quality. Patellids are generally larger than lottiids, and the largest species of lottiids (such as *Lottia gigantea*) occur in parts of the world where patellids are absent. Siphonariids are sometimes confused with patellogastropods, but can be easily distinguished by the muscle scar, which opens toward one side rather than toward the front end.

References: Powell (1973), Kilburn & Rippey (1982).

. . . .

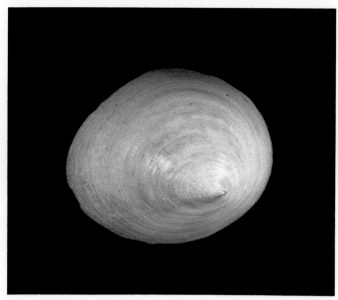

Addisonia paradoxa

Order: Cocculiniformia Haszprunar, 1987
Superfamily: Lepetellacea Dall, 1881
Family: ADDISONIIDAE Dall, 1882
Species: *Addisonia paradoxa* Dall, 1882
Common Name: Paradoxical Blind Limpet
Size: 0.8 inches (20 mm)
Distribution: Nova Scotia to Jamaica

Addisonia paradoxa is the largest of the three known species in the family, reaching about twice the size of the Eastern Atlantic *A. lateralis* (Requien, 1848) and the Eastern Pacific *A. brophyi* McLean, 1985. Addisoniids can be recognized by their thin, white, asymmetric limpetlike shells. Juveniles are symmetric but become increasingly asymmetric as they mature; the protoconch breaks off at an early stage. The apex in adults is positioned to the left and curves toward the posterior end of the shell. The animals are simultaneous hermaphrodites—they are able to produce eggs and sperm at the same time. Addisoniids lack eyes and occur at depths from 300 to 3,800 feet (90 to 1,170 meters). They live inside of and feed on spent egg cases of sharks and skates. Collectors who find such egg cases on the beach should open them to search for these limpets. The egg cases, sometimes called mermaids' purses, are 2 to 6 inches (50 to 150 millimeters) long, brown or black, and rectangular with long filaments projecting from the corners. The only other gastropod associated with these egg cases is the coiled snail of the related family Choristellidae.

Other families of cocculiniform limpets also feed on unusual resources in the deep sea: Cocculinidae feed on wood; Pseudococculinidae on algal holdfasts—the root-like part of the algae attached to the bottom—and the carapaces of crabs; Bathysciadiidae on cephalopod beaks; Bathyphytophilidae on the roots of sea grass; Lepetellidae on the tubes of marine worms; Cocculinellidae on fish bones; and Osteopeltidae on whale bones.

References: Haszprunar (1988), McLean (1985).

. . . .

that sometimes become obsolete on the body whorl. The animals live intertidally on rocky coasts exposed to the open ocean. They lay small dome-shaped egg capsules, which release planktonic larvae.

Neritid shells range from globular to flattened and caplike in shape. The inner walls of the whorls are reabsorbed completely in adults, leaving the spire hollow. The operculum is calcified, paucispiral, and has a lateral peg (except in *Neritilia*). There are about 200 species, which live in the marine intertidal or in brackish or fresh water. *Neritina granosa* Sowerby, 1825, native to Hawaii, has larvae that develop in the ocean. The young, however, migrate up streams and live in fresh water at elevations up to 1,300 feet (400 meters). Genera include *Nerita, Neritilia, Neritina, Smaragdia,* and *Theodoxus.* The family dates back to the Middle Triassic.

References: Kay (1979), Moore (1960), Russell (1941).

. . . .

Nerita peloronta

Order: Neritoida Franc, 1968
Superfamily: Neritacea Rafinesque, 1815
Family: NERITIDAE Rafinesque, 1815
Species: *Nerita peloronta* Linné, 1758
Common Name: Bleeding Tooth
Size: 2 inches (50 mm)
Distribution: Bermuda, Florida, Bahamas, Caribbean

Nerita peloronta is distinguished from the other three species of *Nerita* in the Western Atlantic by the reddish orange blotch in the center of the parietal area. The shell has zigzags of black and red, and rounded spiral cords

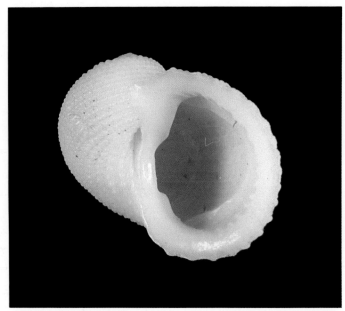

Neritopsis atlantica

Family: NERITOPSIDAE Gray, 1847
Species: *Neritopsis atlantica* Sarasua, 1973
Common Name: Atlantic Neritopsis
Size: 0.5 inches (12 mm)
Distribution: Cuba

There are only two living species in the family Neritopsidae: a common Indo-Pacific species, *Neritopsis radula* (Linné, 1758), which has been known for more than 200 years, and a rare, Western Atlantic species that was not discovered until the 1970s and then received two names in two years. A Cuban scientist named the species *Neritopsis atlantica* in 1973; the next year an American researcher working independently named it *Neritopsis finlayi* Hoerle, 1974, because the Cuban publication was not yet available to him. The dearth of neritopsids in the recent fauna belies their past diversity, with an extensive fossil record reaching to the Middle Devonian. Neritopsids have a distinctive notch in the columella that allows them to be easily separated from neritids and vanikorids. The heavy, calcareous, somewhat trapezoidal operculum has a projection that fits into this notch. Unlike the neritids, the inner walls of the whorls are not reabsorbed and, therefore, the spire in adult shells is not hollow.

References: Hoerle (1974), Moore (1960).

. . . .

Family: PHENACOLEPADIDAE Thiele, 1929
Species: *Phenacolepas crenulata* (Broderip, 1834)
Common Name: Crenulate Phenacolepas
Size: 0.6 inches (16 mm)
Distribution: Tropical Indo-Pacific

Phenacolepas crenulata is one of the largest members of its genus. It has strong radial and concentric ribs, with raised nodes at the intersections. The number of radial ribs increases with shell growth by the introduction of new ribs between the old. The animal lives among rocks intertidally and in depths to 50 feet (15 meters). The shell margin is somewhat concave, suggesting that the animal cannot tightly seal to the surface upon which it lives, unlike the patellogastropod limpets. There are only about twenty species of phenacolepadids, all having white or brownish white porcelaneous, limpetlike shells. The muscle scar is horseshoe-shaped and opens anteriorly as in the patellogastropods, but the apex is at the posterior end of the shell, rather than being central or

anterior, and curves posteriorly as well. The operculum is greatly reduced and imbedded in the foot. *Phenacolepas* is not known as a fossil, but the only other genus in the family, *Plesiothyreus*, with one living species, dates from the Eocene.

References: Fretter (1984), Moore (1960).

. . . .

Phenacolepas crenulata

Order: Neomphalida Haszprunar, 1988
Superfamily: Neomphalacea McLean, 1981
Family: NEOMPHALIDAE McLean, 1981
Species: *Neomphalus fretterae* McLean, 1981
Common Name: Rift Limpet
Size: 1.2 inches (30 mm)
Distribution: Galapagos Rift

Neomphalus fretterae was discovered at the Galapagos deep-sea rifts in 1977 by researchers on the submersible research vessel ALVIN. The animals live on lava rocks and on the large tube worm *Riftia* at the hydrothermal vents in depths around 8,000 feet (2,500 meters). The shell has a periostracum and is porcelaneous internally. The body whorl of the shell is greatly expanded and limpetlike, but the initial coiled whorls can still be seen at the apex. *Neomphalus* has developed independently from but has similar characteristics to members of the Calyptraeidae. They

Neomphalus fretterae (paratype)

have a similar shell shape and an interior shell ridge; both *Neomphalus* and calyptraeids use the gill for filter feeding. Two additional neomphalid genera from Eastern Pacific hydrothermal vents were named in 1989, *Cyathermia* and *Lacunoides*. These have coiled, rather than limpetlike shells. Since the discovery of Neomphalidae, six other new families of gastropods have been found at hydrothermal vents: Lepetodrilidae, Gorgoleptidae, Peltospiridae, Neolepetopsidae, Pyropeltidae, and Clypeosectidae. In contrast, new species of bivalves discovered at the vents have all been readily classified in known families; many are mytilids or vesicomyids.

References: Fretter et al. (1981), McLean (1981), Warén & Bouchet (1989).

. . . .

Order: Vetigastropoda Salvini-Plawén, 1980
Superfamily: Pleurotomariacea Swainson, 1840
Family: PLEUROTOMARIIDAE Swainson, 1840
Species: *Mikadotrochus hirasei* (Pilsbry, 1903)
Common Name: Emperor's Slit Shell
Size: 4 inches (100 mm)
Distribution: Japan and the Philippines

Slit shells are highly desired collector's items; most species are rare and known from only a few specimens. *Mikadotrochus hirasei* is one of the most common species; it lives at depths of 430 to 600 feet (130 to 180 meters). Its common name honors Emperor Hirohito of Japan, who was a skilled marine biologist. It is similar to another Japanese species, *Mikadotrochus beyrichii* (Hilgendorf, 1877), but differs in having finer sculpture and a longer slit situated higher on the body whorl. The operculum is multispiral, corneous, and is too small to fill the aperture. In contrast, in some species, such as *Entemnotrochus rumphii* (Schepman, 1879), the operculum does fill the aperture.

Pleurotomariids have broad-based shells with nacreous interiors; a slit extends from the aperture one-tenth to one-half around the body whorl. As the shell grows, the slit is filled in from the rear, leaving a characteristic trace called the *selenizone.* The base of the slit lies over the

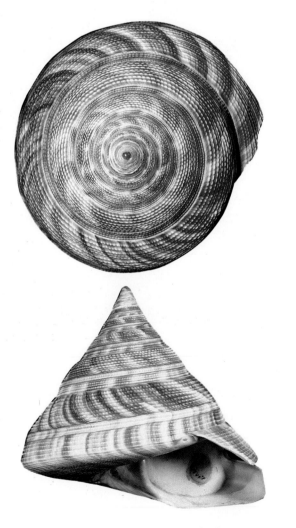

Mikadotrochus hirasei

excretory and reproductive openings. More than twenty species of pleurotomariids are known, more than half of which have been discovered since 1960. Pleurotomariids are highly specialized predators on sponges and not evolutionary relics as has often been assumed. The family was thought to be extinct until the discovery in 1855 in the French West Indies of *Perotrochus quoyanus* (Fischer & Bernardi, 1856). The superfamily Pleurotomariacea is one of the oldest groups of gastropods, with an extensive fossil record dating back to the Upper Cambrian. Many of the living species were named in the genus *Pleurotomaria,* which is now considered to have gone extinct by the end of the Cretaceous. Three living genera are recognized, *Entemnotrochus, Mikadotrochus,* and *Perotrochus,* although these are placed as subgenera of *Pleurotomaria* by some researchers. Pleurotomariids range in size from 2 to 9 inches (50 to 230 millimeters) and occur in the Western Atlantic and Indo-Pacific in depths from 330 to 3,000 feet (100 to 900 meters).

References: Abbott (1972), Harasewych et al. (1988), Moore (1960).

. . . .

Family: SCISSURELLIDAE Gray, 1847
Species: *Anatoma regia* (Mestayer, 1916)
Common Name: Regal Scissurella
Size: 0.1 inches (3 mm)
Distribution: New Zealand

Anatoma regia differs from the similar *Anatoma mantelli* (Woodward, 1859) in having a lower spire and finer axial sculpture. It is sometimes placed in the genus *Schizotrochus,* a synonym of *Anatoma.* It occurs in depths of 300 to 500 feet (90 to 160 meters). There are perhaps sixty species of scissurellids known worldwide; most are less than 0.2 inches (5 millimeters) in length.

Most scissurellids resemble miniature white slit shells, but a few deep-sea forms are limpetlike. The slit is sometimes closed off at the aperture of the shell, forming a circular or elongate hole; the selenizone formed by shell growth filling in the slit is often keeled. The shell is porcelaneous except for a thin interior nacreous layer.

Most species have axial and spiral sculpture; in some the axial ribs are quite pronounced. The operculum is round and multispiral. Scissurellids range from intertidal to abyssal, occurring in depths of up to 7,000 feet (2,200 meters). Some species live and feed on algae. The oldest known scissurellid fossils are Upper Cretaceous, but the group presumably originated during the Paleozoic. Eight genera are recognized in the family: *Scissurella, Anatoma, Incisura, Sinezona, Sukashitrochus, Sutilizona, Temnocinclis,* and *Temnozaga.* The last three were recently discovered at deep-sea hydrothermal vents in the Eastern Pacific.

References: Haszprunar (1988), Herbert (1986), McLean (1989), Powell (1979), Schirò (1986).

. . . .

Anatoma regia

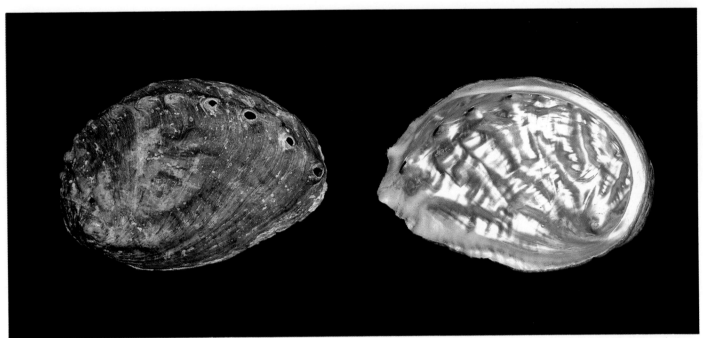

Haliotis kamtschatkana

Family: HALIOTIDAE Rafinesque, 1815
Species: *Haliotis kamtschatkana* Jonas, 1845
Common Name: Pinto Abalone
Size: 5 inches (130 mm)
Distribution: Japan to California

Haliotis kamtschatkana is one of the smaller of the eight species of abalone that occur in California. In the southern part of its range it lives at depths of 20 to 50 feet (6 to 15 meters), but north of Washington it can be found on intertidal rocks. *Haliotis assimilis* Dall, 1878 was formerly considered a southern subspecies of *H. kamtschatkana,* but is now considered a distinct species that replaces it south of Point Conception, California. *Haliotis kamtschatkana* lacks the distinct corded sculpture of and has a straighter growing edge than does *H. assimilis,* and is thus not as ovate.

Abalones are also known as ormers, a contraction from the French *oreille-de-mer* (sea ear). The shell is spirally coiled, but greatly flattened, with a large body whorl in which there is a series of holes. These holes correspond to the slit in pleurotomariids and scissurellids, allowing water to exit the mantle cavity. As the shell grows, the holes are closed off, with only the four to nine nearest the aperture remaining open. As with other limpetlike forms, abalones lack opercula. The interior of the shell is nacreous and often strongly iridescent. Abalones have separate sexes; fertilization is external, and there is a short planktonic larval stage. Most species graze on vegetation intertidally or in shallow water, but some occur in depths as great as 650 feet (200 meters). There are about seventy species worldwide, mostly in the Indian and Pacific Oceans, all currently placed in the genus *Haliotis.* Many species are economically important and are harvested commercially; they are used as food and in making jewelry.

References: Howorth (1978), Owen et al. (1971).

. . . .

Superfamily: Fissurellacea Fleming, 1822
Family: FISSURELLIDAE Fleming, 1822
Species: *Fissurella picta* (Gmelin, 1791)
Common Name: Painted Keyhole Limpet
Size: 4 inches (100 mm)
Distribution: Southern Chile and Argentina

Fissurella picta has sculpture of narrow radial ribs, with primary ribs that are stronger than the secondary and tertiary ribs between them. The ground color of the shell is white; rays of black or dark red highlight some of the

Fissurella picta

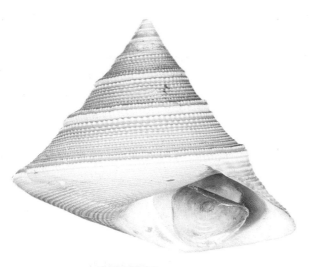

Calliostoma scotti

ribs so that the shell has regular radial stripes. The interior is white and the keyhole is elongate or oval. The species lives on hard substrata in the middle to lower intertidal zone. Thirteen species of *Fissurella* occur in Chile, twelve of which have overlapping ranges in the central coast of the country. All these species are used as food in Chile, where they are known as "lapas." The Patagonian fissurellids are unusually large; most fissurellids are less than 2 inches (50 millimeters) in length.

Fissurellids have a dorsal foramen (the "keyhole") or an anterior notch through which water is expelled after passing through the mantle cavity. The interior of the shell is porcelaneous, with a horseshoe-shaped muscle scar that opens anteriorly. The exterior usually has radial ribs and often has concentric sculpture. The protoconch is spiral, but is often eroded away, or is obliterated by the keyhole, which expands as the animal grows. This expansion is accomplished by reabsorption of shell material by mantle tissue at the border of the hole. The family contains about thirty genera and several hundred species worldwide. In some instances, the animal is bizarre: *Medusafissurella* has a mass of tentacles on either side of the head, and *Buchanania onchidioides* Lesson, 1830 lacks a shell, thereby resembling the marine slug *Onchidium*. Most fissurellids are herbivores, but some *Emarginula* and *Diodora* are known to feed on sponges. The fossil record of fissurellids dates from the Middle Triassic, although it has been proposed that they are derived from the Paleozoic bellerophontaceans.

Reference: McLean (1984).

. . . .

Superfamily: Trochacea Rafinesque, 1815
Family: TROCHIDAE Rafinesque, 1815
Subfamily: Calliostomatinae
Species: *Calliostoma scotti* Kilburn, 1973
Common Name: Scott's Top
Size: 1.3 inches (34 mm)
Distribution: South Africa and Mozambique

Calliostoma scotti has notably concave spire whorls and a convex base. Despite the beaded sculpture on the spiral cords, the surface of the shell has a silky iridescence.

There are nine teleoconch whorls; the number of spiral cords increases on each whorl by the introduction of new cords between existing ones, so that on the body whorl there are thirteen to sixteen cords. The cord at the base is stronger than the others. The species resembles *Calliostoma formosense* E. A. Smith, 1907, which differs in having flat-sided whorls and a less convex base. *Calliostoma scotti*, which occurs in depths of 1,400 to 1,800 feet (420 to 550 meters), is placed in the subgenus *Kombologion*, which has its highest diversity in deep water in the Western Atlantic.

Calliostomatinae includes the genera *Astele, Calliostoma, Maurea, Otukaia, Photinula, Venustatrochus* and about thirty subgenera. There are more than 200 species worldwide, occurring in all oceans and from the intertidal zone to the deep sea. They usually live near their invertebrate prey, which includes soft corals, sponges, and tunicates. When feeding, some rear up on the back of the foot and lunge at their prey. A characteristic feature of the subfamily is the honeycombed or netlike protoconch sculpture. The oldest undoubted calliostomatine fossils are from the Upper Cretaceous.

References: Clench & Turner (1960), Hickman & McLean (1990).

. . . .

Stomatella auricula

Subfamily: Stomatellinae Gray, 1840
Species: *Stomatella auricula* Lamarck, 1816
Common Name: Ear-shaped Stomatella
Size: 0.7 inches (18 mm)
Distribution: Tropical Indo-Pacific

The initial whorls of *Stomatella auricula* are relatively circular, but the last whorl is greatly expanded and elongate. Sculpture on the initial whorls consists of spiral cords, but these are lost on the body whorl, which has numerous axial growth lines. The shell is variable in color, ranging from cream to black, with spots and stripes of green, pink, or white. The aperture is nacreous. The species lives under rocks on coral reefs intertidally and in depths to 50 feet (15 meters).

Stomatellines have low-spired shells with large apertures; genera include *Microtis, Pseudostomatella, Stomatella*, and *Stomatia*. They lack an operculum and shed the posterior part of the foot when disturbed, a process known as autotomy. They are similar to *Granata* and *Hybochelus*, members of the trochid subfamily Eucyclinae, which have an operculum and more beaded sculpture. The oldest known fossils are from Pliocene deposits on Pacific Islands.

References: Cernohorsky (1972), Hickman and McLean (1990).

. . . .

Subfamily: Trochinae Rafinesque, 1815
Species: *Clanculus pharaonius* (Linné, 1758)
Common Name: Strawberry Top
Size: 1 inch (25 mm)
Distribution: Arabian Peninsula

Clanculus pharaonius is often confused with *C. puniceus* (Philippi, 1846), with which it co-occurs, but which also ranges down the East African coast as far south as Natal. *Clanculus pharaonius* has seventeen to nineteen beaded cords on the body whorl. Six or seven of the cords have alternating white and black beads; the remaining cords are red. *Clanculus puniceus* has twenty-two to twenty-eight beaded cords on the body whorl, two to five of which have black beads with one to three (usually two) white beads in between; there are also several cords with some white but no black beads. In both species, the ends of the cords are marked with black at the aperture. *Clanculus pharaonius* live under rocks and coral rubble in shallow water, often occurring in clusters. Young individuals are reported to frequent the umbilicus of adults.

Well-known genera in the subfamily Trochinae include *Cantharidus, Clanculus, Cittarium, Diloma, Gib-*

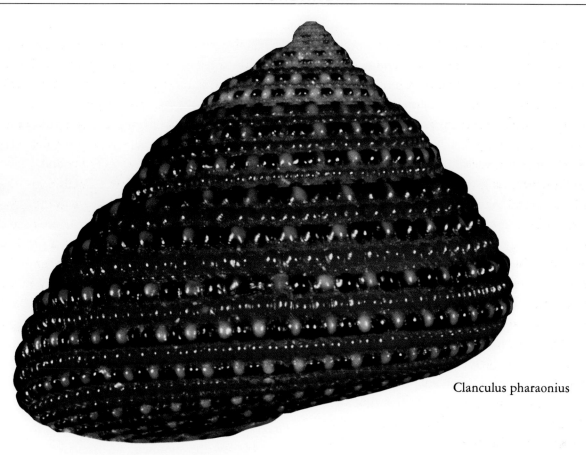

Clanculus pharaonius

bula, Jujubinus, Monodonta, Tectus, Thalotia, and *Trochus.* There are several hundred species worldwide in the tropical and semitropical Indo-Pacific and Eastern Atlantic. There are no Eastern Pacific trochines; species of the genera *Agathistoma, Chlorostoma, Norrisia,* and *Tegula* are now placed in the Tegulinae. *Cittarium pica* (Linné, 1758) is the only Western Atlantic trochine. Most trochines live in the intertidal to shallow subtidal zones on hard surfaces, but some, such as *Cantharidus,* live on sea grass or macroalgae. The oldest known members of the group occur in Middle Triassic rocks.

References: Bosch & Bosch (1982, 1989), Hickman & McLean (1990), Sharabati (1981).

. . . .

Family: TURBINIDAE Rafinesque, 1815
Subfamily: Turbininae Rafinesque, 1815
Species: *Turbo petholatus* Linné, 1758
Common Name: Tapestry Turban
Size: 3 inches (75 mm)
Distribution: Tropical Indo-Pacific

The aptly named Tapestry Turban has complex coloration. Typically the shell is brown with paler blotches or streaks; this pattern is overlain by dark green spiral bands dashed with numerous lighter-colored stripes.

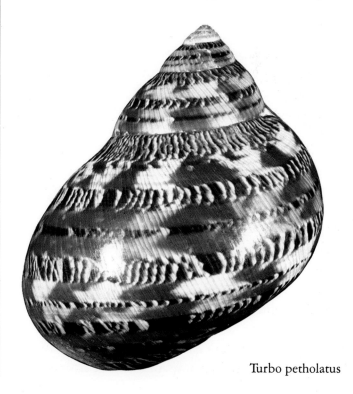

Turbo petholatus

Less frequently, specimens may be primarily orange, green, or tan, or covered with fine white zigzags. The shell is shiny but in some specimens is not totally smooth because of the regularly spaced axial growth lines, of which there can be more than 120 on the body whorl. The aperture is circular and nacreous. The operculum, sometimes called a "cat's eye" in this species, is calcareous, thick, and shiny. Usually it is bluish green at the center and brown toward the margins, except along the growing edge, where it is white. The species lives intertidally on tropical coral reefs.

Calcification of the operculum has previously been used to distinguish the turbinids (turban shells) from the trochids (top shells). This criterion does not hold up, however, because Angariinae and Liotiinae do not have calcified opercula, but have turbinid anatomy. Another opercular feature does help in distinguishing the families: the growing edge of the operculum is long in turbinids but short in trochids. Even though angariines and liotiines have multispiral opercula like those of the trochids, the growing edge is angled so that it is much longer than the width of the whorl. The subfamily Turbininae includes about twenty-five extant genera and subgenera, including *Astraea, Astralium, Bolma, Guildfordia, Lithopoma,* and *Turbo;* members occur worldwide in tropical and subtropical seas, primarily on hard substrata. The oldest unquestioned turbinine fossils are Upper Cretaceous.

References: Beu & Ponder (1979), Hickman & McLean (1990).

. . . .

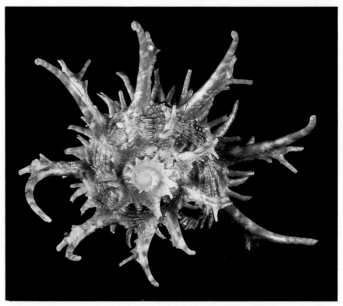

Angaria vicdani

extraordinary length among the mollusks, rivaled only by the spines of some *Guildfordia, Murex, Spondylus,* and *Pitar* species. There are seven to nine rows of short spines below the shoulder. As discussed above, despite being turbinids, *Angaria* have a horny operculum. The shell has a nacreous interior. *Angaria* is the only living genus in the subfamily Angariinae, which has a fossil record extending to the Upper Triassic. There are only a few living species, all in the tropical Indo-Pacific and all restricted to rock and coral substrata.

Reference: Hickman & McLean (1990).

. . . .

Subfamily: Angariinae Thiele, 1921
Species: *Angaria vicdani* Kosuge, 1980
Common Name: Victor Dan's Delphinula
Size: 3 inches (75 mm)
Distribution: Philippines

Angaria vicdani is one of many new species discovered in the Philippines since the 1970s with the advent of the commercial collection of mollusks by use of tangle nets set in deep water. The whorls bear spectacular curved spines at the shoulder; those on the body whorl are of

Subfamily: Liotiinae Adams & Adams, 1854
Species: *Arene cruentata* (Megerle von Mühlfeld, 1824)
Common Name: Star Arene
Size: 0.6 inches (16 mm)
Distribution: Florida, Bahamas, and Caribbean

Arene cruentata has complex sculpture best appreciated under magnification. There are strong, hollow, triangular spines at the shoulder, with two rows of smaller, more closely spaced spines beneath. Above the shoulder are rounded, regularly spaced axial ribs, which can number seventy or eighty on the body whorl of a large specimen. Five to ten fine axial ridges are visible between and sometimes on the ribs. The color pattern consists of pink or brown blotches above the shoulders of the whorls. The species lives under rocks intertidally and to depths of 12 feet (4 meters).

Liotiines characteristically have a thickened lip around the aperture and strong sculpture. The axial sculpture consists of fine incremental ridges and more widely spaced axial ribs. The corneous, multispiral operculum has calcareous granules aligned radially on each whorl. The shell is non-nacreous. Genera include *Arene, Cyclostrema, Dentarene, Liotia, Liotina,* and *Macrarene.* This is the oldest group among the Trochacea; the earliest fossils are from the Permian. Liotiines occur worldwide in tropical and temperate seas, except for the Mediterranean and northeastern Atlantic. The family name Cyclostrematidae is a synonym of Liotiinae. Many species that have been called cyclostrematids actually belong in the Skeneidae.

Reference: Hickman & McLean (1990).

. . . .

Subfamily: Phasianellinae Swainson, 1840
Species: *Phasianella australis* (Gmelin, 1791)
Common Name: Australian Pheasant Shell
Size: 2.5 inches (60 mm)
Distribution: Southern Australia and Tasmania

Phasianella australis has a highly variable color pattern. The ground color of the shell is usually light—beige, tan, pink, or yellowish—with darker axial zones that are brown, greenish, or slate gray. These are interrupted by lighter spiral lines or bands (ten to thirteen on the body whorl) that contain pink flammules. The operculum is white and calcareous. The animals live among seaweed on reefs, usually below the low-tide level. They feed on seaweed and on detritus and foraminifera in its surface.

Shells of members of the Phasianellinae and the related subfamily Tricoliinae can be difficult to tell apart, as both lack interior nacre and are usually smooth and glossy with complex color patterns. Phasianellines, particularly juveniles, which are most likely to be confused with the tricoliines, have spiral lines that interrupt the axial color pattern. These lines are lacking in tri-

coliines. Under mixed wavelength ultraviolet light, tricoliines fluoresce with a red glow, whereas phasianellines do not fluoresce. Fluorescence has been observed in Eocene *Tricolia.* The oldest known phasianellines are from the Miocene of Java and Australia.

References: Coleman (1975), Hickman & McLean (1990), Robertson (1958, 1985).

. . . .

Arene cruentata

Phasianella australis

Family: SKENEIDAE Clark, 1851
Species: *Haplocochlias swifti* Vanatta, 1913
Common Name: Swift's Haplocochlias
Size: 0.2 inches (5 mm)
Distribution: Florida, Bahamas, and Caribbean

Haplocochlias swifti is one of the largest known skeneids. It has four strong spiral cords—one at the shoulder, one at the periphery, and two in between—and numerous weaker cords. Between the cords are many fine, forward-leaning axial lines. The umbilicus is broad and bounded by a spiral cord. The species lives under rocks and dead shells intertidally and to depths of 80 feet (25 meters).

Skeneidae is a large, cosmopolitan family represented mainly in deep water. The shell is non-nacreous, sometimes has a thickened apertural lip, and is rarely higher than wide; the operculum is horny and multispiral. The largest members of the group do not exceed 0.25 inches (6 millimeters) in length. Genera found in shallow water include *Haplocochlias, Parviturbo,* and *Skenea.* Some of the deep-water genera, such as *Dillwynella,* live on decaying wood along with cocculiniform limpets and xylophagaid bivalves.

References: Hickman & McLean (1990), Marshall (1988).

. . . .

Haplocochlias swifti

Seguenzia nitida

Order: Seguenziida Haszprunar, 1988
Superfamily: Seguenziacea Verrill, 1884
Family: SEGUENZIIDAE Verrill, 1884
Species: *Seguenzia nitida* Verrill, 1884
Common Name: Glossy Seguenzia
Size: 0.14 inches (3.5 mm)
Distribution: Northwestern Atlantic

Seguenzia nitida was described as a variety of *Seguenzia formosa* (Jeffreys, 1876) from the northeastern Atlantic, and it may prove to be the same species. The body whorl has eleven sharp spiral cords, the eight on the base being weaker than those at the periphery and above. There are fine spiral lines between the cords. The aperture is sinuous, which is shown in the curvature of the axial lamellae. The species has been dredged at depths of 11,000 to 12,000 feet (3,300 to 3,700 meters).

Few species of seguenziids live in depths of less than 1,000 feet (300 meters) and the greatest diversity of the family is below 3,000 feet (1,000 meters). Species are thought to feed on detritus; most are smaller than 0.3 inches (8 millimeters). There are fifteen genera including *Ancistrobasis, Basilissa,* and *Seguenzia* and about seventy-five extant species. The family occurs in all oceans. Seguenziids resemble trochaceans and have nacreous shells, but unlike trochaceans have penises. There are usually two or three sinuses in the outer lip;

the operculum is corneous and paucispiral. Seguenziids are probably derived from trochacean ancestors, but the fossil record gives no evidence of this; the oldest known seguenziids are from the Eocene.

References: Marshall (1983), Quinn (1983, 1987).

. . . .

Abyssochrysos melanioides

Order: Caenogastropoda Cox, 1959
Suborder: Neotaenioglossa Haller, 1882
Infraorder: Discopoda Fischer, 1884
Superfamily: Loxonematacea Koken, 1889
Family: ABYSSOCHRYSIDAE Tomlin, 1927
Species: *Abyssochrysos melanioides* Tomlin, 1927
Common Name: Melanioid Abyssal Snail
Size: 2 inches (50 mm)
Distribution: South Africa

Abyssochrysos is the only genus in its family, and only two species are known, *A. melanioides* and *A. melvilli* (Schepman, 1909). Both species occur off South Africa, and *A. melvilli* is also found in the Philippines and Indonesia. *Abyssochrysos melvilli* differs from *A. melanioides* ("melanoides" is a frequent misspelling) in being more slender and having nodules at the tops and bottoms of the axial ribs. *Abyssochrysos* are blind, living in depths of 1,600 to 9,000 feet (500 to 2,700 meters) on muddy or sandy bottoms. They are probably deposit feeders. The classification of the Abyssochrysidae has been controversial. Some authors, noting the presence of a penis, have excluded it from the Cerithiacea. They opt instead to ally it, on the basis of shell morphology, with the Loxonematacea, a group thought otherwise to have gone extinct in the Upper Jurassic. Others have stated that the so-called penis is actually a pallial tentacle, and that relationships with Cerithiacea should be re-evaluated.

References: Houbrick (1979), Ponder and Warén (1988).

. . . .

Superfamily: Campanilacea Douvillé, 1904
Family: CAMPANILIDAE Douvillé, 1904
Species: *Campanile symbolicum* Iredale, 1917
Common Name: Bell Clapper
Size: 9.5 inches (240 mm)
Distribution: Southwestern Australia

Campanile symbolicum is the only living member of the family Campanilidae, which first appears in the fossil record in the late Cretaceous and was abundant in the Paleocene and Eocene. It has a high-spired, chalky shell. The sculpture is usually obscured by erosion and the shell often has scars from the attachment of hipponicid gastropods. The operculum is brown, corneous, and paucispiral. *Campanile symbolicum* reaches almost 10 inches (250 millimeters) in length, but is dwarfed by some Eocene campanilids that could be as long as 3 feet (0.9 meters). Judging by the habits of the living species, campanilids were herbivores in shallow, sandy subtidal flats. It is possible that their decline is due to competition with the strombids, which are also grazers in shal-

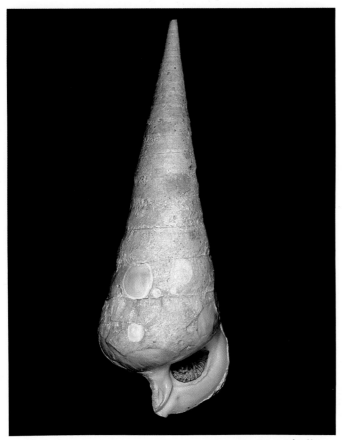

Campanile symbolicum

low, sandy areas, and which began diversifying in the late Eocene. Campanilids resemble some cerithiids in shell form, but differ in having a calcified periostracum, lacking a glassy capsule around the eggs and in a variety of anatomical features.

References: Haszprunar (1988), Houbrick (1981, 1988).

. . . .

Superfamily: Cerithiacea Férussac, 1819
Family: DIASTOMATIDAE Cossmann, 1893
Species: *Diastoma melanioides* (Reeve, 1849)
Common Name: Melanioid Diastoma
Size: 2 inches (50 mm)
Distribution: South Australia

Diastoma melanioides is the only living member of the Diastomatidae, fossil species of which are known from Paleocene through Pleistocene. It has a high-spired shell of ten to thirteen whorls with spiral cords and slanting axial ribs. The shell resembles that of some members of the freshwater family Thiaridae, and it is possible that early diastomatids gave rise to the thiarids. The periostracum is thin and tan in color; it appears fuzzy because of rows of tiny projecting hairs corresponding in position to the underlying spiral sculpture. The operculum is dark brown, corneous, ovate, and paucispiral. Living animals burrow in sandy bottoms and feed on algae and detritus in shallow water. Because of historical misunderstandings of the limits of the family, many species and genera have been erroneously assigned to the Diastomatidae, including *Alaba, Alabina, Diala, Finella, Scaliola,* and some *Bittium* species. These are now placed in various families including Litiopidae, Dialidae, Obtortionidae, Scaliolidae, and Cerithiidae.

References: Houbrick (1981, 1988).

. . . .

Family: DIALIDAE Ludbrook, 1941
Species: *Diala flammea* (Pease, 1868)
Common Name: Flame Diala
Size: 0.1 inches (3 mm)
Distribution: Tropical Indo-Pacific

The shell of *Diala flammea* has seven or eight teleoconch whorls and does not have an umbilicus. There are numerous alternating brown and white spiral lines interrupted by white streaks originating from the suture. Some specimens have spiral rows of white dots at the suture and periphery, those at the suture being partially hidden by the white streaks. The species is abundant, and can be the dominant micromollusk in patch reefs in tropical lagoons, where it lives in mats of red algae and in floating brown algae. It can occur at densities as high as ten individuals per cubic centimeter. Some researchers have placed *Diala* with *Litiopa* and *Alaba* in Litiopidae, but it lacks tentacles on the side of the foot and axial ribs on the protoconch. Diala have been recorded as Miocene fossils on some Pacific islands.

References: Kay & Switzer (1974), Luque et al. (1988), Ponder (1985).

. . . .

Diastoma melanioides

Litiopa melanostoma

Family: LITIOPIDAE Gray, 1847
Species: *Litiopa melanostoma* Rang, 1829
Common Name: Sargassum Snail
Size: 0.25 inches (6 mm)
Distribution: Tropical Atlantic

Litiopa melanostoma leads a pelagic existence, living and feeding in the open sea on floating seaweed, to which it attaches by means of threads of mucus. The shell ranges from white to brown; in lighter colored specimens there are brown spots below the suture and sometimes a row of similar spots at the periphery of the body whorl. Some researchers consider the species to be circumtropical. The only other genus that has been confidently assigned to Litiopidae is *Alaba*, which lives on filamentous algae. Both *Litiopa* and *Alaba* have a gland in the base of the foot that produces anchoring threads of mucus that prevent dislodgement. Litiopids have strongly ribbed protoconchs with 3.5 to 4 whorls. They differ from other cerithiaceans in having long tapering tentacles on the hind part of the foot. The operculum is corneous and paucispiral. About forty species have been named in *Alaba* or *Litiopa*, but few of these have been studied, and the true diversity of the group is unknown. The family is circumtropical in distribution and dates from the Eocene.

References: Houbrick (1987), Luque et al. (1988).

· · · · · · · · · · · · ·

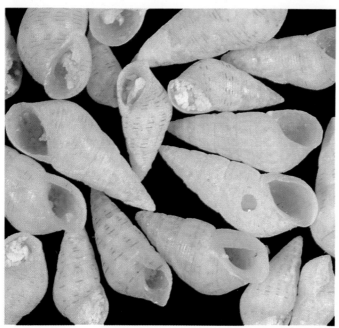

Diala flammea

Finella dubia

Family: OBTORTIONIDAE Thiele, 1925
Species: *Finella dubia* (d'Orbigny, 1842)
Common Name: Dubious Finella
Size: 0.1 inches (3 mm)
Distribution: Bermuda to Brazil

Finella dubia is a common micromollusk that lives on various types of algae subtidally to depths of 100 feet (30 meters). Specimens range from white to brown, or occasionally are spirally banded with these colors. The shell has three smooth protoconch whorls and six to seven teleoconch whorls. The first few teleoconch whorls are angular in outline due to strong peripheral ridges; later whorls are rounded. There are twenty to thirty-five curved axial ribs on the body whorl; occasionally a few ribs are swollen into rounded varices. The body whorl has twelve to fourteen spiral cords. There are perhaps a dozen species of *Finella* worldwide; *Obtortio* is a synonym. Because the family was first named Obtortionidae, it goes by that name rather than the later Finellidae.

References: Ponder (1985), Ponder & Warén (1988).

. . . .

Family: SCALIOLIDAE Iredale & McMichael, 1962
Species: *Scaliola glareosa* A. Adams, 1862
Common Name: Gravelly Scaliola
Size: 0.1 inches (3 mm)
Distribution: Tropical Indo-Pacific

Scaliolids are unusual in that they cement grains of sand to their shells in the manner that xenophorids attach shells and stones. In *Scaliola glareosa* the shell, which is white, can be completely obscured by the attached sand. It differs from *Scaliola bella* A. Adams, 1860 in having a narrower shell. *Scaliola gracilis* A. Adams, 1862 is distinguished in attaching fewer sand grains and having a partly detached body whorl. Scaliolids can be abundant in sediments at depths from 3 to 60 feet (1 to 20 meters) in the Indo-Pacific. They have high-spired shells with round apertures; usually the first protoconch whorl is smooth, the second is axially ribbed, and the third has a single keel.

References: Kay (1979), Ponder & Warén (1988).

. . . .

Scaliola glareosa

Rhinoclavis sinensis

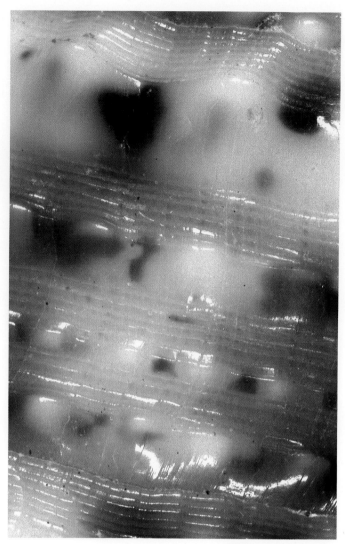

Rhinoclavis sinensis

Family: CERITHIIDAE Fleming, 1822
Species: *Rhinoclavis sinensis* (Gmelin, 1791)
Common Name: Obelisk Vertagus
Size: 3 inches (75 mm)
Distribution: Tropical Indo-Pacific

Rhinoclavis sinensis is the most widespread of the eleven Indo-Pacific *Rhinoclavis* species, ranging from South Africa and the Red Sea to Hawaii and the Tuamotus Archipelago. It has three or four nodular spiral cords per whorl. The shell is usually creamy white, mottled, and spotted with brown. Like other *Rhinoclavis,* it has a columellar fold and a siphonal canal that curves dorsally. The animals live from the intertidal to 75 feet (23 meters); they burrow in sandy patches on reef flats and in lagoons with sandy coral rubble bottoms and feed on algae.

Rhinoclavis obeliscus (Bruguière, 1792), the basis of the common name of this species, is a synonym.

Although most cerithiaceans have an anterior siphonal notch, the cerithiids (ceriths) are the only group with a pronounced siphonal canal. Cerithiids have ovate, paucispiral opercula, whereas cerithideids, potamidids, and batillariids have circular, multispiral ones. Cerithiid genera include *Argyropeza, Bittium, Cerithium, Clypeomorus, Fastigiella, Pseudovertagus,* and *Varicopeza;* there are several hundred species. Cerithiids occur in all oceans, mainly on soft bottoms from intertidal areas to the deep sea. The family has an extensive fossil record reaching at least to the late Cretaceous.

References: Houbrick (1974, 1978, 1985, 1988).

· · · · · · · · · · · · · ·

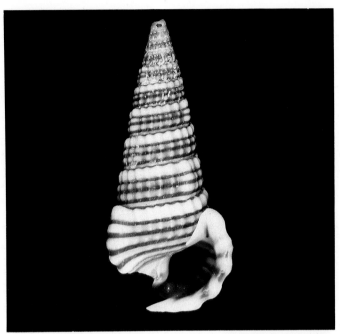

Cerithidea cingulata

Family: CERITHIDEIDAE Houbrick, 1988
Species: *Cerithidea cingulata* (Gmelin, 1791)
Common Name: Banded Horn Shell
Size: 2 inches (50 mm)
Distribution: Indian Ocean and Western Pacific

Cerithidea cingulata has a high-spired shell with eight to twelve whorls. The axial ribs are cut into nodules by deep spiral grooves and the outer lip of the aperture is flared. Members of the species live on intertidal sand and mud flats in mangrove swamps and estuaries. Large individuals occur farther upshore than small ones do. *Cerithidea* is the only genus in the Cerithideidae; *Cerithideopsis* and *Cerithideopsilla* are subgenera. Population densities as high as 11,500 individuals per square yard (13,800 per square meter) have been recorded for one species. The family is unusual in that members have a third eye on the siphon, in addition to the normal eyes on the tentacles. When the animal retracts into the shell, this third eye peers around the operculum from within the siphonal notch. The operculum is thin, corneous, round, and multispiral. The first fossil *Cerithidea* appeared in the Miocene. The Cerithideidae might also be ranked as a subfamily of Potamididae.

References: Houbrick (1984, 1988).

. . . .

Family: POTAMIDIDAE Adams & Adams, 1854
Species: *Tympanotonos fuscatus* (Linné, 1758)
Common Name: Dusky Creeper
Size: 3 inches (75 mm)
Distribution: Cape Verde Islands, Senegal to Angola

Tympanotonos fuscatus is relatively constant in color, with its uniform shades of brown, but is quite variable in sculpture. Some individuals have a row of heavy triangular spines on each whorl, while others have rows of smaller nodules. The latter form was formerly known as *Tympanotonos radula* (Linné, 1758), a synonym. ("Tympanotonus" and "Tympanotomus" are common misspellings.) Members of the species, like other potamidids, live in mangroves, mud flats, and estuaries, where they feed on detritus in the high intertidal zone. The family is most diverse in the tropical Indo-Pacific and is not represented in the Western Atlantic and Eastern Pacific (unless Cerithideidae is included as a subfamily). Living potamidid genera are *Pirenella, Pyrazus, Telescopium,* and *Terebralia; Potamides* is extinct. Potamidids differ from batillariids in the radular conformation, lacking denticles on the base of the central tooth, and in other anatomical features.

References: Bernard (1984), Houbrick (1988).

. . . .

Tympanotonos
fuscatus

Batillaria minima

Family: BATILLARIIDAE Thiele, 1929
Species: *Batillaria minima* (Gmelin, 1791)
Common Name: West Indian False Cerith
Size: 0.8 inches (20 mm)
Distribution: Bermuda to Brazil

Batillaria minima

Batillaria minima is a highly variable species. Color ranges from white and light gray to black; the shell is often spirally banded in black and white. The white bands sometimes contain a fine, spiral brown line; black areas can have white speckles. The sculpture is nodular, with spiral cords crossing strong axial ribs. Members of the species feed on detritus on tidal flats in mangroves and estuaries where they can live at densities of greater than 830 individuals per square yard (1,000 individuals per square meter). They resemble small cerithiids, but can be recognized by the lack of an extended siphonal canal and by the circular, paucispiral operculum. The family has recently been separated from the Potamididae on the basis of characteristics of the radula, spermatozoa, reproductive system, and other anatomical features. Batillariids are primarily temperate and subtropical in distribution, whereas potamidids are tropical. Genera include *Batillaria, Rhinocoryne,* and *Zeacumantus.*

References: Abbott (1974), Houbrick (1988).

· · · · · · · · · · · · ·

· 49 ·

Fossarus orbignyi

Planaxis sulcatus

Family: FOSSARIDAE Troschel, 1861
Species: *Fossarus orbignyi* Fischer, 1864
Common Name: Orbigny's Fossarus
Size: 0.1 inches (3 mm)
Distribution: Bermuda to Brazil

Fossarus orbignyi has a white, trochoid shell, with height about equal to width, and a tall, brown protoconch of about three whorls, with axial ribs and fine spiral cords. The teleoconch consists of about three whorls, with four strong spiral carinations. In between these are seven to nine spiral cords, which serrate the lip at the aperture. The shell is umbilicate, and there is no siphonal notch. The operculum is corneous, paucispiral, and has an excentric nucleus. The species lives in depths of 0 to 6 feet (0 to 1.8 meters) in algae on rocks. The fossarids were classified near the vanikorids and hipponicids until the recent discovery that they have a cephalic brood pouch like that of the planaxids. However, *Megalomphalus* and *Macromphalus* (and *Couthouyia,* a synonym) which have been placed in Fossaridae are actually vanikorids.

References: Boss (1982), Houbrick (1988), Ponder (1980), Warén & Bouchet (1988).

. . . .

Family: PLANAXIDAE Gray, 1850
Species: *Planaxis sulcatus* (Born, 1778)
Common Name: Sulcate Clusterwinkle
Size: 1.2 inches (30 mm)
Distribution: Tropical Indo-Pacific

Planaxis sulcatus occurs abundantly throughout the tropical Indo-Pacific in rocky, intertidal areas. It feeds on microalgae on hard substrata in the low to midtidal zone where surf action is low to moderate. These snails are conspicuous as they cluster together in crevices and depressions when exposed by the tide. The shell is solid and has heavy spiral cords. The color pattern consists of dark blotches and zigzags on a white background; occasionally specimens are entirely black. The periostracum is thin and brown; the operculum fills the aperture and is paucispiral with the nucleus near the base.

Planaxids occur worldwide on tropical seacoasts. The

family contains about twenty species in six genera: *Angiola, Fissilabia, Hinea, Holcostoma, Planaxis,* and *Supplanaxis.* (*Hinea* should not be confused with *Hinia,* a nassariid). Some species, including the Caribbean *Angiola lineata* (da Costa, 1778), have bioluminescent areas in the mantle, but it is not known if these serve for recognition of other members of the species or as warning to predators. Some planaxids resemble members of the family Littorinidae, but can be readily distinguished in having an anterior siphonal notch. As with most cerithiaceans, male planaxids lack a penis, whereas male littorinids are phallate. Eggs develop in a brood pouch in the head. In some cases the embryos hatch as planktonic larvae, in others they are retained in the brood pouch until the crawling stage. In some species females are larger than males.

Reference: Houbrick (1987).

. . . .

Family: MODULIDAE Fischer, 1884
Species: *Modulus modulus* (Linné, 1758)
Common Name: Atlantic Modulus
Size: 0.6 inches (16 mm)
Distribution: Bermuda to Brazil

Modulus modulus has a low-spired, trochoid shell of five to six whorls and a small fold on the columella. The protoconch consists of two whorls, which have thin spiral cords. The early teleoconch whorls are sharply angled, but the shell develops a more rounded profile as it grows. The shell is usually covered with algae. The operculum is corneous, round, and multispiral. The animal feeds primarily on minute algae attached to marine grasses. There are seven or eight species of *Modulus,* which is the only genus in the family. *Modulus* occurs worldwide in tropical and subtropical seas. The only other cerithiaceans with trochoid shells are the fossarids, which lack the columellar fold of *Modulus.* The columellar fold marks one side of the otherwise indistinct siphonal notch. Like the great majority of cerithiaceans, male modulids lack a penis.

Reference: Houbrick (1980).

. . . .

Modulus modulus

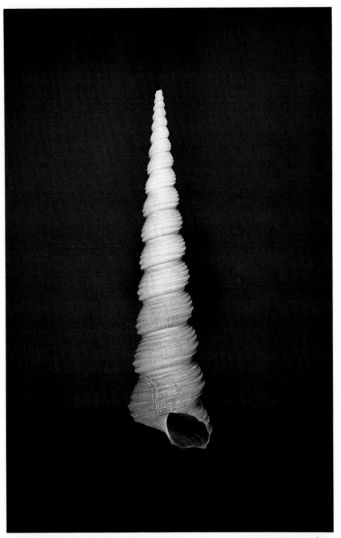

becomes increasingly rounded, with the first cord marking the periphery throughout. There can be as many as thirty whorls. The species lives in depths of 6 to 60 feet (2 to 20 meters) on soft bottoms.

Most turritellids are thought to be filter feeders, but some are also deposit feeders. They usually live in depths of 30 to 330 feet (10 to 100 meters), but range from intertidal to 5,000 feet (1,500 meters). Local population densities higher than 417 individuals per square yard (500 individuals per square meter) have been recorded. Some species brood eggs in the mantle cavity and release crawling juveniles; others lay egg masses that release planktonic larvae. There are probably more than 150 living species of turritellids, and more than 1,000 names have been given to fossil forms from the Mesozoic through the Pleistocene. Genera in the family include *Gazemeda, Haustator, Mesalia, Protoma, Turritella, Zeacolpus,* and *Vermicularia.* The last has a shell in which the later whorls are irregularly coiled and do not touch each other. Lack of a siphonal canal distinguishes turritellid shells from the superficially similar shells of some cerithiaceans and terebrids.

Reference: Allmon (1988).

. . . .

Turritella terebra

Superfamily: Turritellacea Lovén, 1847
Family: TURRITELLIDAE Lovén, 1847
Species: *Turritella terebra* (Linné, 1758)
Common Name: Screw Turritella
Size: 6 inches (150 mm)
Distribution: Burma and Taiwan to Australia

The early whorls of *Turritella terebra* differ markedly from the later ones. The protoconch is smooth and paucispiral; there is not a marked transition to the teleoconch. Initial sculpture consists of a single weak spiral cord which strengthens so that the whorls become sharply angled. About 1.5 to 2 whorls after the first cord appears, a second cord arises above it; after a similar interval, a third cord starts above that. Farther down the shell, additional cords arise above and below these three, and are introduced between them. As a result, the whorl profile

Family: SILIQUARIIDAE Anton, 1838
Species: *Siliquaria squamata* Blainville, 1827
Common Name: Scaly Slit Worm-shell
Size: 6 inches (150 mm)
Distribution: North Carolina to Brazil

Siliquaria squamata lives imbedded in sponge at depths from 80 to 2,000 feet (25 to 600 meters). The whorls are completely detached and irregularly coiled, with a slit running the length of the shell. The slit is smooth-edged when first formed, but its top margin becomes scalloped by ingrowing protuberances that give it the appearance of a series of connected holes. The slit is also closed off from within the initial whorls. The layer of shelly material that closes the slit lies below the scalloped margin. The slit easily differentiates siliquariids from vermetids and the turritellid *Vermicularia,* both of which have long irregularly coiled shells, but not all siliquariids have a slit: *Pyxipoma* and *Siliquaria* do, but *Stephopoma* do not. In

Vermicularia, the early whorls are regularly coiled, forming a high spire; in siliquariids if the early whorls are regularly coiled, they are low-spired.

References: Gould (1966), Morton (1971).

. . . .

Superfamily: Vermetacea Rafinesque, 1815
Family: VERMETIDAE Rafinesque, 1815
Species: *Petaloconchus innumerabilis* Pilsbry & Olsson, 1935
Common Name: Innumerable Worm-shell
Size: 4 inches (100 mm)
Distribution: Mexico to Peru

Petaloconchus innumerabilis live in dense colonies in which series of individuals coil in concert. Sometimes growth of the colony is so rapid that the snails have no time to coil, lest their apertures become buried within the colony. Vermetids are suspension feeders that capture food with mucous nets. Members of the family cement the shell to hard surfaces making themselves immobile. They can be solitary or colonial. In some species the foot is vestigial and the operculum lacking. The columellar muscle is long and straplike, allowing the animal to retract far into its shell. Many species inhabit the intertidal zone; the irregularly coiled shell conforms to the substratum allowing it to withstand wave action. Males lack a penis but have pelagic packets of sperm that enable internal fertilization. Embryos are brooded on the inner shell wall or free in the mantle cavity. In vermetids, the initial teleoconch whorls coil at right angles to the protoconch whorls, as in members of the order Heterostropha. Genera include *Dendropoma, Petaloconchus, Serpulorbis, Tripsycha,* and *Vermetus.* Vermetid shells that have lost the protoconch are often confused with the irregularly coiled tubes of annelid worms. They can be distinguished by the vermetids' three-layered shell that is glossy within, as opposed to the worms' two-layered shell that is dull within.

References: Houbrick (1988), Keen (1971), Morton (1971).

. . . .

Siliquaria squamata

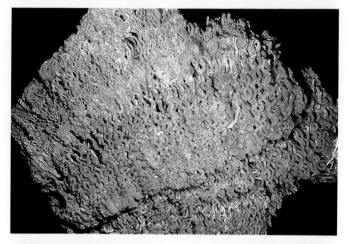

Petaloconchus innumerabilis (syntype)

Littoraria angulifera

Superfamily: Littorinacea Gray, 1840

Family: LITTORINIDAE Gray, 1840

Species: *Littoraria angulifera* (Lamarck, 1822)

Common Name: Angulate Periwinkle

Size: 1 inch (25 mm)

Distribution: Bermuda to Brazil, also West Africa

Littoraria angulifera typically lives well above the high-tide line on mangrove trees or pilings. Despite its supratidal habitat, it produces planktonic egg capsules and larvae, as do most littorinids. Some species of littorinids, mostly those at high latitudes, brood their young, releasing them at the crawling stage. Littorinids are commonly known as periwinkles or winkles. About 173 species are currently recognized worldwide; most live intertidally or supratidally. The family is defined anatomically in having a spiral pallial oviduct and an anterior bursa copulatrix. All species have spiral sculpture to some degree, although in some cases such as *Lacuna*, it is faint. Some have nodulose sculpture, such as

Cenchritis, Tectarius, and some *Nodilittorina.* Members of a few genera—*Bembicium, Peasiella,* and *Risellopsis*—have trochoid shells. The aperture is simple and lacks a siphonal notch. There are three subfamilies, Littorininae, Laevilitorininae, and Lacuninae. The operculum is corneous and can have few to many whorls. The oldest fossils attributed with certainty to the family date from the Upper Paleocene.

References: Abbott (1974), Reid (1986, 1989).

· · · · · · · · · · · · · ·

Family: SKENEOPSIDAE Iredale, 1915

Species: *Skeneopsis planorbis* (Fabricius, 1780)

Common Name: Flat Skeneopsis

Size: 0.06 inches (1.5 mm)

Distribution: Greenland to Florida and Iceland to the Azores

Skeneopsis planorbis lives on weeds in tide pools on the lower part of rocky shores, and subtidally to depths of

100 feet (30 meters), often among sponges and old oyster shells. The minute shell is disk-shaped with four whorls, brown periostracum, a round aperture, and a deep umbilicus. The operculum is circular and multispiral. Breeding can occur year-round, but is usually in the spring. Egg capsules are attached to filaments of algae; they measure about 0.016 inches (0.4 millimeters) and contain one or two eggs, which hatch at the crawling stage in three to four weeks. An abnormally left-handed form has been reported in the Eastern Atlantic. The systematic position of the Skeneopsidae is uncertain; it has been placed in both the Littorinacea and the Rissoacea. Only a few species are known.

References: Abbott (1974), Graham (1988), Ponder (1988).

. . . .

Skeneopsis planorbis

Superfamily: Cingulopsacea Fretter & Patil, 1958
Family: CINGULOPSIDAE Fretter & Patil, 1958
Species: *Eatonina pulicaria* (Fischer, 1873)
Common Name: Flealike Eatonina
Size: 0.04 inches (1 mm)
Distribution: Mauritius

Eatonina pulicaria has a distinctive color pattern that is not visible except under magnification. The minute shell is ovately conic, solid, smooth, and non-umbilicate. The animals live on algae and debris in partially exposed areas around the low-tide line.

There are about sixty species of cingulopsids in five genera: *Eatonina, Pickenia, Pseudopisanna, Skenella,* and *Tubbreva. Cingulopsis,* on which the family name is based, is a synonym of *Coriandria,* which is a subgenus of *Eatonina.* Species live worldwide in shallow water. Development is direct and the protoconch is paucispiral and virtually smooth. Cingulopsids are difficult to separate from rissoids and eatoniellids on the basis of shells alone, as some members of each group have smooth, ovate-conic shells. All three groups have an operculum with a lateral peg; distinctions are based on anatomical and radula characters. Because of the lack of distinctive characteristics allowing assignment of shells to Cingulopsidae, the fossil record of the group has been traced only to the Pliocene.

Reference: Ponder & Yoo (1980).

. . . .

Eatonina pulicaria

Eatoniella huttoni

Family: EATONIELLIDAE Ponder, 1965
Species: *Eatoniella huttoni* (Pilsbry, 1888)
Common Name: Hutton's Eatoniella
Size: 0.3 inches (8 mm)
Distribution: New Zealand

Eatoniella huttoni was first named *Rissoa flammulata* Hutton, 1878. Ten years later, H. A. Pilsbry transferred it to the genus *Phasianella,* where it was a junior homonym of *Phasianella flammulata* Philippi, 1848. Because two species in a genus cannot have the same name, Pilsbry renamed Hutton's species *Phasianella huttoni.* Although the species is no longer placed in *Phasianella,* the replacement name is still used in accordance with the rules of zoological nomenclature, which state that a name rejected as a junior secondary homonym (before 1961) cannot be used. The species was thought to be a phasianelline because of its striking color pattern and size; other eatoniellids are from 0.04 to 0.12 inches (1 to 3 millimeters) long.

There are about ninety species of eatoniellids known, placed in the genera *Crassitoniella, Eatoniella, Liratoniella,* and *Pupatonia.* Most are from southern Australia and New Zealand, where they are the dominant small algal dwelling mollusks. They feed on algae and detritus. Eatoniellids can be distinguished from littorinids in having a peg on the operculum and lacking a penis in males. Pha-

sianellids have a calcareous operculum without a peg, whereas the eatoniellid operculum is corneous.

References: Ponder & Yoo (1978), Powell (1979), Robertson (1985).

. . . .

Pisanna micronema (syntype)

Superfamily: Rissoacea Gray, 1847
Family: ANABATHRIDAE Coan, 1964
Species: *Pisanna micronema* (Suter, 1898)
Common Name: Finely Threaded Pisanna
Size: 0.1 inches (3 mm)
Distribution: New Zealand

Pisanna micronema is one of the more colorful species in the Anabathridae. Characteristically, it is purplish red on the spire and tan or yellowish white on the body whorl. Sculpture consists of numerous curved axial ribs and very fine spiral grooves. It lives in moderately deep water off southern New Zealand. Many other species of *Pisanna* live on algae or the undersides of rock or coral blocks in the lower intertidal zone.

The Anabathridae are worldwide in distribution; there are about 120 known species in eight genera, *Afriscrobs, Amphithalamus, Anabathron, Badepigrus, Microdryas, Nodulus, Pisanna,* and *Pseudestea.* Most of the species occur in Australia and New Zealand. The most common anabathrid in the eastern United States is the minute 0.04 inches (1 millimeter) *Amphithalamus vallei* Aguayo and Jaume, 1947, which can be collected in the Florida Keys on the red algae *Bostrychia* on intertidal rocks, mangrove roots, and pilings. Anabathridae was, until recently, classified as a subfamily of Barleeidae; they are known as fossils from the Oligocene.

References: Abbott (1974), Ponder (1983, 1988), Ponder & Yoo (1976).

. . . .

Family: BARLEEIDAE Gray, 1857
 **Species:** *Lirobarleeia kelseyi* (Dall & Bartsch, 1902)
Common Name: Kelsey's Barley Snail
Size: 0.3 inches (8 mm)
Distribution: California and Baja California

Lirobarleeia kelseyi was described as a *Rissoa,* then placed in *Rissoina* (Rissoidae); it was assigned only recently to the Barleeidae. The shell is high-spired, having five to six teleoconch whorls, with oblique, sometimes obsolete axial ribs and incised spiral grooves. The family Barleeidae includes about fifty living species in five genera: *Barleeia, Caelatura, Fictonoba, Lirobarleeia,* and *Protobarleeia.* All species have direct development; the protoconch has few whorls, is dome-shaped and has a microsculpture consisting of minute pits. The only other rissoaceans with this type of microsculpture are the Anabathridae and Emblandidae. In barleeids, the operculum has a prominent peg that projects beyond its inner margin and has a ridge on the middle part of its inner surface. The peg and ridge are reduced or absent in anabathrids and emblandids. Barleeids are worldwide in distribution, with highest diversity in Western North America. Their fossil record starts in the Eocene, but they are thought to have originated in the Mesozoic.

References: Ponder (1983, 1988).

. . . .

Lirobarleeia kelseyi

Emblanda emblematica

Family: EMBLANDIDAE Ponder, 1985
Species: *Emblanda emblematica* (Hedley, 1906)
Common Name: Emblematic Emblanda
Size: 0.08 inches (2 mm)
Distribution: Southeastern Australia

Emblanda emblematica is the only known member of its family. It lives on algae in shallow water in New South Wales, Australia. The shell is solid and lacks an umbilicus. The protoconch has 1.25 whorls; the teleoconch has two to three. There are ten to twelve axial ribs, which are nodulose where crossed by a spiral cord at the periphery. The operculum is transparent yellow and paucispiral with the nucleus off-center. The shell is similar to that of anabathrids, barleeids, and rissoids, and it is possible that other members of this family have gone unrecognized because of this. The most important feature distinguishing the Emblandidae is the radula, which has only three teeth per row. In contrast, all other rissoaceans have radulae with seven teeth per row.

References: Ponder (1985, 1988).

. . . .

Caecum imbricatum

Family: CAECIDAE Gray, 1850
Species: *Caecum imbricatum* Carpenter, 1858
Common Name: Imbricate Caecum
Size: 0.1 inches (3 mm)
Distribution: Florida, Bahamas, and Caribbean

Specimens of *Caecum imbricatum* are usually white, but can be tan, pink, or mottled. Sculpture consists of ring-like ribs with the four or five anterior ones being heavier and more widely spaced, and lengthwise ridges with fine striations in between. The species occurs in sediments in depths of 3 to 400 feet (1 to 183 meters). Specimens from deep water tend to be larger and more finely sculptured than those from shallow water.

Caecids have a normally coiled protoconch, but the teleoconch is an elongate, curved tube. The animal forms a plug (septum) in the tube and loses the protoconch. A second plug is formed later, and the early parts of the tube are lost. The plug often bears a pointed projection, called the mucro, extending past the posterior end of the tube. The tubular adult shells can be superficially similar to scaphopod shells, but are distinguished by the plug; scaphopods are open at both ends. In one genus, *Strebloceras,* the early whorls remain attached. There are about a dozen genera of caecids and perhaps 300 species. They occur in temperate and tropical regions throughout the world, living in sediment or mats of algae. In many shallow-water areas in the Caribbean, caecids constitute 10 to 20 percent of the micromollusk fauna.

References: Boss (1982), Moore (1972).

. . . .

Family: ELACHISINIDAE Ponder, 1985
Species: *Elachisina floridana* (Rehder, 1943)
Common Name: Florida Cingula
Size: 0.08 inches (2 mm)
Distribution: Florida, Bahamas, and Caribbean

The shell of *Elachisina floridana* is white under a thin, brown periostracum and has a low, smooth, paucispiral protoconch and a narrow umbilicus. There are about thirty-five spiral cords on the body whorl; there is no axial sculpture. The type specimens of the species were collected in the Florida Keys, where they live gregariously under large slabs of rock imbedded in sticky clay on silt in the intertidal zone. *Elachisina* is the only known member of its family. Ten living species are recognized as well as one extinct species from the Pliocene of Florida. Species of *Elachisina* have previously been placed in

Naticidae and Rissoidae. *Microdochus* is a synonym of *Elachisina*. Recent anatomical studies have demonstrated the distinctiveness of the family Elachisinidae, which was not named until 1985 when its members were brought together. Externally, living elachisinids are characterized by the presence of tentacles on the mantle edge and the rear of the foot.

References: Ponder (1985, 1988).

Elachisina floridana

Family: EPIGRIDAE Ponder, 1985
Species: *Epigrus cylindraceus* (Tenison-Woods, 1878)
Common Name: Cylindrical Epigrus
Size: 0.2 inches (5 mm)
Distribution: South Australia

Epigrus is the only member of its family; only three or four species are known, all from Australia. The family is characterized by a distinctive type of radula, with a minute central tooth and somewhat rectangular lateral and marginal teeth. The shell of *Epigrus cylindraceus* is white, solid, smooth, and shiny; it also lacks periostracum and umbilicus. The protoconch has 1.5 whorls; the teleoconch four or five. The teleoconch has fine axial growth lines. About one-third of the aperture lies to the left of the shell axis, which is a greater proportion than in most rissoaceans. The species probably lives in coarse sediments subtidally and on the continental shelf.

References: Ponder (1985, 1988).

. . . .

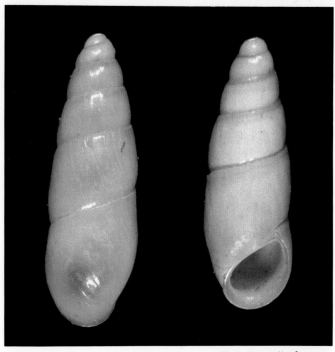

Epigrus cylindraceus

Family: FALSICINGULIDAE Slavoshevskaya, 1976
Species: *Falsicingula kurilensis* (Pilsbry, 1905)
Common Name: Kurile Cingula
Size: 0.15 inches (4 mm)
Distribution: Japan and the Kurile Islands

The shell of *Falsicingula kurilensis* is simple, with rounded whorls and a brown periostracum. The protoconch is paucispiral and has fine spiral cords. The spire whorls are often eroded. The egg capsules are minute and lens-

Falsicingula
kurilensis

shaped; each contains a single embryo that hatches as a crawling juvenile. The species is unusual in that sperm is stored in the pericardium, the membrane enclosing the heart. Sperm storage in the kidney has also been reported in falsicingulids. Falsicingulids can be difficult to tell from rissoids and hydrobiids that have simple shells, but they have distinctive reproductive anatomy. There are about half a dozen species known, all in the northern Pacific. They live in shallow marine waters and in estuaries.

References: Ponder (1985, 1988).

. . . .

Iravadia quadrasi

Family: IRAVADIIDAE Thiele, 1928
Species: *Iravadia quadrasi* (Boettger, 1893)
Common Name: Quadras's Iravadia
Size: 0.15 inches (4 mm)
Distribution: Southeast Asia to Australia

Iravadia quadrasi lives in brackish water in mud flats, mangrove swamps, and estuaries. Some *Iravadia* species are similar to the rissoids *Alvania* and *Merelina,* but are distinguished by the forward-leaning outer lip. Some *Iravadia* live in brackish water, whereas others are fully marine. Members of the Iravadiidae are all relatively high-spired, but vary considerably in sculpture, ranging from smooth to nodular. They can be recognized by the flat-topped, smooth protoconch with a small initial whorl; most rissoaceans have a sculptured protoconch. About fifty living species of iravadiids are known, most in the Indo-Pacific and some in the Eastern Atlantic. There are about a dozen genera. No living species have yet been reported from North or South America, although a couple of extinct species are known. The earliest recorded member of the group is from the Upper Cretaceous.

References: Ponder (1984, 1988).

. . . .

Family: RISSOIDAE Gray, 1847
Species: *Rissoina ambigua* (Gould, 1849)
Common Name: Ambiguous Rissoina
Size: 0.3 inches (8 mm)
Distribution: Tropical Indo-Pacific

Rissoina ambigua is the most common of the many members of its genus in the Indo-Pacific. Shells range from white to tan in color; some are spirally banded. The protoconch is smooth and white and has three whorls. The teleoconch has seven whorls; the shell from whorls one to five is concave in profile, but convex from five to seven. The shell is axially ribbed, with twenty or more ribs on the body whorl; under high magnification, numerous fine spiral lines can be seen between the ribs. The columella is cut short by a shallow sinus. The operculum has a lateral peg. The species is abundant on reefs and in tide pools in depths up to 10 feet (3 meters).

The Rissoidae is one of the largest families of gastropods, with more than thirty genera and at least 500 species, most under 0.4 inches (10 millimeters). Better known genera include *Alvania, Cingula, Manzonia, Onoba, Pusillina, Rissoa, Rissoina, Schwartziella, Setia,* and

Rissoina ambigua

live on mud and vegetation in the upper reaches of salt marshes and are normally submerged only by high spring tides. Egg capsules are laid in heaps and covered with fecal pellets to prevent them from drying up; planktonic larvae emerge during the spring tides or floods.

The family Assimineidae is divided into two subfamilies: Assimineinae, with about ten genera, which live in estuaries and supratidal environments worldwide in tropical and subtropical areas, and Omphalotropidinae, with about nine genera, which are primarily terrestrial, occurring in Southeast Asia and on some Pacific islands. Members of the family have simple, ovate shells, often with spiral sculpture. The operculum is corneous and paucispiral and sometimes has calcareous deposits.

References: Boss (1982), Graham (1988).

. . . .

Zebina. Rissoids occur worldwide, ranging from boreal to tropical regions. The great range of shapes and sculpture precludes identification of shell features characterizing the family, which is defined, instead, on the basis of internal anatomy. A few generalizations, however, can be made. Protoconch sculpture varies considerably, but is never primarily axial. The shell is at least as tall as it is wide, and the columella is simple, usually straight or slightly concave. The earliest known rissoids are from the Middle Jurassic of Europe.

References: Kay (1979), Ponder (1985).

. . . .

Assiminea grayana

Family: ASSIMINEIDAE Adams & Adams, 1856
Species: *Assiminea grayana* Fleming, 1828
Common Name: Gray's Assiminea
Size: 0.25 inches (6 mm)
Distribution: Britain and Holland to Denmark

The shell of *Assiminea grayana* is yellowish or tan, sometimes with a brown spiral band at the periphery of the body whorl. There are six to seven whorls, which are smooth except for many fine growth lines. The animals

Family: TRUNCATELLIDAE Gray, 1840
Species: *Truncatella pulchella* Pfeiffer, 1839
Common Name: Beautiful Truncatella
Size: 0.2 inches (5 mm)
Distribution: Bermuda, Bahamas, Florida, and the Caribbean

Truncatella pulchella often occurs together with *Truncatella caribaeensis* Reeve, 1842, a species with which it has been confused. They live in and under mats of cast-up vegetation at the top of the intertidal zone. *Truncatella pulchella* is more resistant to drying out, and is able to live beyond the high-tide line in the storm strand and terrestrial leaf litter. It is smaller than *T. caribaeensis,* has a ribbed protoconch, and has a narrower aperture, which is reinforced by a varix behind the lip; *T. caribaeensis* lacks this varix and has a smooth protoconch. *Truncatella bilabiata* Pfeiffer, 1840 is a synonym of *T. pulchella.*

There are about eighty species of truncatellids worldwide. The first few whorls of the shell are cut short, or truncated, in all members of the family. They form an internal plug (septum) and lose the whorls above it, having weakened the shell in a line just above the plug. Although many gastropods lose the initial whorls of the shell, this is usually due to erosion rather than by the process of truncation. Only a few marine gastropods—mostly members of *Caducifer* (Buccinidae) and the Caecidae—truncate the shell. Truncatellids are also unusual because they crawl in a way unique among the gastropods. They extend the snout and place it on the surface in front of them, then step the foot up behind, thus moving rather like an inchworm does. Other snails crawl on a layer of mucus secreted by the foot. One-third of truncatellid species are amphibious, living in sheltered areas at the top of the intertidal zone in tropical and semitropical coasts throughout the world. The remainder of the species are terrestrial, occurring in Trinidad, Barbados, the Cayman Islands, the Greater Antilles, and many islands in the Pacific, including New Guinea and Guam.

Reference: Rosenberg (1989).

. . . .

Truncatella pulchella

Tornus subcarinatus

Family: TORNIDAE Sacco, 1896
Species: *Tornus subcarinatus* (Montagu, 1803)
Common Name: Keeled Tornus
Size: 0.1 inches (3 mm)
Distribution: Mediterranean to British Isles

The shell of *Tornus subcarinatus* is semitransparent, low-spired, and umbilicate. The body whorl has six spiral keels, two of them at the base, and about forty axial ribs. The growth lines lean strongly forward, crossing the axial ribs at angles of up to forty-five degrees. The animal is blind and has two tentacles on the right edge of the mantle. An unusual feature is that the anterior end of the gill can project from the mantle cavity. Members of the species live under boulders imbedded in yellow, well-oxygenated sand, rather than in black sand with little or no oxygen.

Tornids are often confused with vitrinellids, but there are several distinguishing features. Vitrinellids have eyes; a corneous, round, multispiral operculum; and a penis without glands. Tornids lack eyes; have an oval, paucispiral operculum; and have several glandular processes on the penis. *Adeorbis* often has been confused with *Tornus;* it is now thought to belong in the Vitrinellidae. The scope and distribution of the family Tornidae are unknown because most species have not been studied anatomically to confirm their membership in the group.

References: Bieler & Mikkelsen (1988), Graham (1982, 1988), Ponder & Warén (1988).

. . . .

Family: VITRINELLIDAE Bush, 1897
Species: *Cochliolepis parasitica* Stimpson, 1858
Common Name: Parasitic Scale Snail
Size: 0.15 inches (4 mm)
Distribution: North Carolina, Bahamas, and Caribbean

The name *Cochliolepis parasitica* is a misnomer, because the species is not parasitic. Stimpson, who named the species, discovered specimens living under the scales of a marine worm, and assumed that it was a parasite. The species is now known to be a herbivore or detritus feeder that lives with the worm in its tube but does not parasi-

tize it. The brick red tissues can be seen through the transparent shell, which rapidly becomes opaque white after the animal has died. The shell is smooth except for fine growth lines, virtually flat, and has a broad umbilicus. *Cochliolepis nautiliformis* (Holmes, 1860), described as a fossil, is a synonym.

There are probably several hundred species of vitrinellids worldwide, most of them minute, but until many of these species are studied anatomically, the limits of the family will be unknown. Adeorbidae and Circulidae are now considered synonyms of Vitrinellidae rather than Tornidae. Vitrinellid genera include *Adeorbis, Circulus, Cochliolepis, Cyclostremiscus, Pleuromalaxis, Teinostoma,* and *Vitrinella.* In addition to associations with worms, some vitrinellids are known to live in the burrows of stomatopod crustaceans. The family is thought to have originated by the Cretaceous.

References: Bieler & Mikkelsen (1988), Moore (1972).

. . . .

Cochliolepis parasitica

Superfamily: Strombacea Rafinesque, 1815
Family: APORRHAIDAE Gray, 1850
    Species: *Aporrhais pespelicani* (Linné, 1758)
Common Name: Common Pelican's-foot
Size: 2 inches (50 mm)
Distribution: Mediterranean to northern Norway and
                Iceland

There are only five living species in the family Apor-rhaidae, one in the northwestern Atlantic and four in the Eastern Atlantic. *Aporrhais pespelicani* is the most common of these. It has eight to ten whorls, axial ribs, and fine spiral sculpture; the aperture is flared and has long projections. The operculum is corneous and does not fill the aperture. The animal is a browser and a detritus feeder that lives partly buried in sediment subtidally and to depths of 600 feet (180 meters). Breeding occurs in spring or summer; the larvae have planktonic develop-ment. The Aporrhaidae have an extensive fossil record from the Jurassic to the Recent. Many extinct species had projections of the aperture far surpassing the length of those of the living species.

Reference: Graham (1988).

. . . .

Aporrhais
pespelicani

Lambis violacea

Family: STROMBIDAE Rafinesque, 1815
Species: *Lambis violacea* (Swainson, 1821)
Common Name: Violet Spider Conch
Size: 4.5 inches (110 mm)
Distribution: Western Indian Ocean

Lambis violacea is a classic rare shell. The species has been known for more than 200 years, and specimens are occa-sionally collected in Mauritius and surrounding islands, but it is still considered rare and is highly prized. It has ten or eleven fingerlike projections on the lip posterior to the so-called stromboid notch, where an eye pro-trudes, and four or five anterior to it. The deep purple color within the aperture is stable; specimens that have been in museums for more than 100 years have faded only modestly.

There are nine species of *Lambis,* all restricted to the tropical Indo-Pacific. They have from five to sixteen long projections around the aperture. The number of digits in each species is relatively constant. All species are active grazers in shallow water around coral reefs. The most abundant species, *Lambis lambis,* is used as food in the Philippines. Female *Lambis* are usually larger than males of the same species. Hybrids have been reported between some species.

References: Abbott (1961), Dance (1969), Walls (1980).

. . . .

Family: STROMBIDAE Rafinesque, 1815
Species: *Strombus listeri* T. Gray, 1852
Common Name: Lister's Conch
Size: 6 inches (150 mm)
Distribution: Gulf of Oman to the Bay of Bengal

Strombus listeri has been known since the 1600s, but only a half dozen specimens had been collected by 1960. Research vessels dredged several specimens in the Northern Indian Ocean in the 1960s and, in 1969, Thai and Burmese fishermen trawled more than 500 specimens. As late as 1970, specimens brought as much as $1,000 from uninformed collectors, but by 1972 the price had dropped to $10, and the species is now considered moderately common.

Fifty-four species of *Strombus,* or conchs, are known worldwide in tropical and subtropical seas. There are forty-two in the Indo-Pacific, four in the Eastern Pacific, seven in the Western Atlantic, and one in the Eastern Atlantic. They range in size at maturity from less than 1 inch (2.5 millimeters) to more than 13 inches (330 millimeters). The adult shell is usually heavy with a flaring aperture; juvenile shells usually have rounded varices on the early teleoconch whorls. The operculum is long and clawlike, with a serrated edge. It is used for leverage during locomotion, which is a leaping motion with the muscular foot, and in defense against marauding crabs and fish. The eyes are set on long stalks, with the right eye protruding through the stromboid notch, which is a sinus in the outer lip, and the left eye protruding through the siphonal canal. All species are herbivores, living mostly in shallow, sandy areas. Some species are harvested commercially for food.

References: Abbott (1960, 1972), Dance (1969), Walls (1980).

. . . .

Strombus listeri

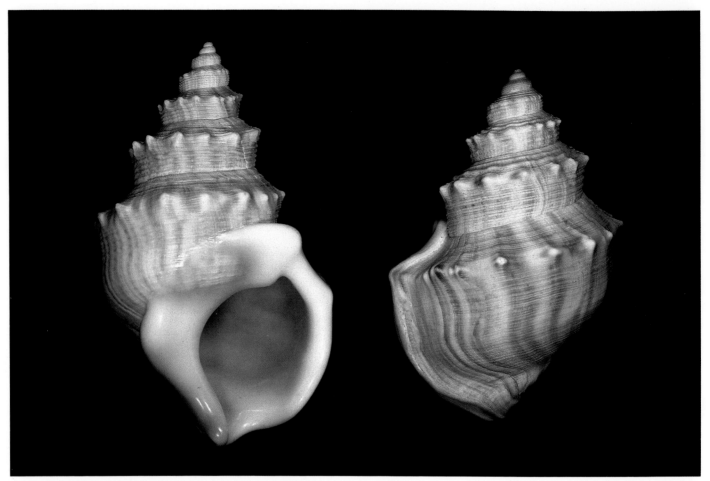

Struthiolaria papulosa

Family: STRUTHIOLARIIDAE Gabb, 1868
Species: *Struthiolaria papulosa* (Martyn, 1784)
Common Name: Large Ostrich-foot
Size: 3 inches (75 mm)
Distribution: New Zealand

Struthiolaria papulosa has a solid shell with shouldered, nodular whorls, fine spiral cords, and brown axial streaks. The outer lip and parietal area are usually heavily calloused. In the southern part of its range, shells are larger, with weaker nodules on the shoulder and deeper grooves between the spiral cords. It is common in shallow water on sand and mud flats in estuaries and along the open coast. *Struthiolaria vermis* (Martyn, 1784) is similar, but smaller, reaching only about 2 inches (50 millimeters) in height; it usually has a channeled suture and often has two smaller keels below the primary one at the shoulder.

Only four living species of struthiolariids are known. In addition to the two from New Zealand, there is one species in southeastern Australia, and one on Kerguelen Island and South Georgia (genus *Perissodonta*). The family was more diverse in the early Tertiary, and the oldest known fossils are from the Upper Cretaceous of New Zealand. Struthiolariids are ciliary feeders, using the gill to trap particles of food in mucus. Food is transferred from the gill to the food groove, a ciliated gutter on the mantle cavity floor that carries the mucous-bound particles forward, so the animal can reach back with its snout to ingest them. The operculum in *Struthiolaria* does not fill the aperture and has a terminal spike. The animal digs this spike into the bottom to right itself when overturned.

References: Morton (1971), Powell (1979).

· · · · · · · · · · · · · ·

Family: SERAPHIDAE Gray, 1853
Species: *Terebellum terebellum* (Linné, 1758)
Common Name: Terebellum
Size: 2 inches (50 mm)
Distribution: East Africa to Samoa

Terebellum terebellum is the only surviving member of the family Seraphidae. Its streamlined shape is an adaptation for its habit of rapid burrowing just below the surface of the sand. The animal uses its eyes, which are on long stalks, as periscopes; one eye is kept stationary at the surface of the sand as the animal crawls forward, then the other eye is pushed to the surface through the siphon and the eye behind is withdrawn. This alternate advancement of the eyes is somewhat like the movement of an ape's arms when it swings from branch to branch. The shell has a channeled suture and is extremely variable in color pattern. The operculum has four sawteeth and is partially imbedded in the foot. The animal lives in sand just subtidally to depths of 100 feet (30 meters). The species is known from the Miocene, and the family from the Paleocene. Highest diversity was during the Eocene, when there were four genera.

References: Jung (1974), Jung & Abbott (1967).

. . . .

Superfamily: Xenophoracea Troschel, 1852
Family: XENOPHORIDAE Troschel, 1852
Species: *Xenophora neozelanica* Suter, 1908
Common Name: New Zealand Carrier Shell
Size: 3 inches (75 mm)
Distribution: North Island, New Zealand

Xenophora neozelanica is quite similar to *Xenophora peroniana* (Iredale, 1929), the Australian Carrier Shell, but it has coarser sculpture on its base and is bigger as an adult (up to 1.5 times larger). The spire angle varies from 62 to 84 degrees. The umbilicus is slightly open in juveniles, but closed in adults. Up to 70 percent of the dorsal part of the shell can be hidden by attached shells and stones, and up to fifteen objects can be attached per whorl. Where objects are not attached, the dorsal surface is furrowed. The aperture is white to light brown; the base has

Terebellum terebellum

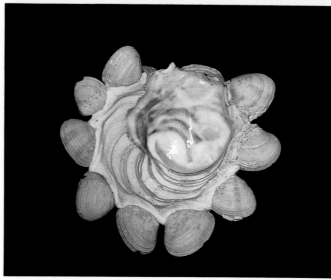

Xenophora neozelanica

irregularly spaced brown stripes that follow the curve of the aperture. The species lives on the continental shelf in depths of 115 to 300 feet (35 to 90 meters). A subspecies, *Xenophora neozelanica kermadecensis* Ponder, 1983 has been described from the Kermadec Islands.

Shells of xenophorids are broad-based; most of the twenty-two living species attach foreign objects to the shell. The most recent revision of the group recognized only one genus, *Xenophora*, with subgenera *Xenophora, Onustus,* and *Stellaria.* The Xenophoridae are probably more closely related to the Calyptraeidae than the Strombidae. *Xenophora* crawling has been described as "galumphing," "leaping," or a "one-legged stomp." The animal places the foot on the bottom, lifts the shell, and throws itself forward about half a shell length. Probably all species are deposit feeders. The *Oxford English Dictionary* records that *Xenophora* that attach stones to the shell are called "mineralogists," whereas those that attach shells are called "conchologists." The oldest undoubted xenophorid fossils are from the Cretaceous; the group diversified in the Paleocene.

References: Ponder (1983), Powell (1979).

. . . .

Superfamily: Calyptraeacea Lamarck, 1809
Family: CALYPTRAEIDAE Lamarck, 1809
Species: *Calyptraea calyptraeformis* (Lamarck, 1822)
Common Name: Australian Shelf Limpet
Size: 1 inch (25 mm)
Distribution: Southern Australia

The shell of *Calyptraea calyptraeformis* looks like that of a normally coiled, globular gastropod such as a moon snail (Naticidae) that has lost the lower part of each whorl. The early whorls are somewhat pronounced, but the shell becomes flatter with growth. Members of the species live in depths of 6 to 65 feet (2 to 20 meters) on small stones and shells. Their shape can be variable, depending on how they conform to the underlying surface. The species is sometimes placed in the genus *Sigapatella.*

Many calyptraeids have lost the spirally coiled form and are cap-shaped, with a porcelaneous internal shelf or cup. Calyptraeids are ecologically more similar to oysters than to other gastropod limpets in being sedentary filter feeders. Members of the family are sequential hermaphrodites, starting life as males and later changing to females. Some species of *Crepidula* form stacks, with the large individuals at the bottom being female and smaller ones at the top being male. The calyptraeids began diversifying during the Cretaceous. More than 100 living species are known worldwide; major genera include *Calyptraea, Cheilea, Crepidula,* and *Crucibulum.*

References: Coleman (1975), Hoagland (1977).

. . . .

Family: CAPULIDAE Fleming, 1822
Species: *Capulus ungaricus* (Linné, 1758)
Common Name: Fool's Cap
Size: 2 inches (50 mm)
Distribution: Greenland to Florida, Iceland to the Mediterranean

Capulus ungaricus has a cap-shaped shell with a spirally coiled apex. The straw-colored periostracum is fringed at the edge of the aperture. The aperture is broad and ovate; an operculum is lacking. Individuals up to 0.16 inches (4 millimeters) in length are males; larger ones are females, with the penis being reduced to a nub. *Capulus ungaricus* often live on the shells of other ciliary-feeding mollusks, feeding on material rejected from their gills in the form of mucus-bound particles. They also can collect food with their own gills. Some species of capulids bore holes in the shells of their hosts in order to extract fluids and food particles.

Although they have spirally coiled rather than cap-shaped shells, the Trichotropidae have recently been included in the Capulidae, because of anatomical similarities. Both groups have heavy periostracum, are ciliary feeders, and are sequential hermaphrodites, being male first. Most capulids are temperate or boreal in distribution.

References: Graham (1988), Ponder & Warén (1988).

. . . .

Calyptraea calyptraeformis

Capulus ungaricus

Vanikoro cancellata

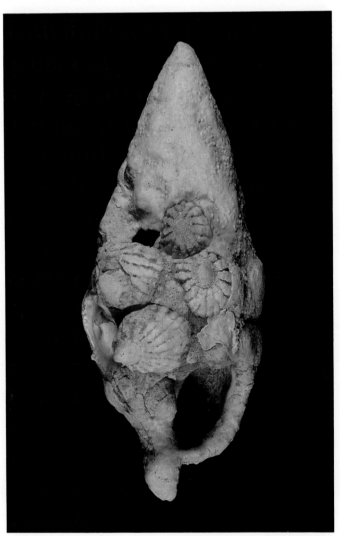

Sabia conica

Superfamily: Vanikoracea Gray, 1840
Family: VANIKORIDAE Gray, 1840
Species: *Vanikoro cancellata* (Lamarck, 1822)
Common Name: Cancellate Vanikoro
Size: 1 inch (25 mm)
Distribution: Tropical Indo-Pacific

Vanikoro cancellata has both axial ribs and spiral cords; the axial ribs are weak or absent on the body whorl of large individuals. The periostracum is straw-colored and the shell is umbilicate. The species lives in and among rubble on reefs in shallow water, where it feeds on detritus. In some *Vanikoro* species, sculpture changes or becomes obsolete on the body whorl of adults; as a result, juveniles and adults have been named as different species. Most vanikorids can attach to the substratum with a suckerlike structure on the rear of the foot. The family includes the genera *Macromphalus, Megalomphalus, Talassia,* and *Vanikoro,* and perhaps forty species. The operculum is corneous and paucispiral, or non-spiral. There is no siphonal notch. *Merria* and *Narica* are synonyms of *Vanikoro; Couthouyia* is a synonym of *Macromphalus.*

References: Boss (1982), Cernohorsky (1972), Kay (1979), Warén & Bouchet (1988).

. . . .

Family: HIPPONICIDAE Troschel, 1861
Species: *Sabia conica* (Schumacher, 1817)
Common Name: Conical Hoof-shell
Size: 0.8 inches (20 mm)
Distribution: Tropical Indo-Pacific

Sabia conica lives attached to the shells of shallow-water gastropods, such as *Strombus, Conus,* and *Turbo,* usually near the aperture, presumably feeding on the fecal pellets of its host. It is irregular in shape as it conforms to the contours of the host shell, in which it digs out noticeable scars. Some hipponicids secrete an attachment plate from the bottom of the foot; the shell muscles are attached to this plate and can pull the other valve down, shutting the animal inside. They are thus convergent on bivalves, meaning that they share similar traits, but have evolved independently of each other. Hipponicids have dorsal and ventral valves, however, rather than left and right valves. Most of the muscle of the foot is lost, in keeping with their sedentary habit. The animals often live in dense colonies and have long snouts used to search for food that drifts into their vicinity. The penis is greatly extensible, allowing internal fertilization of neighboring snails to occur, even though the animals are immobile. They are sequential hermaphrodites, being male first. Genera include *Hipponix, Pilosabia,* and *Sabia.*

References: Cowan (1974), Kay (1979), Yonge (1960).

. . . .

Superfamily: Cypraeacea Rafinesque, 1815
Family: CYPRAEIDAE Rafinesque, 1815
Species: *Cypraea fultoni* Sowerby, 1903
Common Name: Fulton's Cowrie
Size: 3 inches (75 mm)
Distribution: South Africa and Mozambique

Until recently, *Cypraea fultoni* was one of the world's rarest seashells; it is still one of the most desirable. The first specimen was collected from the stomach of a mussel-cracker fish, and for many years all available shells were *ex piscibus* (from fish). Specimens have sold for as much as $24,000, although only a few have brought more than $10,000. Several hundred specimens are now known, many taken in the past few years by Soviet trawlers operating off Mozambique, and they have been available for less than $2,000. The dorsal pattern of *Cypraea fultoni* is considerably variable, with no two specimens alike. The color pattern is deposited by folds of the mantle that overlie the shell. As layers of wavy lines are superimposed, the shell develops its characteristic, asymmetric pattern. The living animal is a translucent, ghostly white, with short, slender papillae tipped in opaque white. Analysis of the stomach contents has shown that the species feeds on sponges. *Cypraea fultoni* is sometimes placed in the genus *Bernaya.*

Members of the family Cypraeidae are known as cowries; currently 204 species are recognized. Most researchers place all species in the genus *Cypraea,* but many subgeneric names are available and eventually, as anatomical knowledge of the group increases, it will be divided. Members of the family occur in tropical and subtropical seas worldwide, with the highest diversity in the Indo-Pacific. Most species have planktonic larvae and broad geographic ranges. Those that have direct development tend to be restricted to a particular region. The greatest number of endemics occurs in South Africa, with fifteen such species. Cypraeids feed on marine vegetation, sponges, and other sedentary invertebrates. The fossil record of the group extends to the Lower Cretaceous.

References: Burgess (1985), Dance (1969), Liltved (1989).

. . . .

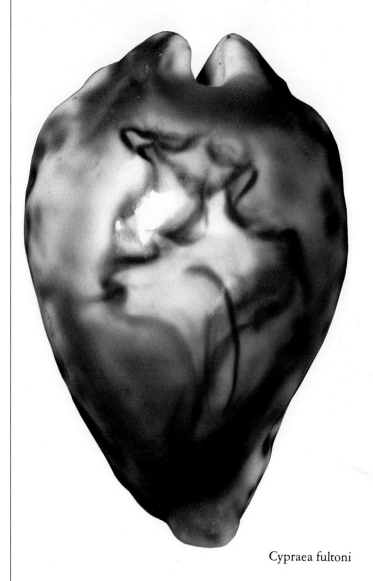

Cypraea fultoni

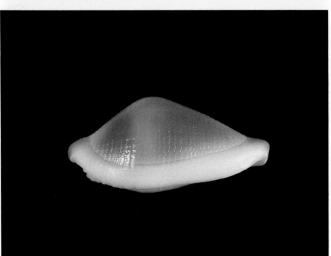

Crenavolva rosewateri

Family: OVULIDAE Fleming, 1822
Subfamily: Ovulinae Fleming, 1822
Species: *Crenavolva rosewateri* Cate, 1973
Common Name: Rosewater's Egg Cowrie
Size: 0.4 inches (10 mm)
Distribution: South Africa to Japan and Australia

Constant features in the coloration of the rather variable *Crenavolva rosewateri* are its orange terminals and white base. Dorsal color ranges from white through pink and tan to reddish purple, with a lighter band at the widest part of the shell. The shell is usually rounded at the sides, but some individuals develop an angled keel at the widest part. The living animal has a pattern of brown to red blotches and orange pustulate spots on the mantle; it occurs in depths of 10 to 100 feet (3 to 30 meters) on soft corals.

There are about 170 species of ovulids worldwide in tropical and subtropical seas. All species for which larval types are known have long-term planktonic larvae, and most species have broad geographic ranges. In recent years many species previously known only from Japan have been found in the Philippines, Australia, and South Africa. All ovulids are external parasites on octocorals, including gorgonaceans (horny corals such as sea fans and sea whips), alcyonaceans (soft corals), and pennatulaceans (sea pens). A broad range of shell morphologies occurs in the subfamily Ovulinae, from globular to elongate as reflected by the numerous genera, including *Calpurnus, Crenavolva, Cyphoma, Neosimnia, Ovula, Phenacovolva, Primovula, Prionovolva, Prosimnia, Pseudosimnia, Simnia, Volva,* and *Xandarovula.* The other subfamilies of Ovulidae are Eocypraeinae and Pediculariinae. The oldest known ovuline fossils are from the Upper Eocene.

References: Cate (1973), Liltved (1989).

. . . .

Subfamily: Eocypraeinae Schilder, 1924
Species: *Pseudocypraea exquisita* Petuch, 1979
Common Name: Exquisite Egg Cowrie
Size: 0.4 inches (10 mm)
Distribution: South Africa to Guam and the Philippines

Pseudocypraea exquisita is sometimes mistaken for *Pseudocypraea adamsonii* (Sowerby, 1832), from which it differs in having only spiral sculpture on the dorsum, rather than both spiral and longitudinal sculpture, and in having the central base smooth and shiny, rather than ridged. *Pseudocypraea exquisita* lives in depths of 160 to 820 feet (50 to 250 meters) on substrata with sponge and soft coral. *Pseudocypraea adamsonii* is a widespread Indo-Pacific species that can be found under coral rocks intertidally and in shallow water.

The two species of *Pseudocypraea* along with one species of *Jenneria* are the only living representatives of the Eocypraeinae. They resemble cypraeids, but are distinguished by the spirally striate juvenile shell. They differ from ovulines in having teeth on both the inner and outer lip; most ovulines have teeth only on the outer lip or lack them altogether. The Eocypraeinae have a more extensive fossil record than the Ovulinae, dating to the Middle Cretaceous.

References: Cate (1973), Liltved (1989).

. . . .

Superfamily: Velutinacea Gray, 1840
Family: TRIVIIDAE Troschel, 1863
Subfamily: Triviinae Troschel, 1863
Species: *Trivirostra exigua* (Gray, 1831)
Common Name: Exiguous Trivia
Size: 0.2 inches (5 mm)
Distribution: Tropical Indo-Pacific

Trivirostra exigua is patterned in pink and white with strong transverse ribs, some of which bifurcate. There is a dorsal furrow of variable strength; the ribs are usually continuous across it. The interspaces between the ribs are slightly granular at high magnification (25×). The species is widespread in the Indo-Pacific but is most common in the Hawaiian Islands.

About 150 species of triviines are currently recog-

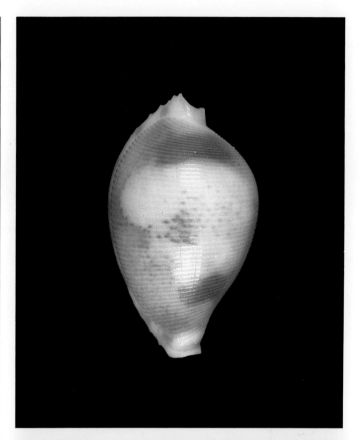

Pseudocypraea exquisita

nized; genera include *Niveria, Pseudotrivia, Pusula, Trivia, Triviella,* and *Trivirostra.* They resemble cypraeids in shape but differ in that most species have transverse ribs and a longitudinal dorsal furrow, which are characters that very few cypraeids have. Cypraeids and ovulids differ from triviids and velutinids in having a triaxial rather than monaxial osphradium. Neither cypraeaceans nor velutinaceans have an operculum. Triviids feed on ascidians (sea squirts), which are invertebrates of the phylum Chordata. In some species the coloration of the mantle closely resembles that of their prey, thereby serving as camouflage; other species mimic anemones or toxic nudibranchs that are avoided by predators. The family Triviidae is divided into two subfamilies, Eratoinae and Triviinae. Eratoinae has the longer fossil record, dating from the Lower Paleocene; triviines date from the Lower Eocene.

References: Cate (1979), Liltved (1989).

. . . .

Trivirostra exigua

Subfamily: Eratoinae Gill, 1871
Species: *Erato voluta* (Montagu, 1803)
Common Name: Volute Erato
Size: 0.5 inches (12 mm)
Distribution: Mediterranean to Norway

The shell of *Erato voluta* is glossy white or tan and has a flattened protoconch. The outer lip is thickened and has fifteen to eighteen denticles on its inner edge. The living animal is speckled with brown, red, orange, and yellow on white. It occurs in depths of 65 to 330 feet (20 to 100 meters) on hard bottoms in association with ascidians (sea squirts) on which it feeds. There are about thirty living species of eratoines, placed in the genera *Alaerato, Erato, Hesperato,* and *Proterato.* They occur worldwide, mostly in tropical and subtropical seas. Eratoine shells are sometimes confused with those of marginellids, but can be distinguished by the type of dentition on the inner lip of the aperture. Many eratoines form apertural denticles or short folds at maturity, but these do not extend inside the shell. In marginellids, the folds are present in juveniles and wrap around the columella into the interior of the shell.

References: Cate (1977), Graham (1988).

. . . .

Family: VELUTINIDAE Gray, 1840
Species: *Velutina velutina* (Müller, 1776)
Common Name: Velvety Velutina
Size: 0.7 inches (18 mm)
Distribution: Arctic Ocean, North Atlantic, North Pacific

Velutina velutina has a swollen body whorl covered by brown periostracum. The aperture is large and almost circular. The calcareous part of the shell is thin and white or pink with fine spiral cords and growth lines. The animal occurs in depths of 16 to 300 feet (5 to 90 meters), where it feeds on solitary ascidians (sea squirts). This species used to be known as *Velutina laevigata* (Linné, 1767), but the identity of Linné's species cannot be determined from his description and no type material or illustrations exist for verification.

Velutinids have fragile, globular-to ear shaped shells

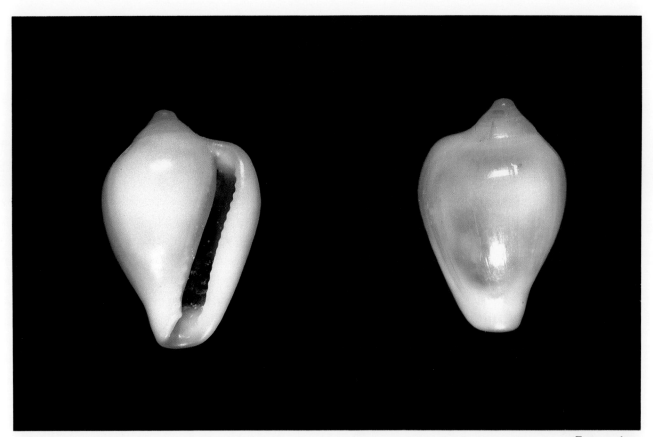

Erato voluta

Velutina velutina

with rapidly expanding whorls. They occur worldwide, but are more diverse in cold seas than in the tropics. Genera include *Capulacmaea, Lamellaria, Marsenina, Mysticoncha,* and *Velutina.* The family name Velutinidae has one year's priority over the synonymous Lamellariidae (1840 versus 1841). In some species, the shell is smooth and completely enclosed in folds of the mantle. The mantle provides camouflage with pattern and texture that mimic ascidians, sponges, barnacles, and other invertebrates. This passive avoidance of predation by protective resemblance is supplemented by mantle glands that produce acid secretions for active deterrence of predators.

References: Behrens (1980), Graham (1988).

. . . .

Natica euzona

Superfamily: Naticacea Forbes, 1838
Family: NATICIDAE Forbes, 1838
Species: *Natica euzona* Récluz, 1844
Common Name: Beautifully-banded Moon
Size: 1.2 inches (30 mm)
Distribution: Tropical Indo-Pacific

Natica euzona is one of the most beautiful of the moon snails, having an intricate pattern of caramel-colored wavy lines and blocks arranged in spiral bands. The white parietal callus extends into the umbilicus. The calcareous operculum has one marginal rib. The species is rather

rare, occurring in sand at depths of 65 to 230 feet (20 to 70 meters). The naticids are a cosmopolitan group of perhaps 200 living species divided into several subfamilies. Members of Naticinae have a hard, calcareous operculum, Polinicinae and Ampullospirinae a corneous one, and the ear-shaped Sininae lack an operculum.

Naticids feed on mollusks that live in soft, sandy bottoms. They have an accessory boring organ on the proboscis that secretes chemicals that soften and dissolve the shell of their prey, allowing the radula to cut it away, forming a circular borehole. (Muricids have an independently evolved accessory boring organ that is located in the sole of the foot.) Prey tissue is removed by the proboscis through the borehole and digested internally. Boring is a slow process, proceeding at rates of 0.024 inches (0.6 millimeters) per day or less; several days can elapse between capture and consumption of prey. Some naticids, rather than boring their prey, suffocate them by wrapping them in mucus and holding them within the voluminous foot. Members of more than eighty families of bivalves and gastropods have been documented as prey of naticids. Naticid boreholes can be distinguished by their beveled sides; those of muricids and capulids are straight-sided. Octopuses inject venom into shelled prey through an irregular or oval, but not circular, borehole; they do not feed through the hole. The oldest undoubted naticid fossils and boreholes are from the Cretaceous, about 100 million years ago. Triassic boreholes attributed to naticids need further study.

References: Marincovich (1977), Kabat (1990).

. . . .

Superfamily: Tonnacea Suter, 1913
Family: CASSIDAE Latreille, 1825
Species: *Cassis tuberosa* (Linné, 1758)
Common Name: King Helmet
Size: 8 inches (200 mm)
Distribution: North Carolina to Brazil

As do most cassids, *Cassis tuberosa* feeds nocturnally on echinoids (sea urchins and sand dollars). It holds its prey with its bilobed foot and penetrates the test (shell) by the combined action of sulfuric acid, secreted by glands in the proboscis, and the radula. The proboscis is highly extensible and can reach the test of the long-spined sea urchin *Diadema* before the rest of the animal is in range of the spines. It is thought that the proboscis administers a toxic or anaesthetic substance that prevents the urchin from escaping.

Cassidae is divided into three subfamilies: Cassinae (helmet shells), Phaliinae (bonnet shells), and Oocorythinae (false tuns). Cassids have mainly large, thick, low-spired shells with anterior siphons twisted to point dorsally. The outer lip is strongly thickened; in many species varices mark the position of the previous lips deposited during growth pauses. A corneous operculum is always present; the periostracum is weak or absent. There are about seventy species worldwide in tropical and temperate seas. The family dates from the mid-Cretaceous.

References: Abbott (1968), Beu (1981), Hughes & Hughes (1981), Taylor et al. (1980).

. . . .

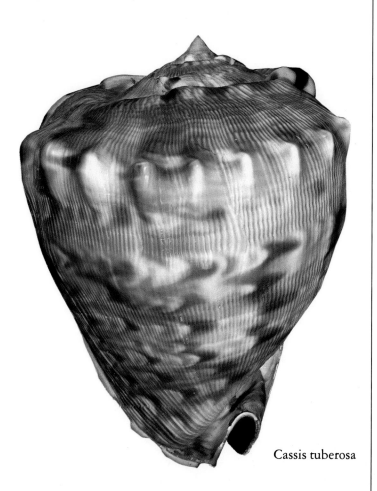

Cassis tuberosa

Bufonaria lamarckii

Family: BURSIDAE Thiele, 1925
Species: *Bufonaria lamarckii* (Deshayes, 1853)
Common Name: Lamarck's Frog Shell
Size: 2 inches (50 mm)
Distribution: Tropical Indo-Pacific

Bufonaria lamarckii is a widespread species, having been found from the Red Sea to the Line Islands, but is nowhere common. It is characterized by the dark brown lining in the aperture, with light orange denticles and folds. The denticles on the outer lip are divided into four groups of one to three each. The posterior siphonal canals are exceptionally long in this species, and the apex is usually eroded. The animal lives on coral reefs subtidally and to depths of 65 feet (20 meters).

The bursids are also known as frog shells; there are about fifty species worldwide in tropical and subtropical seas. Most are coarsely sculptured; they can be distinguished from ranellids by the siphonal canal at the posterior end of the aperture. This canal in some species is rather elongate. In most species, varices are spaced a half-whorl apart; in some they are separated by up to two-thirds of a whorl. A corneous operculum is present; periostracum is weak or absent. Bursids feed on ophiuroids (brittle stars), echinoids (sea urchins and sand dollars), and crinoids (sea lilies). The oldest known fossil bursids are from the Albian of the mid-Cretaceous.

References: Beu (1981, 1985, 1988).

. . . .

Distorsio burgessi (holotype)

Cymatium pileare

Family: PERSONIDAE Gray, 1854
Species: *Distorsio burgessi* Lewis, 1972
Common Name: Checkerboard Distorsio
Size: 2.5 inches (60 mm)
Distribution: Hawaiian Islands

Although some species of *Distorsio* are circumtropical in distribution, *Distorsio burgessi* is endemic to the Hawaiian Islands. It can be distinguished from the common *Distorsio anus* (Linné, 1758) by the dark brown grooves in its parietal shield and the white shell, lightly stained with orange. *Distorsio anus* has no pattern on the parietal shield, but the rest of shell is richly patterned in brown and white. *Distorsio burgessi* is found in depths of up to 280 feet (85 meters).

There are about a dozen species of personids in three genera, *Distorsio, Distorsionella,* and *Personella.* In general, the sculpture is knobby and the aperture constricted. Varices are spaced slightly less than every three-quarters of a whorl; the shell bulges asymmetrically between the varices. *Persona* is a synonym of *Distorsio,* but the family name Personidae is older than Distortionidae. The personids were, until recently, placed in the Ranellidae. Some *Distorsio* feed on polychaete worms. They have an extremely long proboscis, which would help in hunting polychaetes in crevices narrower than the shell could enter. The fossil record of Personidae extends to the Upper Cretaceous.

References: Beu (1981, 1985, 1988), Lewis (1972), Warén & Bouchet (1990).

. . . .

Family: RANELLIDAE Gray, 1854
Species: *Cymatium pileare* (Linné, 1758)
Common Name: Common Hairy Triton
Size: 4 inches (100 mm)
Distribution: Tropical Indo-Pacific

Cymatium pileare was long regarded as a circumtropical species, but is now thought to be restricted to the Indo-Pacific. *Cymatium aquatile* (Reeve, 1844), which had been considered a synonym of it, occurs in the Indo-Pacific and the Eastern and Western Atlantic. Eastern Pacific shells identified as *Cymatium pileare* are *Cymatium macrodon* (Valenciennes, 1832). *Cymatium pileare* is distinguished by having the ridges on the outer lip extending well inside the aperture. The interior of the outer lip is red and the parietal area is dark with light folds. In *Cymatium aquatile,* the aperture is pale orange, and the ridges are short and paired. Two other species in this complex are *Cymatium martinianum* (d'Orbigny, 1845) from the Atlantic, and *Cymatium intermedium* (Pease, 1869) from the Indo-Pacific, but common only in Hawaii.

There are about 115 species of ranellids, which are also known as triton shells. The family was formerly called Cymatiidae, but Ranellidae is the older name. Most species have thick, coarsely sculptured shells with varices every half to two-thirds of a whorl. The operculum is corneous and, in most genera, the periostracum is heavy and bristly. Many species occur in more than one ocean basin because their larvae have planktonic stages lasting as long as a year. Ranellids feed on a wide variety of invertebrates, including mollusks, polychaetes, crustaceans, echinoderms, ascidians, and brachiopods. They use the proboscis to apply an anaesthetizing fluid to their prey. The oldest known fossil ranellids are of Aptian age, from the mid-Cretaceous.

References: Beu (1985, 1988), Beu & Cernohorsky (1986), Beu & Kay (1988).

. . . .

Family: FICIDAE Meek, 1864
Species: *Ficus ventricosa* (Sowerby, 1825)
Common Name: Swollen Fig Shell
Size: 5 inches (125 mm)
Distribution: Baja California to Peru

The shell of *Ficus ventricosa* is tan with brown spots on the twelve to fifteen primary spiral cords on the body whorl. Halfway between each pair of primary cords are weaker secondary cords, between primary and secondary cords are tertiary cords, then quaternary cords, and in some cases quinary cords. There are also fine axial riblets about equal in strength to the tertiary cords. The aperture is a porcelaneous lavender inside. The species occurs in depths of 3 to 160 feet (1 to 50 meters) and is more common offshore.

Ficus ventricosa

About a dozen species of *Ficus* (fig shells) are known. They occur in tropical and semitropical seas except for the Eastern Atlantic and are thought to feed on echinoids and polychaetes. Ficids have lightweight, cancellate shells without varices. The shell is low-spired, the body whorl large with an elongate siphonal canal. Unlike other tonnaceans, they have small, inconspicuous salivary glands, rather than large complex ones. The only other extant genus in the family is *Thalassocyon,* with one species that occurs in abyssal depths from South Africa to the Kermadec Islands. *Thalassocyon* has a small, corneous operculum, unlike *Ficus,* which lacks an operculum. Fossil ficids are known from the Upper Cretaceous.

References: Beu (1981), Keen (1971), Warén & Bouchet (1990).

. . . .

Malea pomum

Family: TONNIDAE Suter, 1913
Species: *Malea pomum* (Linné, 1758)
Common Name: Pacific Grinning Tun
Size: 3 inches (75 mm)
Distribution: Tropical Indo-Pacific

Malea pomum is one of the smallest and most colorful members of the Tonnidae. The shell has ten to thirteen spiral cords on the body whorl. The spaces between the cords correspond to denticles on the inner lip of the aperture, which thickens inwardly. *Malea* differs from *Tonna* in having a constricted aperture, with a thickened lip and several folds in the parietal area. *Malea pomum* lives just subtidally and in depths up to 100 feet (30 meters). A subspecies, *Malea pomum noronhensis* Kempf & Matthews, 1969 was described from oceanic islands off Brazil.

There are about twenty-five living species of tonnids (tun shells). The Oocorythinae, formerly placed in Tonnidae, are now considered to be cassids. Some tonnid species are almost circumtropical in distribution in warm seas; their larvae can remain in the plankton for six to eight months. Tonnids have large, simple shells with spiral sculpture, and a usually wide aperture. An operculum is lacking. They feed on holothurians (sea cucumbers). The oldest known fossil tonnids are from the Maastrichtian in the Cretaceous.

References: Beu (1981), Warén & Bouchet (1990).

. . . .

Akibumia flexibilis

Atlanta peronii

Family: LAUBIERINIDAE Warén & Bouchet, 1990
Species: *Akibumia flexibilis* Kuroda & Habe, 1959
Common Name: Flexible Akibumia
Size: 0.8 inches (20 mm)
Distribution: Tropical Indo-Pacific

Akibumia flexibilis is known from only a few specimens taken off Japan, and one off Tanzania. The shell has seven whorls and is thin and slightly flexible. The protoconch consists of 4.5 to 5 whorls and has a latticed sculpture of spiral and axial threads. The species was originally assigned to the Trichotropidae, but is now placed in the family Laubierinidae, which was named in 1990. Laubierinids differ from other tonnaceans in having a gill with one rather than two rows of filaments and in lacking a well-defined siphonal notch or canal. *Laubierina,* the other known genus in the family is unusual in that the reticulate larval shells can be large (0.2 inches or 5 millimeters), and males are sexually mature at the time of settlement. Laubierinids live in depths below 600 feet (180 meters). Only six species, all rare, are currently known. The family has not as yet been reported in the fossil record.

Reference: Warén & Bouchet (1990).

. . . .

Infraorder: Heteropoda Lamarck, 1812
Superfamily: Carinariacea Blainville, 1818
Family: ATLANTIDAE Rang, 1829
Species: *Atlanta peronii* Lesueur, 1817
Common Name: Peron's Sea Butterfly
Size: 0.4 inches (10 mm)
Distribution: Worldwide

Atlanta peronii has a flattened, dextrally coiled shell consisting of five whorls, with a keel around the shell circumference. The shell is white and the base of the keel is sometimes brown. *Atlanta peronii* is pelagic, spending its entire life floating and swimming in the ocean in tropical and temperate areas. The foot is modified for use as a fin and the keel on the shell acts as a stabilizer when the animal is swimming. The animals are predatory and have well-developed eyes with crystalline lenses. The fin bears a sucker that is used to hold prey, which includes pteropods such as *Hyalocylis,* and other heteropods. There are sixteen species of atlantids in three genera, *Atlanta, Oxygyrus,* and *Protatlanta,* which differ in the degree of calcification of the shell. The oldest undoubted atlantid fossils date from the Miocene, although the group is thought to have originated during the Mesozoic.

References: Lalli & Gilmer (1989), Spoel (1976).

. . . .

Carinaria lamarcki

Family: CARINARIIDAE Blainville, 1818
Species: *Carinaria lamarcki* Péron & Lesueur, 1810
Common Name: Lamarck's Glassy Nautilus
Size: 2 inches (50 mm)
Distribution: Worldwide

Carinaria lamarcki has a cap-shaped shell with a spirally coiled protoconch. The shell is fragile and transparent, with a central keel and concentric corrugations. The shell covers only the viscera of the animal, and is much smaller than the body, which can range in length up to 8.5 inches (220 millimeters). Like the atlantids, carinariids are pelagic throughout life, occurring worldwide in tropical and temperate seas. The shell, although anatomically dorsal, hangs below the body in life. The animals are active predators, and swim using the modified foot as a fin. They feed on salps, small fish, crustaceans, and other planktonic mollusks. There are seven species of carinariids in three genera, *Carinaria*, *Pterosoma*, and *Cardiopoda*. *Carinaria cristata* (Linné, 1767), the largest planktonic gastropod, can reach lengths of 20 inches (0.5 meters). The fossil record of the family dates from the Jurassic.

References: Lalli & Gilmer (1989), Spoel (1976).

. . . .

Mastonia guamensis

Infraorder: Ptenoglossa Gray, 1853
Superfamily: Triphoracea Gray, 1847
Family: TRIPHORIDAE Gray, 1847
Species: *Mastonia guamensis* Kosuge, 1974
Common Name: Guam Triphora
Size: 0.2 inches (5 mm)
Distribution: Guam (Marianas Islands)

Mastonia guamensis is one of the unheralded jewels one finds when studying minute species. The shell has two rows of beads on each spire whorl, the lower row being orange-brown and the upper lavender. The protoconch has four spirally keeled whorls with numerous axial riblets. The teleoconch is slightly concave in outline and has ten whorls. The animals live on encrusting sponges under rocks subtidally in depths to 6 feet (2 meters).

The Triphoridae is a large family, having probably more than 1,000 species. They should not be confused with the homophonous Triforidae. Triphorids are extremely diverse in the Indo-Pacific, and more than eighty species have been found in a single collecting sample; they are specialized for feeding on various types of sponges. Most species are sinistral and have a posterior siphonal canal in addition to the anterior one. However, some triphorids of the subfamilies Adelacerithiinae and Metaxiinae are dextral and lack the posterior siphon, and are difficult to separate from cerithiopsids on the basis of shell characters. Triphorids have five to sixty-three radular teeth per row, whereas cerithiopsids and triforids always have seven teeth per row. The oldest unquestionably triphorid fossils are from the Paleocene.

Reference: Marshall (1983).

. . . .

Family: CERITHIOPSIDAE Adams & Adams, 1853
Species: *Cerithiopsis bicolor* C. B. Adams, 1845
Common Name: Two-toned Cerithiopsis
Size: 0.5 inches (12 mm)
Distribution: South Carolina to the Caribbean

This common, shallow-water species is usually misidentified as *Cerithiopsis emersonii* (C. B. Adams, 1839) from New England, but is distinguished by color and sculpture. *Cerithiopsis bicolor* has a yellowish shell with a reddish brown or pink band at the suture, whereas *C. emersonii* is one color—ocher or reddish brown. *Cerithiopsis bicolor* has five spiral cords on the lower whorls, the second and fourth of which are strongly beaded. The first cord, immediately below the suture, and the fifth cord are slender and smooth. The first cord is appressed to the fifth cord of the whorl above, or partially overlaps it. The third (middle) cord is intermediate in strength and sometimes develops beading, but not as strongly as on the second and fourth. In *C. emersonii*, the first and fifth cords are often faint and the beading on the third cord is stronger. *Cerithiopsis bicolor* has an axially ribbed protoconch of about four whorls.

The Cerithiopsidae contains about 400 species in thirty genera; the largest individuals do not exceed 1 inch (25 millimeters) in length. They occur worldwide in cold, temperate, and tropical seas. Many species live in association with sponges, often burrowing into them. Male cerithiopsids lack a penis.

References: Boss (1982), Lyons (1989).

. . . .

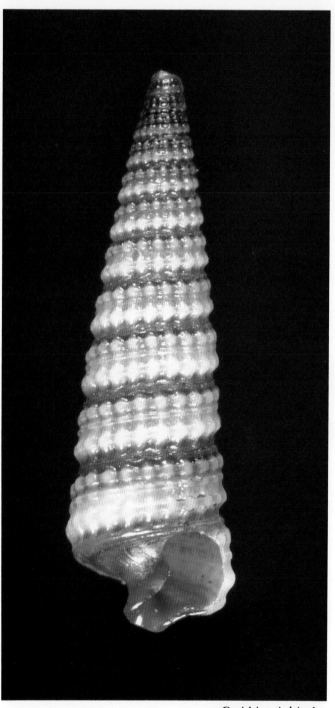

Cerithiopsis bicolor

Family: TRIFORIDAE Jousseaume, 1884

Species: *Cerithiella metula* (Lovén, 1846)

Common Name: Pillar Cerithiella

Size: 0.6 inches (16 mm)

Distribution: Mediterranean to Iceland and Scandinavia

Cerithiella metula has a white, slender shell of fourteen to eighteen whorls. The initial whorl of the protoconch is smooth and rounded; the next two whorls have curved axial ribs. The teleoconch whorls have straight axial ribs. The body whorl has four strong spiral cords, three of which are visible on the spire whorls. The species has been dredged in depths of 130 to 4,000 feet (40 to 1200 meters).

Triforids have high-spired, right-handed shells, usually with a basal spiral cord and an anterior siphonal canal that angles away from the aperture. Some, such as *Triforis,* also have a posterior siphonal notch or tube. The family Triforidae should not be confused with the homophonous Triphoridae, most members of which are left-handed. Most triforids live in cold seas and feed on the outer surfaces of sponges.

References: Boss (1982), Marshall (1983), Thorson (1941).

. . . .

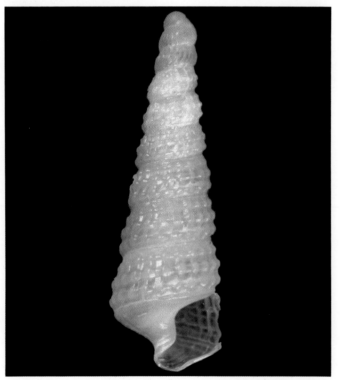

Cerithiella metula

Schwengelia hendersoni

Superfamily: Epitoniacea Berry, 1910

Family: ACLIDIDAE Sars, 1878

Species: *Schwengelia hendersoni* (Dall, 1927)

Common Name: Henderson's Schwengelia

Size: 0.15 inches (4 mm)

Distribution: Florida

Schwengelia hendersoni has a translucent white shell of six to seven whorls, with a smooth, rounded protoconch of about 1.7 whorls. The early whorls have two or three sharp spiral cords, which increase to four or five on later whorls. The cords may become weaker on the lower whorls. The species has been dredged in depths from 30 to 3,100 feet (10 to 950 meters). It is similar to *Schwengelia floridana* (Bartsch, 1911), which has much weaker spiral sculpture. Members of Aclididae generally have small, white, elongate shells with smooth protoconchs. The operculum is thin, corneous, paucispiral, and has the nucleus at the edge. Anatomical investigations on the various genera included in the family will likely show that it is heterogeneous, assembled on the basis of superficial similarities of the shells.

References: Abbott (1974), Boss (1982).

. . . .

trap" is Dutch, and "wendeltreppe" is German for "spiral staircase.") Epitoniids are parasites or predators on coelenterates and can often be found buried in sand around sea anemones. Beachcombers who see charcoal or bits of styrofoam in the driftline should keep an eye out for wentletraps, as the lightweight shells wash to the same level on the shore.

References: Dance (1966, 1969).

. . . .

Epitonium scalare

Family: EPITONIIDAE Berry, 1910
Species: *Epitonium scalare* (Linné, 1758)
Common Name: Precious Wentletrap
Size: 2.5 inches (60 mm)
Distribution: East Africa to Fiji

In the mid-1700s, *Epitonium scalare* was one of the most coveted of all seashells, and drew fabulous prices at auctions. Legend holds that Chinese artisans made rice-paste facsimiles of the shell to satisfy ravenous collectors. Today such a forgery, if any exist, would be worth far more than the shell itself, which can be bought for $10. The species is commonly dredged subtidally in depths to 100 feet (30 meters).

Epitonium scalare is one of the largest of the several hundred species of wentletraps; most epitoniids are less than 1 inch (25 millimeters) in length. It is unusual in that the whorls do not touch each other except at the varices; in most wentletraps the whorls are in contact. ("Wentle-

Janthina janthina

Family: JANTHINIDAE Lamarck, 1812
Species: *Janthina janthina* (Linné, 1758)
Common Name: Common Janthina
Size: 1.5 inches (40 mm)
Distribution: Tropics and subtropics worldwide

Janthina janthina is the largest and most abundant of the five species in its genus. The shell is angled at the periphery and is broader than that of the other species, which are more globular in shape. The shell is lilac on the spire and violet on the base. This coloration serves as camouflage, as *Janthina* float upside-down on bubble rafts at the surface of the ocean. To a predator coming from beneath, the light spire would blend with the sky; similarly, the dark base would blend into the depths for an aerial predator. *Janthina* builds its bubble raft with its foot by encasing air in mucus. The animal has no operculum, and would fall from its raft if it withdrew into its shell. The animal is unable to swim and cannot make a new float underwater and so could not return to the surface. *Janthina* prey mainly on pelagic coelenterates, including *Velella* (the "by-the-wind-sailor") and *Physalia* (the "Portuguese man-of-war"), but are known to eat other *Janthina* also. The only other member of Janthinidae is *Recluzia* with about three species. *Recluzia* are similar in habits to *Janthina,* but have brown, higher-spired shells.

Reference: Lalli & Gilmer (1989).

. . . .

Niso hendersoni

Superfamily: Eulimacea Adams & Adams, 1854
Family: EULIMIDAE Adams & Adams, 1854
Species: *Niso hendersoni* Bartsch, 1953
Common Name: Henderson's Niso
Size: 1.25 inches (32 mm)
Distribution: North Carolina to Florida

Niso hendersoni is one of the largest eulimids, having up to eighteen whorls. The shell is smooth and glossy, except for occasional finely incised microscopic growth lines. The ground color is brownish yellow, with a white band at the periphery. A fine brown line with brown markings runs through the center of the white band. The operculum is yellow, thin, corneous, and paucispiral. The species has been dredged in depths of 80 to 660 feet (25 to 200 meters). *Niso splendidula* (Sowerby, 1834) in the Eastern Pacific is a closely related species.

Eulimids typically have small, glossy, white shells. Most species are parasites on echinoderms such as starfish and sea cucumbers. Many are free-living—able to move from one host to another—but some are permanently attached, or have become endoparasites, losing the shell and living within the tissues of their host. There are probably several thousand species, many of them undescribed. Synonyms of Eulimidae include Stiliferidae and Melanellidae.

References: Boss (1982), Warén (1980).

. . . .

Suborder: Neogastropoda Thiele, 1929
Superfamily: Muricacea Rafinesque, 1815
Family: MURICIDAE Rafinesque, 1815
Subfamily: Muricinae Rafinesque, 1815
Species: *Murex pecten* Lightfoot, 1786
Common Name: Venus Comb Murex
Size: 6 inches (150 mm)
Distribution: East Africa to New Caledonia

Murex pecten is perhaps the most spectacular and the most perplexing of all molluscan shells. On first encounter, people are amazed that such an object exists; then they wonder how the spines are made and what their function is. The most thoughtful observers wonder how the shell grows, because the spines from the previous whorl would block the aperture on the next increment of growth if not somehow removed. The spines are formed by fingerlike projections of the mantle, which excretes calcium carbonate. The mantle can also reabsorb the shell, and cuts off the spines of the preceding whorl as needed. The spines might function to encage prey, to keep the shell from sinking into soft sediment, or to protect against predators.

Many muricids have episodic growth, with the shell remaining one size for a while, followed by rapid growth until the next varix is constructed. There are three varices per whorl in some genera, more in others. Some ranellids resemble muricines in having a long anterior canal, but are easily distinguished as the varices are spaced half a whorl or more apart. The Muricidae contains at least 500 species, most of which are predators on other gastropods, bivalves, and barnacles. There are several subfamilies, two of which are discussed in the following sections. The first muricids appeared in the fossil record during the Aptian in the Cretaceous.

References: Fair (1976), Paul (1981), Ponder & Vokes (1988), Radwin & D'Attilio (1976), Vokes (1971).

. . . .

Murex pecten

Subfamily: Thaidinae Jousseaume, 1888
Species: *Plicopurpura patula* (Linné, 1758)
Common Name: Wide-mouthed Purpura
Size: 3 inches (75 mm)
Distribution: South Florida, Bermuda, and Caribbean

Plicopurpura patula has 4.5 to 5.5 rapidly expanding whorls. The broad aperture allows for a large foot for gripping onto rocks, as the species lives in the surf zone in intertidal areas. The animal feeds on barnacles, tube-dwelling polychaete worms, and other mollusks, including chitons. It secretes a milky fluid that may have an anaesthetizing or paralyzing effect on its prey. This fluid turns purple when exposed to air and has been used as a permanent dye.

As do most muricids, thaidines (rock shells) have an accessory boring organ in the sole of the foot, and can

Plicopurpura patula

bore holes in the shells of their prey by combined chemical and radular action. Naticids also bore holes, but their boring organ is in the proboscis, and they produce beveled boreholes, whereas those of muricids are straight-sided. The Thaidinae includes many genera of tropical and subtropical intertidal predatory gastropods, such as *Drupa, Mancinella, Morula, Purpura, Stramonita,* and *Thais.*

References: Clench (1947), Kool (1987).

. . . .

Babelomurex echinatus

Subfamily: Coralliophilinae Chenu, 1859
Species: *Babelomurex echinatus* (Azuma, 1960)
Common Name: Prickly Latiaxis
Size: 1 inch (25 mm)
Distribution: Japan to the Philippines

Babelomurex echinatus is one of the spiniest coralliophilines; with six or seven spiral rows of spines and ten to twelve varices, it can have more than seventy spines on the body whorl. Color ranges from white to peach and light brown. Coralliophilines are parasites on various kinds of corals. The radula is reduced or lost, and feeding is by suction. Some *Coralliophila* live on hard corals, whereas other genera, such as *Rapa,* live buried in colonies of soft corals. *Magilus* burrows in hard corals and forms a tubelike, uncoiled shell. There are more than 200 species, mainly in tropical and subtropical seas, in nine genera: *Babelomurex, Coralliophila, Emozamia, Hirtomurex, Latiaxis, Magilus, Mipus, Rapa,* and *Rhizochilus.* The oldest known fossils are from the Campanian of the Late Cretaceous.

Reference: Kosuge & Suzuki (1985).

. . . .

Family: TURBINELLIDAE Swainson, 1835
Subfamily: Turbinellinae Swainson, 1835
Species: *Syrinx aruanus* (Linné, 1758)
Common Name: Australian Trumpet
Size: 30 inches (760 mm)
Distribution: North Australia

Syrinx aruanus is the largest of all shelled gastropods; the world record specimen being slightly over 30 inches (760 millimeters) long. It is often referred to as the largest gastropod, but some individuals of *Aplysia vaccaria* Winkler, 1955, the California Black Seahare, which lacks an external shell, also reach lengths of 30 inches (760 millimeters). For years, *Syrinx* was classified in the Melongenidae, but the protoconch, operculum, radula, proboscis, and egg cases are more similar to those of turbinellids. The protoconch of *Syrinx* is tall and multiwhorled; it is almost always broken off in adults. The genus *Perostylus* was named for juvenile shells, which differ markedly in appearance from adults. *Megalatractus* is another synonym of *Syrinx. Syrinx* lives on mudflats intertidally and in depths to 30 feet (10 meters).

The Turbinellidae is divided into four subfamilies, Turbinellinae, Vasinae, Ptychatractinae, and Columbariinae. Some taxa previously placed in Volutidae have recently been transferred to Ptychatractinae, genera of which include *Benthovoluta, Ceratoxancus, Metzgeria, Ptychatractus,* and *Surculina.* Vasinae and Columbariinae are discussed in more detail below. Members of the family are predators on sipunculans (peanut worms) and poly-chaetes. There are more than 100 species worldwide. The fossil record of turbinellids extends to the Albian of the Early Cretaceous.

References: Harasewych & Petit (1989), Quinn (1981), Wagner & Abbott (1990).

. . . .

Columbarium spinicinctum

Subfamily: Columbariinae Tomlin, 1928
Species: *Columbarium spinicinctum* (von Martens, 1881)
Common Name: Spiny Pagoda Shell
Size: 2.5 inches (60 mm)
Distribution: Eastern Australia

Columbarium spinicinctum occurs in depths of 160 to 430 feet (50 to 130 meters) off Eastern Australia. Like many columbariines, the shell resembles that of some *Murex* species in having spines and a long anterior siphonal canal. It differs in having a bulbous protoconch and an operculum with the nucleus at the end, rather than at the side, and in its lack of varices. Columbariines lack the columellar folds seen in most other turbinellids. There are about fifty living species worldwide, all restricted to deep water on the outer continental shelf and upper continental slope. They are thought to feed on tube-dwelling polychaetes. Genera include *Columbarium, Coluzea,* and *Fulgurofusus.* The group first appeared in Maastrichtian of the Late Cretaceous of Europe.

References: Harasewych (1983, 1986).

. . . .

Syrinx aruanus

Tudivasum armigerum

Subfamily: Vasinae Adams & Adams, 1853
Species: *Tudivasum armigerum* (A. Adams, 1856)
Common Name: Armored Vase
Size: 3 inches (75 mm)
Distribution: North Australia

Like the columbariines, *Tudivasum armigerum* resembles species of *Murex* in having a spiny shell with a long anterior canal. It differs from muricines in having a bulbous protoconch and an operculum with a terminal nucleus, and in its lack of varices, and from columbariines in having columellar folds. The animal lives on sand and rubble bottoms from the low-tide line to depths of 115 feet (35 meters).

There are about twenty-five species of vasines (vase shells), which occur worldwide in tropical and subtropical seas, primarily in the intertidal zone and in shallow water. Genera include *Afer, Tudicla, Tudivasum,* and *Vasum. Tudivasum* was previously known as *Tudicula,* which caused confusion with *Tudicla.* The only living species of *Tudicla* is *Tudicla spirillus* (Linné, 1767).

References: Abbott (1959), Rosenberg & Petit (1987).

· · · · · · · · · · · · · ·

Family: BUCCINIDAE Rafinesque, 1815
Subfamily: Buccininae Rafinesque, 1815
Species: *Babylonia ambulacrum* (Sowerby, 1825)
Common Name: Gallery Babylonia
Size: 2 inches (50 mm)
Distribution: Andaman Sea to the Philippines

Babylonia ambulacrum can be distinguished from other members of its genus by its deep sutural canal with a raised margin; the canal becomes distinctly narrower on the body whorl near the aperture. The brown spots on the last whorl are close together, and sometimes fuse, giving a pattern of diagonal bands. The umbilicus is open in subadults, but callused over when the animal is fully mature. Some *Babylonia* are known to eat dead fish.

The Buccinidae is a large group with more than 1,000 species. Some recent classification, followed herein, treat Nassariinae, Fasciolariinae, and Melongeninae as subfamilies of Buccinidae, rather than as full families because there is little anatomical distinction among them, and it can sometimes be difficult to tell by shell alone to which group a specimen belongs. Buccinids are carnivores and scavengers, feeding on bivalves, polychaetes, and carrion. They occur in all oceans, from the intertidal zone to abyssal depths. The genus *Clea* is unusual in having invaded fresh water in southeast Asia. Buccinine genera include *Beringius, Buccinum, Colus, Neptunea,* and *Penion.* The Buccinidae are known as Albian fossils from the Early Cretaceous.

References: Altena & Gittenberger (1981), Boss (1982), Ponder & Warén (1988).

. . . .

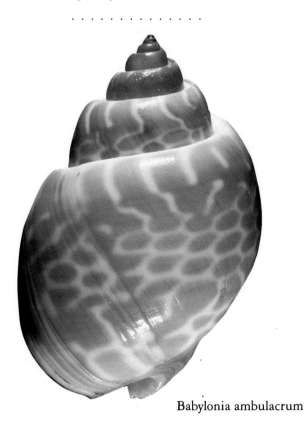

Babylonia ambulacrum

Pleuroploca gigantea

Subfamily: Fasciolariinae Gray, 1853
Species: *Pleuroploca gigantea* (Kiener, 1840)
Common Name: Florida Horse Conch
Size: 24 inches (610 mm)
Distribution: North Carolina to Yucatan

Pleuroploca gigantea is the largest shelled gastropod in the Western Hemisphere, with the world record specimen just over 2 feet (610 millimeters) in length. Typical adults are about 1 foot (305 millimeters) long. The shell is covered with a dark brown periostracum, which flakes off of dried specimens. Young specimens are orange in color, and the living animal is red. *Pleuroploca gigantea* lives in depths of 1 to 20 feet (0.3 to 6 meters) on sandy, muddy grass flats, where it feeds on other mollusks.

Fasciolariines have high-spired shells with well-developed anterior siphonal canals. In some genera, such as *Fusinus,* the canal can be as long as the spire. Many fasciolariines have weak columellar folds. The operculum is corneous, brown, thick, and has a terminal nucleus. There are more than 200 species, which are distributed worldwide in tropical and subtropical seas. They are active predators on bivalves, gastropods, and polychaetes. Members of one genus, *Opeatostoma,* have a strong spine on the outer lip that they use to wedge clams open. The fossil record of fasciolariines reaches the Aptian of the early Cretaceous.

References: Bullock (1974), Wagner & Abbott (1990).

. . . .

Subfamily: Melongeninae Gill, 1871
Species: *Busycotypus canaliculatus* (Linné, 1758)
Common Name: Channeled Whelk
Size: 8 inches (200 mm)
Distribution: Massachusetts to Florida

Busycotypus canaliculatus is a common species in shallow water in bays along the eastern seaboard of the United States, where it feeds on bivalves. It is characterized by a deep, square-sided canal at the suture. The periostracum is a dirty yellow, with small hairs projecting in the area between the ridge and the canal. Egg capsules are laid in a string; each capsule is oval with a scalloped edge. The strings of capsules often wash ashore; they resemble coiled sets of vertebrae. The eggs hatch within the capsules, and the young exit by crawling through a pore on the outer rim.

The Melongeninae tend to be lower spired than the Fasciolariinae, and to have larger body whorls. The columella does not have any folds. The operculum is thick and corneous with a terminal nucleus. There are twenty to twenty-five species in the subfamily, which is tropical in distribution except for *Busycotypus* and *Busycon,* which also occur in temperate waters. They are predators on mollusks in sandy and muddy areas in the intertidal zone and shallow water, and will also feed on carrion. The group originated by the Albian of the Early Cretaceous.

References: Abbott & Dance (1982), Clench & Turner (1956).

. . . .

Busycotypus canaliculatus

Subfamily: Nassariinae Iredale, 1916
Species: *Nassarius gaudiosus* (Hinds, 1844)
Common Name: Gaudy Nassa
Size: 0.8 inches (20 mm)
Distribution: Tropical Indo-Pacific

Nassarius gaudiosus is an abundant species that lives in colonies in pockets of clean coral sand on reefs intertidally and in depths to 65 feet (20 meters). The color pattern is quite variable, but is usually white or cream with blotches of tan, brown, or orange. Brown spiral lines are usually visible on the body whorl, especially near the outer lip. The spire is concave and axially ribbed, with an inflated penultimate whorl.

Nassariines (mud snails) occur worldwide in tropical and temperate seas but are most diverse in the tropical Indo-Pacific. More than 300 living species are known.

Genera include *Bullia, Buccinanops, Cyllene, Demoulia, Dorsanum,* and *Nassarius.* In some species tentacles project from the posterior end of the foot. The operculum is thin and corneous, and often has a serrated edge. Many nassariines are scavengers, feeding on carrion, but they are also known to eat opisthobranch eggs, detritus, and algae. Fossil nassariines are known from the Campanian of the Late Cretaceous.

References: Allmon (1990), Cernohorsky (1984).

. . . .

Family: COLUMBELLIDAE Swainson, 1840
Species: *Columbella mercatoria* (Linné, 1758)
Common Name: Common Dove-shell
Size: 0.8 inches (20 mm)
Distribution: Florida and Bermuda to Brazil

Columbella mercatoria comes in an abundance of colors, ranging from almost pure white, through yellow and orange, to dark brown, or speckled with various combinations of them. Sculpture consists of numerous spiral cords and shallow axial ribs. The outer lip is thickened in adults and bears a dozen or more denticles. The periostracum is thin and flaxen; the operculum is smaller than the aperture. The animal lives under rocks intertidally and in depths to 12 feet (4 meters).

The Columbellidae (dove-shells) are a diverse family represented in all oceans worldwide. There are perhaps as many as 500 species. Although conchologically diverse, they are united by features of the radula. They are unusual for muricaceans in having no cusp on the central tooth of the radula (except in two species). The lateral teeth apparently can rotate together and function like tweezers. Individuals of most species are less than 0.4 inches (10 millimeters) in length and few exceed 2 inches (50 millimeters). Columbellids have been reported to feed on a wide variety of items including polychaetes, small crustaceans, ascidians, hydroids, algae, and carrion. The oldest fossil columbellids are from the Lower Paleocene.

References: Boss (1982), Jung (1989).

. . . .

Nassarius gaudiosus

Columbella mercatoria

Harpa costata

Harpa costata has long been one of the most desirable of seashells. Although many hundreds of specimens are known, the species has a restricted geographic range in the western Indian Ocean. The current market value is $300 to $500, depending on the size and quality of the specimen. It is easily distinguished from other *Harpa* species by the large number of axial ribs, thirty or more on the body whorl. The species lives on sand banks in depths to 6 feet (2 meters). The living animal has a large foot which, when fully extended, is twice the length of the shell.

The family Harpidae includes three genera, *Austroharpa, Harpa,* and *Morum* and about thirty-seven species. Most species of *Harpa* live in the tropical Indo-Pacific, but there is one species in the Eastern Pacific and one in the Eastern Atlantic. The fossil record dates to the Paleocene, in the form of the extinct genus *Eocithara.* More information on the family is provided under the next species, *Morum dennisoni.*

References: Dance (1969), Rehder (1973), Walls (1980).

. . . .

Family: HARPIDAE Bronn, 1849
Subfamily: Harpinae Bronn, 1849
Species: *Harpa costata* (Linné, 1758)
Common Name: Imperial Harp
Size: 4 inches (100 mm)
Distribution: Mauritius, Rodrigues, and northern Madagascar

Subfamily: Moruminae Hughes & Emerson, 1987
Species: *Morum dennisoni* (Reeve, 1842)
Common Name: Dennison's Morum
Size: 2 inches (50 mm)
Distribution: Florida, Bahamas, and Caribbean

Morum dennisoni has long been considered one of the great rarities among seashells. Of the perhaps thirty specimens known by the 1960s, all but a few were in museums. During the 1980s, dredging off Barbados and Colombia produced numerous specimens, but the species still commands a high price. *Morum dennisoni* is closely related to *Morum veleroae* Emerson, 1968 from the Eastern Pacific; the latter differs in having more delicate axial sculpture and a mauve rather than orange parietal callus. They are considered "twin" or cognate species that presumably diverged from a common ancestral stock that was divided into separate populations by the closing of the Isthmus of Panama about three million years ago. *Morum dennisoni* lives in depths from 200 to 460 feet (60 to 140 meters) in coral, rock, and sponge substrata.

Until recently, *Morum* was considered a member of the family Cassidae on the basis of shell morphology. Anatomical studies have now demonstrated that it is actually a member of the Harpidae. Both *Harpa* and *Morum* share the unusual behavior of losing the rear part of the foot when disturbed, presumably to distract predators. The self-inflicted loss of a body part in this manner is called autotomy. *Harpa* and *Morum* both have reduced radulae sometimes with only one tooth per row; they feed on crustaceans, probably by sucking semidigested fluids from their prey. *Morum* have a reduced, corneous operculum, whereas *Harpa* lack an operculum altogether. *Morum* have direct development whereas *Harpa* have planktonic development. Twenty-three living species of *Morum* are known from the tropical Western Atlantic and Indian and Pacific Oceans. The fossil record of *Morum* dates to the Eocene.

References: Dance & Emerson (1967), Dance (1969), Hughes (1986), Hughes & Emerson (1987).

. . . .

Morum dennisoni

Marginella goodalli

Family: MARGINELLIDAE Fleming, 1828
Species: *Marginella goodalli* Sowerby, 1825
Common Name: Goodall's Marginella
Size: 1.5 inches (40 mm)
Distribution: Senegal

Marginella goodalli is often confused with a recently named, but commoner species, *Marginella sebastiani* Marche & Rosso, 1979. The latter is larger, reaching 2 inches (50 millimeters), and is orange-red in color, whereas *M. goodalli* is orange-yellow. *Marginella goodalli* has a proportionately shorter, narrower aperture than *M. sebastiani*, and the shoulder of the last two whorls is concave, whereas the shoulder in *M. sebastiani* is convex.

There are several hundred species of marginellids, mostly in tropical and subtropical waters, with highest diversity in West and South Africa. Most species have direct development, and geographical ranges can be quite restricted. Marginellids have smooth, glossy shells and lack an operculum. In most species, the shell forms a thickened lip at maturity. The family is divided into three subfamilies, Marginellinae, Marginelloninae, and Cystiscinae. Most species are under 1 inch (25 millimeters) in length, but *Afrivoluta* and *Marginellona* both can exceed 5 inches (130 millimeters). One genus, *Rivomarginella*, occurs in fresh water in Thailand. Marginellids have been reported to feed on other gastropods, foraminifera, and carrion. Some species lack a radula and presumably feed suctorially. The family is first seen in Maastrichtian deposits in the Late Cretaceous.

References: Coovert (1988), Coovert & Coovert (1990).

. . . .

Pleioptygma helenae

Family: PLEIOPTYGMATIDAE Quinn, 1989
Species: *Pleioptygma helenae* (Radwin & Bibbey, 1972)
Common Name: Helen's Miter
Size: 4.5 inches (110 mm)
Distribution: Atlantic Honduras

Pleioptygma helenae is the only known living representative of the genus *Pleioptygma,* which is well-represented in the form of Pliocene fossils from the Carolinas and Florida. The living species has a beautiful marbled pattern of brown and white with about twenty dashed spiral lines, which are raised as cords on the spire and lower body whorl. There are six folds on the columella. The upper whorls have axial lines between the spiral cords. The protoconch is white and smooth, consisting of 2.3 whorls. The animals have been dredged in depths of 330 to 500 feet (100 to 150 meters).

The systematic position of *Pleioptygma* has long been controversial. The genus was named as a member of the Volutidae, but *P. helenae* was named in the Mitridae. Recent anatomical studies have demonstrated that *Pleioptygma* has unique features of the proboscis, buccal mass, and radula that justify placing it in its own family, but it is probably more closely related to the Mitridae than the Volutidae. Pleioptygmatids probably feed on soft-bodied prey such as polychaetes and sipunculans.

Reference: Quinn (1989).

. . . .

Family: MITRIDAE Swainson, 1831
Species: *Mitra sanguinolenta* Lamarck, 1811
Common Name: Bloody Miter
Size: 1.2 inches (30 mm)
Distribution: Mozambique to Oman

Mitra sanguinolenta is a rare species that until recently was known only from Somalia. The shell has spiral cords and axial ribs, with small pits at the intersections of their interspaces. In some specimens the axial sculpture is weak. The cords and ribs are light orange, their interspaces blood red. A broad white band encircles the body whorl and a narrow band lies below the suture. There are four columellar folds.

The Mitridae and Costellariidae collectively are known as the miter shells. In most mitrids the spiral sculpture is dominant, whereas axial sculpture dominates in costellariids. Most costellariids have numerous sharp spiral cords (lirations) in the aperture on the inner surface of the outer lip. These lirations are absent in mitrids. There are about 250 species of mitrids, which occur worldwide in tropical and temperate seas. Diversity is highest in the tropical Indo-Pacific. Species live in sand or under rocks in coral reefs. They feed primarily on sipunculans (peanut worms) and gastropods. The fossil record of mitrids extends to the Turonian of the Late Cretaceous.

References: Cernohorsky (1970, 1976, 1991), Pechar et al. (1980), Turner (1989).

. . . .

Family: COSTELLARIIDAE MacDonald, 1860
Species: *Vexillum stainforthii* (Reeve, 1842)
Common Name: Stainforth's Miter
Size: 2 inches (50 mm)
Distribution: Tropical Western Pacific

Vexillum stainforthii has ten to twelve strong axial ribs per whorl; there are five red spiral bands on the body whorl, with two visible on the spire whorls. The red is primarily on the axial ribs and not in the interspaces. There are numerous fine spiral grooves. The columella has four folds and the area around the siphonal canal is stained bluish black.

The Costellariidae and Mitridae together are known as the miter shells. In costellariids, axial sculpture is dominant, but most have spiral sculpture, particularly on the early whorls. In mitrids spiral sculpture dominates. Almost all costellariids, except *Austromitra,* have apertural lirations, which mitrids lack. Costellariids also differ from mitrids in having simple, curved lateral radular teeth, rather than multicuspid ones, and in lacking an epiproboscis (snout), so that the head appears to be truncated just in front of the tentacles. There are about 250 species of costellariids worldwide, with highest diversity in the tropical Indo-Pacific. They feed mainly on gastropods. The oldest known fossils are from the Cenomanian of the Late Cretaceous.

References: Cernohorsky (1970, 1976), Pechar et al. (1980), Turner (1989).

. . . .

Mitra sanguinolenta

Vexillum stainforthii

Oliva porphyria

Family: OLIVIDAE Latreille, 1825
Subfamily: Olivinae Latreille, 1825
Species: *Oliva porphyria* (Linné, 1758)
Common Name: Tent Olive
Size: 4.5 inches (110 mm)
Distribution: Gulf of California to Panama

Oliva porphyria is the largest of the living olive shells, and is one of the most distinctive and instantly identifiable of all seashells. The pattern of chestnut zigzags on a pink background is like that of the tented cone shells, and calls to mind maps of mountain ranges in fantasy kingdoms. The animal lives intertidally and in depths to 65 feet (20 meters) in sand.

There are several hundred species of olive shells worldwide, with highest diversity in tropical and subtropical regions. Most live in sand, where they feed mainly on bivalves, and also on gastropods and polychaetes. The family is divided into four subfamilies: Ancillinae (treated in more detail below), Agaroninae, Olivellinae, and Olivinae. Olivines lack opercula; most members of the other subfamilies have them. Olivid shells are usually smooth and highly polished. The fossil record of the group begins in the Campanian of the Late Cretaceous.

References: Greifeneder et al. (1981), Petuch & Sargent (1986), Zeigler & Porreca (1969).

. . . .

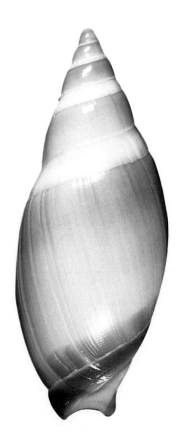

Ancillista cingulata

Scaphella junonia

Subfamily: Ancillinae Swainson, 1835
Species: *Ancillista cingulata* (Sowerby, 1830)
Common Name: Girdled Ancilla
Size: 3 inches (75 mm)
Distribution: Northern Australia

Ancillista cingulata is similar to *A. velesiana* Iredale, 1936, also from Australia, which reaches sizes of 4 inches (100 millimeters). *Ancillista velesiana* has a more inflated, cylindrical body whorl than *A. cingulata,* and its spire has a glossy, golden brown callus. The spire in *A. cingulata* lacks the callus, and is pink or bluish gray in color. The species lives on intertidal and subtidal sandflats. There are about 100 species of Ancillinae, which occur in temperate and tropical seas worldwide. Almost all species have an operculum, which is thin, corneous, and has a nearly terminal nucleus. The foot is expansible, and has

flaplike extensions that almost completely cover the shell when the animal is crawling.

References: Kilburn (1981), Wilson & Gillett (1971).

. . . .

Family: VOLUTIDAE Rafinesque, 1815
Species: *Scaphella junonia* (Lamarck, 1804)
Common Name: Junonia or Juno's Volute
Size: 5 inches (130 mm)
Distribution: North Carolina to Florida to Yucatan

For many years *Scaphella junonia* was considered one of the rarest of the volutes. In the 1820s only four specimens were known in Europe. As with most "rare" shells, rarity was due to lack of knowledge of the habitat—living in depths from 60 to 260 feet (20 to 80 meters), specimens rarely wash up on beaches. Thousands have been taken by shrimp trawlers operating out of the Florida Keys, and specimens have been available for as little as $10. *Scaphella junonia* is now considered the commonest of the species of *Scaphella*.

The Volutidae contains about 250 species worldwide, with highest diversity in Australia. Most species lack an operculum; those that have one tend to have higher spires or constricted apertures. Most species have strong columellar folds; these, however, are weak or absent in some. A few species are live-bearers, with the eggs hatching internally and releasing crawling juveniles. Volutids are predators on bivalves and gastropods. Late Cretaceous Cenomanian deposits hold the earliest volutid fossils.

References: Dance (1969), Weaver & duPont (1970).

Family: VOLUTOMITRIDAE Gray, 1854
Species: *Waimatea obscura* (Hutton, 1873)
Common Name: Cloudy Volutomitra
Size: 1 inch (25 mm)
Distribution: Southern Australia, Tasmania, and New Zealand

The shell of *Waimatea obscura* has incised spiral lines below the suture and on the lower part of the body whorl, and some forms have axial ribs. The color is dark brown or olive, with a white band below the suture and spiral rows of flecks of white on the body whorl. The species has been dredged in depths of 30 to 200 feet (9 to 64 meters).

Volutomitrids resemble mitrids but have an operculum, and a second columellar fold that is as strong or stronger than the first one. In mitrids, the first fold is strongest. The radula differs from that of mitrids in having a wishbone-shaped central tooth, rather than a

Waimatea obscura

cusped plate, and in lacking lateral teeth in some cases. There are about twenty-five living species of voluto-mitrids, most in deep or cold water. The fossil record of the group has been traced to the Maastrichtian of the Late Cretaceous.

References: Cernohorsky (1970), Powell (1979).

. . . .

Sveltia gladiator

Superfamily: Cancellariacea Forbes & Hanley, 1851
Family: CANCELLARIIDAE Forbes & Hanley, 1851
Species: *Sveltia gladiator* (Petit, 1976)
Common Name: Gladiator Nutmeg
Size: 2 inches (50 mm)
Distribution: Galapagos Islands

Sveltia gladiator is unusually spiny for a cancellariid. It has five to seven varices per whorl, each with a prominent spine at the periphery, and sometimes a second spine on the spiral cord below where it intersects the varix. The animal has been dredged in depths of 650 feet (200 meters) in the Galapagos. Most cancellariids have rough sculpture of intersecting spiral and axial elements. Most species have three or four columellar folds, but some have smooth columellae. An operculum is lacking. There are more than 150 species of cancellariids, also known as nutmeg shells, with high diversity in the Eastern Pacific. Most species are tropical or subtropical, but the genus *Admete* inhabits cold seas. The radula is unusual in its long, bladelike central teeth and lack of marginal and lateral teeth. Cancellariids are thought to use the radula to penetrate tissues of living prey, from which they suck fluids. The fossil record of the family extends to the Cenomanian of the Late Cretaceous.

References: Beu & Maxwell (1987), Petit & Harasewych (1986, 1990).

. . . .

Superfamily: Conacea Rafinesque, 1815
Family: CONIDAE Rafinesque, 1815
Species: *Conus gloriamaris* Chemnitz, 1777
Common Name: Glory-of-the-Sea
Size: 5 inches (130 mm)
Distribution: Indonesia to the Solomon Islands

The most famous of all seashells, *Conus gloriamaris* has been sought by collectors ever since its discovery in the eighteenth century, and has been surrounded by legends of its rarity and possible extinction. About a dozen specimens were known by 1900, and more than fifty had been recorded by 1970 when scuba divers in the Solomon Islands collected more than 150 specimens. The record price paid for this shell was $2,000 in 1964. The largest known specimen is 6.4 inches (162 millimeters) in length. Even today, when thousands are known, specimens taken in tangle nets in the Philippines can bring hundreds of dollars. The enormous desirability of the shell is somewhat hard to account for, as it has never been the rarest of shells, nor the most beautiful—large specimens of the common textile cone are as pretty. Perhaps the great allure lies in the name itself, *gloriamaris,* Glory-of-the-Sea.

There are as many as 500 species of cone shells in tropical and semitropical seas worldwide. The radula in cones lacks central and lateral teeth, and the marginal teeth have been modified as ''harpoons'' that inject venom into the cone's prey. Cones feed mainly on gastropods, polychaetes, and fish; species that are poisonous to fish can be dangerous to humans, and human fatalities have been caused by some Indo-Pacific species. Collectors must exercise caution in handling live cone shells. Despite the large number of species, a satisfactory generic classification of the cones has not been established, because of the relative uniformity of shell shapes in the family. Most classifications place all species in the genus *Conus,* pending availability of anatomical information that might allow generic revision. Fossil cones are known from the Maastrichtian of the Late Cretaceous.

References: Abbott (1972), Dance (1966), Walls (1978).

. . . .

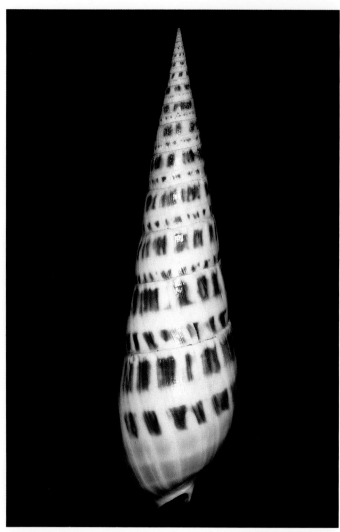

Terebra maculata

Family: TEREBRIDAE Mörch, 1852
Species: *Terebra maculata* (Linné, 1758)
Common Name: Marlinspike
Size: 10 inches (250 mm)
Distribution: East Africa to the Eastern Pacific

Terebra maculata is the largest and heaviest of the terebrids. The shell is yellow-white in color, with two spiral bands of bluish black maculations. On the early whorls, the upper band is bordered below by a spiral groove, and there are numerous axial ribs. Both spiral and axial sculpture are lost on later whorls, which have only fine axial growth lines. The animal lives subtidally in sand to depths of 650 feet (200 meters).

There are about 270 species of terebrids (auger shells). Terebrid shells resemble those of turritellids, but

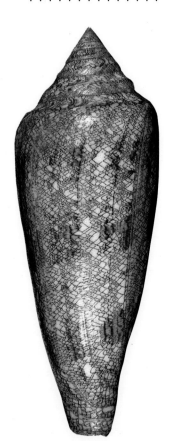

Conus gloriamaris

are easily distinguished by possession of an anterior siphonal notch. Terebrids are most diverse in the tropical Indo-Pacific, and only a few species occur in temperate waters. They are nocturnal, sand-dwelling predators, feeding mainly on polychaetes. It is likely that the Terebridae will be divided into two families. True terebrids have hypodermic radular teeth with which they inject venom into prey; the other group has two rows of solid teeth and no venom apparatus. Many terebrids lack a radula and could be members of either group. The fossil record of terebrids (in the broad sense) extends to the Maastrichtian of the Late Cretaceous.

References: Bratcher and Cernohorsky (1987), Taylor (1990).

. . . .

Family: TURRIDAE Adams & Adams, 1853
Subfamily: Turrinae Adams & Adams, 1853
Species: *Turris babylonia* (Linné, 1758)
Common Name: Babylonian Turrid
Size: 3 inches (75 mm)
Distribution: Philippines and Indonesia to the Solomon Islands

Turris babylonia has a striking color pattern of squarish black blotches on white with some streaks of brown. The sculpture consists of strong rounded spiral cords alternating with weak cords in the interspaces. The strongest cord is the one immediately below the anal sinus. As the shell grows, the anal sinus is filled in by a narrow cord that has closely spaced brown or black dots on it that are often smaller than the black blotches below. On the spire whorls, this cord can easily be mistaken for the subsutural cord above it, making it difficult to accurately count the whorls. However, the subsutural cord is thicker and has the largest blotches of any of the cords. Members of the species live in fine coral sand in depths to 20 feet (6 meters).

The Turridae are the most speciose family of mollusks, with several thousand living species and several hundred genera. All species are carnivorous, preying mainly on polychaete worms. The shells characteristically have a "turrid notch," an anal sinus on the outer lip

near the suture. The family has been divided into more than a dozen subfamilies, some of which are treated individually herein. Members of the typical subfamily, Turrinae, have a moderately long siphonal canal, lack a parietal callus, and have smooth columella and protoconch. The radula may lack the central tooth; the marginal tooth is wishbone-shaped, but sometimes missing the outer part. Turrines differ from Cochlespirinae in that the anal sinus forms a keel, often at the periphery, as the shell grows, whereas cochlespirines form a smooth, sometimes slightly sunken area on the shoulder above the periphery. The oldest known turrids date from the Turonian of the Late Cretaceous.

References: Kilburn (1983), McLean (1971), Powell (1964, 1966).

. . . .

Turris babylonia

Tropidoturris
scitecostata

The Borsoniinae includes spindle-shaped shells, some of which have one to three columellar folds. The operculum can be present or absent. The radula is toxoglossate, with hollow marginal teeth; lateral and ventral teeth are lacking. The marginals are often barbed, and are used to inject poison into prey. Some of the genera included in the subfamily are *Bathytoma, Borsonia, Cordieria, Inodrillia, Tomopleura,* and *Tropidoturris.* Some authors synonymize the subfamily Mitromorphinae with Borsoniinae. The fossil record of the subfamily extends to the Paleocene.

References: Kilburn (1986), McLean (1971), Powell (1966).

. . . .

Subfamily: Borsoniinae Bellardi, 1875
Species: *Tropidoturris scitecostata* (Sowerby, 1903)
Common Name: Elegantly Ribbed Turrid
Size: 0.8 inches (20 mm)
Distribution: South Africa

Tropidoturris scitecostata occurs in depths of 650 to 1,600 feet (200 to 500 meters) off South Africa. There are ten or eleven spiral cords and twenty to twenty-six opisthocline (backward leaning) axial ribs on the body whorl. It is similar to *Tropidoturris anaglypta* Kilburn, 1986, but differs in having the spiral cords on the body whorl restricted to the base and in having longer axial ribs. The protoconch is smooth and blunt, consisting of 1.5 whorls. Color is a moderate pink in fresh shells, but fades to light brown or yellowish pink.

Cochlespira elegans

Subfamily: Cochlespirinae Powell, 1942
Species: *Cochlespira elegans* (Dall, 1881)
Common Name: Elegant Star-turris
Size: 2 inches (50 mm)
Distribution: Florida

Cochlespira elegans is an extremely rare species that occurs in depths of 160 to 1,150 feet (50 to 350 meters) off both coasts of Florida. It is similar to *Cochlespira radiata* (Dall, 1889), but is larger, has two rather than one spiral row of spines at the periphery, and the spines are more closely spaced. The shell has about ten whorls and is off-white with numerous beaded spiral cords. The area below the suture is smooth, marked only by the faint, curved growth lines of the anal sinus. Cochlespirines resemble turrines in having an elongate anterior siphonal canal, but differ in the characteristics of the anal sinus, as discussed above. Cochlespirine genera include *Aforia*, *Antiplanes*, *Cochlespira*, *Fusiturricula*, *Knefastia*, and *Megasurcula*. This is one of the oldest groups of turrids, extending back to the Cretaceous.

References: McLean (1971), Powell (1966).

. . . .

Subfamily: Crassispirinae Morrison, 1966
Species: *Crassispira quadrifasciata* (Reeve, 1845)
Common Name: Four-banded Turrid
Size: 0.4 inches (10 mm)
Distribution: Caribbean

The distinctive color pattern of *Crassispira quadrifasciata* makes it perhaps the most easily identified of the many species of *Crassispira*. The shell is a deep chocolate brown to black, with a strong, white subsutural cord and about twenty white axial ribs on the body whorl. The ribs are bound below by additional white spiral cords. The protoconch has about two whorls; the second whorl develops axial ribs. The teleoconch has about seven whorls. The aperture is reinforced by a varix as in other crassispirines and drilliines. Crassispirines differ in radular characters from drilliines. They usually have only marginal teeth of wishbone type, but with the outer part lacking; or of duplex type, with a smaller part superim-

posed on a larger one. The fossil record of the group extends to the Eocene.

References: Kilburn (1988), McLean (1971), Powell (1966).

. . . .

Crassispira quadrifasciata

Thatcheria mirabilis

Subfamily: Daphnellinae Deshayes, 1863

Species: *Thatcheria mirabilis* Angas, 1877

Common Name: Thatcher's Wonder Shell

Size: 4 inches (100 mm)

Distribution: Japan to Australia

The elegant, sweeping lines of *Thatcheria mirabilis* have long evoked images of Japanese architecture, and for many years the species was thought to be endemic to Japan. In recent years, however, trawlers have recovered specimens from northern Australia. There is a story, perhaps apocryphal, that Frank Lloyd Wright would give a specimen of this shell to his students to remind them to remain humble before the matchless designs of nature. The species lives in depths from 200 to 2,000 feet (60 to 600 meters) on fine sand and muddy bottoms.

Thatcheria has sometimes been classified in its own subfamily, Thatcheriinae. Except for its exaggerated peripheral keel, it does not differ significantly from other daphnellines. Daphnellines can be distinguished from other turrids in having the protoconch sculptured with diagonal lines that form a cross-hatching of diamonds. Also, the anal sinus is at the suture, rather than at the shoulder or periphery, with its base intersecting the suture nearly at right angles. The previous whorl thus forms one side of the anal sinus. Daphnellines lack an operculum, and lack central and lateral radular teeth. The marginal teeth are hollow and are not barbed. The oldest reported fossil daphnellines are from the Eocene.

References: McLean (1971), Powell (1966).

. . . .

Clavus lamberti

Subfamily: Drilliinae Olsson, 1964
Species: *Clavus lamberti* (Montrouzier, 1860)
Common Name: Lambert's Clavus
Size: 0.8 inches (20 mm)
Distribution: Tropical Indo-Pacific

Clavus lamberti has a shell of about eight whorls, with a ground color ranging from orange-brown to tan. There are four white spiral bands outlined with brown on the body whorl. The upper two bands cross the axial ribs, which, on the spire, lie just above the suture. The upper spire is concave in outline. Members of the species live intertidally and subtidally on coral reefs. The subfamily Drilliinae was formerly called Clavinae, but that name had been used first for a group of insects. Drilliines have solid shells with short siphonal canals and live primarily on reefs and under rocks. The aperture in most species is reinforced by a swollen varix on the body whorl behind the anal sinus. There are five teeth per radular row, with the central tooth being reduced and the laterals broad and comblike. Drilliine genera include *Agladrillia*, *Bellaspira*, *Clavus*, *Imaclava*, *Iredalea*, *Splendrillia*, and *Tylotiella*. The fossil record of the subfamily extends to the Oligocene.

References: Kilburn (1988), McLean (1971), Powell (1966).

. . . .

Subfamily: Mangeliinae Fischer, 1883
Species: *Lienardia rubida* (Hinds, 1843)
Common Name: Ruby Lienardia
Size: 0.5 inches (12 mm)
Distribution: Tropical Pacific

Lienardia rubida is one of the commoner species of turrids on tropical Pacific islands, where it lives under coral rocks intertidally. The shell has about twenty spiral cords and ten to thirteen axial ribs on the body whorl. The protoconch has about two whorls, which have a single spiral keel; the teleoconch has about five whorls. The shell is pink to rose with brown spiral bands. Like many mangeliines, it has apertural denticles. Mangeliines lack central and lateral radular teeth and have hollow mar-

ginal teeth. Most lack an operculum, although it is present in some boreal genera. The fossil record dates from the Paleocene, but the highest diversity of the subfamily is Miocene to Recent.

References: Cernohorsky (1972), McLean (1971), Powell (1966).

. . . .

Lienardia rubida

Orbitestella toreuma

Order: Heterostropha Fischer, 1885
Superfamily: Valvatacea Gray, 1840
Family: ORBITESTELLIDAE Iredale, 1917
Species: *Orbitestella toreuma* Powell, 1930
Common Name: Embossed Orbitestella
Size: 0.03 inches (0.7 mm)
Distribution: North Island, New Zealand

Orbitestella toreuma has a minute, disklike shell with a broad umbilicus. The whorls are strongly keeled and have nodules. It resembles some members of the Omalogyridae, from which it differs in having a sinuous rather than a rounded aperture. Omalogyrids differ anatomically from orbitestellids in many ways, including lacking a pallial tentacle and a style sac. The Orbitestellidae includes two genera, *Orbitestella* and *Microdiscula*. The animals live under rocks and on various intertidal and subtidal algae, particularly coralline algae. They appear to be distantly related to the freshwater Valvatidae and the marine Cornirostridae. The fossil record of Orbitestellidae extends to the Eocene, and possibly to the Jurassic.

References: Ponder (1990, 1991).

. . . .

Superfamily: Rissoellacea Gray, 1850
Family: RISSOELLIDAE Gray, 1850
Species: *Rissoella caribaea* Rehder, 1943
Common Name: Caribbean Rissoella
Size: 0.07 inches (1.7 mm)
Distribution: Florida, Bahamas, and Caribbean

Rissoella caribaea has a simple, white, umbilicate shell, through which the black body is clearly visible. The animal lives intertidally on various types of algae, often among mangroves, but has also been taken in depths to 80 feet (25 meters). *Rissoella galba* Robertson, 1961 is similar, but is half the size of *R. caribaea* at maturity, and has a white band on the shell and a yellow body.

About forty species of rissoellids are known; they occur worldwide in tropical and temperate waters. The simple shells are similar to those of some rissoaceans, however, live rissoellids can be easily distinguished in having two pairs of cephalic tentacles instead of one. Rissoellids lack osphradium, ctenidium, and style sac. The operculum is corneous and translucent and has a lateral peg. The animals are simultaneous hermaphrodites. They have direct development—there is no planktonic larval stage.

References: Ponder & Yoo (1977), Robertson (1961).

. . . .

Rissoella caribaea

Superfamily: Omalogyracea Sars, 1878
Family: OMALOGYRIDAE Sars, 1878
Species: *Ammonicera binodosa* Sleurs, 1985
Common Name: Binoded Ammonicera
Size: 0.03 inches (0.7 mm)
Distribution: Maldive and Seychelles Islands

Although it is less than 0.04 inches (1 millimeter) long, *Ammonicera binodosa* is larger than most species in its genus. The flat shell has about three whorls and is virtually symmetrical about the plane perpendicular to the shell axis. It is characterized by a double row of nodes on both sides of the shell; there are thirteen to seventeen nodes per row on the body whorl. The operculum is round, corneous, and paucispiral, with about four whorls; it is unusual for the genus in having a strong central peg on the inner surface.

The family Omalogyridae includes the smallest known gastropods, some of which are fully mature at sizes less than 0.02 inches (0.5 millimeters). They occur worldwide in temperate and tropical seas, living on various types of algae. The best way to collect these minute snails and the similar orbitestellids is to wash handfuls of filamentous algae in fresh water and sort the resulting debris under a microscope. Omalogyrids are sequential hermaphrodites, being male first. They have direct development, lacking a planktonic larval stage. Many species in this family probably remain undiscovered because of their small size.

References: Boss (1982), Sleurs (1985).

. . . .

Superfamily: Architectonicacea Gray, 1850
Family: ARCHITECTONICIDAE Gray, 1850
Species: *Architectonica perspectiva* (Linné, 1758)
Common Name: Clear Sundial
Size: 2 inches (50 mm)
Distribution: Tropical Indo-Pacific

Architectonica perspectiva has a flat, slightly convex base bordered by a white peripheral keel with light brown spots. On each side of the keel is a white spiral cord with brown spots. The suture forms between the keel of the

Ammonicera binodosa

Architectonica perspectiva

preceding whorl and the spiral cord above it. A white spiral cord lies immediately below the suture; it is broader than the ones by the keel and is bordered below by a brown band. The middle of the whorls is beige or grayish brown. Axial sculpture consists of oblique grooves across the whorls that become weaker on the body whorl. The animal is often trawled subtidally on sandy-mud bottoms in depths to 160 feet (50 meters).

There are about 130 species of architectonicids worldwide; they are also known as sundial shells. They have flattened, low-spired shells and heterostrophic protoconchs, with the apex pointing toward the base of the teleoconch. Thus, the protoconch spirals up the axis of coiling, and the teleoconch spirals back down. This results in a left-handed protoconch attached to a right-handed teleoconch. The animals feed on various coelenterates such as sea anemones and coral polyps. The fossil record of the family extends to the Late Cretaceous.

References: Bieler (1988), Garrard (1977).

. . . .

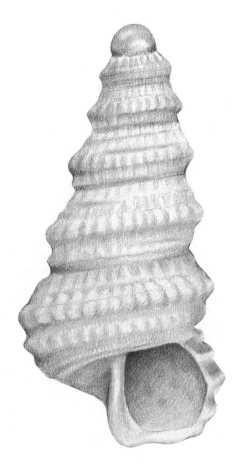

Mathilda barbadensis

Family: MATHILDIDAE Dall, 1889
Species: *Mathilda barbadensis* Dall, 1889
Common Name: Barbadan Mathilda
Size: 0.25 inches (6 mm)
Distribution: Florida, Bahamas, and Caribbean

Mathilda barbadensis has a brown shell with about seven teleoconch whorls. The protoconch is heterostrophic, being left-handed, and carried at a 120-degree angle to the right-handed teleoconch. There are four spiral cords on the spire whorls, the lower two being stronger. These are crossed by numerous axial ribs, giving a beaded or cancellate appearance. The animal is common in depths up to 1,300 feet (400 meters). Mathildids have high-spired shells, usually with heterostrophic protoconchs, but the heterostrophy is virtually lost in some species that have direct development. Most inhabit deep water, where they feed on coelenterates.

References: Boss (1982), Haszprunar (1985).

. . . .

Superfamily: Pyramidellacea Gray, 1840
Family: PYRAMIDELLIDAE Gray, 1840
Species: *Pyramidella acus* (Gmelin, 1791)
Common Name: Needle Pyram
Size: 2 inches (50 mm)
Distribution: Tropical Indo-Pacific

Pyramidella acus, one of the largest pyramidellids, has an elongate shell of up to twenty whorls. The sutures are angulate and impressed. The shell is smooth except for fine axial growth lines. There are five rows of brown spots on the body whorl, two or three of which are visible on the spire. The columella has three folds, the posterior one being the largest, and there is a small anterior siphonal notch. The animal lives in shallow water in sand.

There are probably more than 1,000 species of pyramidellids, most with shells less than 0.4 inches (10 millimeters) in length. They occur in all oceans from intertidal to abyssal depths. The protoconch is usually heterostrophic and left-handed and is set at an angle to the teleoconch. The operculum is thin, corneous, and paucispiral. The animals are hermaphroditic and most have planktonic larvae. Ctenidium and radula are lacking. Pyramidellids are suctorial parasites or predators on many kinds of invertebrates, including mollusks, worms, sponges, and crustaceans. The fossil record of the family extends to the Upper Cretaceous.

References: Boss (1982), Ponder (1987).

. . . .

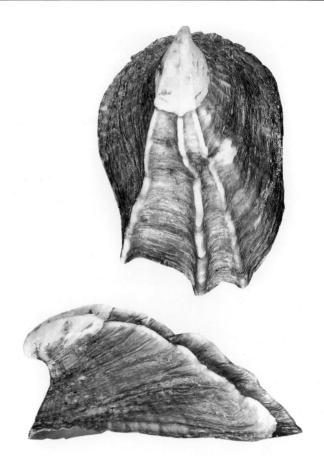

Amathina tricarinata

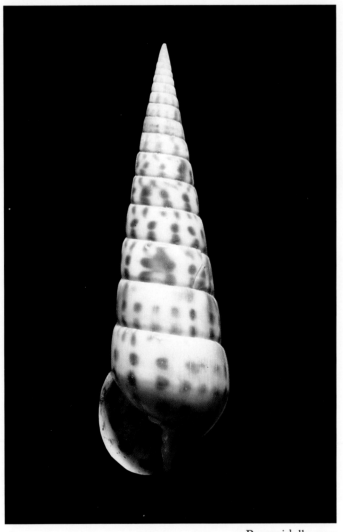

Pyramidella acus

Family: AMATHINIDAE Ponder, 1987
Species: *Amathina tricarinata* (Linné, 1767)
Common Name: Three-ridged Cap Shell
Size: 0.8 inches (20 mm)
Distribution: Tropical Indo-Pacific

Amathina tricarinata is another example of convergence on the limpet form that has been arrived at independently by many groups of gastropods. The species has usually been placed in the Hipponicidae or Capulidae, but recently has been shown to be anatomically similar to the Pyramidellidae. The animal lives on the shells of large bivalves such as pinnids, pteriids, and ostreids, feeding suctorially with its proboscis on the fluids of its host. Other probable members of Amathinidae include the limpetlike *Amathinoides* and *Cyclothyca,* and the normally coiled *Clathrella* and *Iselica.*

Reference: Ponder (1987).

. . . .

Ringicula pilula

Order: Opisthobranchia Milne Edwards, 1848
Suborder: Cephalaspidea.Fischer, 1883
Superfamily: Ringiculacea Philippi, 1853
Family: RINGICULIDAE Philippi, 1853
Species: *Ringicula pilula* Habe, 1950
Common Name: Pill Ringicula
Size: 0.25 inches (6 mm)
Distribution: Japan

Ringicula pilula is rather large for a ringiculid. The fat, globelike shell has about forty finely incised grooves on the body whorl and traces of axial sculpture on the early teleoconch whorls. It is occasionally dredged in depths of 330 to 1,000 feet (100 to 300 meters). Ringiculids, which resemble miniature cassids, typically have a thickened varix on the outer lip, two strong columellar folds, and an anterior siphonal notch. There is usually a parietal nodule. There is no operculum and the radula lacks a central tooth. The animals are hermaphrodites, as are all cephalaspideans. Ringiculids occur worldwide in temperate and tropical seas, usually in soft mud in relatively deep water. Ringiculid fossils are known from the Early Cretaceous.

References: Boss (1982), Habe (1968).

. . . .

Superfamily: Acteonacea d'Orbigny, 1835
Family: ACTEONIDAE d'Orbigny, 1835
Species: *Acteon eloiseae* Abbott, 1973
Common Name: Eloise's Acteon
Size: 1.5 inches (38 mm)
Distribution: Oman and the Persian Gulf

Acteon eloiseae is the largest and most beautiful of the Acteonidae and one of the most recently discovered. The shell is white with three rows of large, crescent-shaped orange blotches outlined in black. The body whorl has more than thirty incised grooves. The animal lives in shallow water in muddy sand in beds of marine grass. Acteonids have relatively sturdy shells with large body whorls and exposed, usually elevated spires; the columella usually has one or two folds. The animal can retract entirely into the shell and an operculum is present. The cephalic shield is divided into a pair of anterior lobes. Some species are known to be carnivorous, feeding on polychaetes. Acteonid fossils have been reported from the Jurassic.

References: Bosch & Bosch (1982, 1989), Marcus (1974), Thompson (1988).

. . . .

Acteon eloiseae

Bullina nobilis

Family: BULLINIDAE Gray, 1850
Species: *Bullina nobilis* Habe, 1950
Common Name: Noble Bubble
Size: 0.8 inches (20 mm)
Distribution: Japan

Bullina nobilis is the largest and most colorful of the bullinids, with sixteen to twenty axial lines and two spiral bands of ruby red on a white background. The shell has more than thirty spiral ribs on the body whorl, with the interspaces spanned by numerous axial riblets. The shell has four whorls and an umbilical opening formed by a small, white callous shield recurved from the columella. The animal lives on fine sandy bottoms in depths of 30 to 330 feet (10 to 100 meters).

Bullinids have ovate, external shells with moderately elevated spires. They can withdraw entirely into the shell, and have an operculum. Bullinids resemble acteonids, but differ in lacking pronounced columellar folds. They tend to have stronger axial sculpture between the spiral cords than do acteonids, in which such sculpture is usually weak or absent.

Reference: Rudman (1971).

. . . .

Family: HYDATINIDAE Pilsbry, 1895
Species: *Hydatina albocincta* (van der Hoeven, 1839)
Common Name: White-banded Paper-bubble
Size: 2 inches (50 mm)
Distribution: South Africa to Australia and Japan

Hydatina albocincta has a thin, fragile, globular shell with four brown spiral bands on a creamy white background. The bands are composed of oblique axial elements of varying degrees of brown. The aperture is white, with the external pattern showing through, and has a white parietal callus. The animal lives on sandy bottoms, in depths of 30 to 330 feet (10 to 100 meters).

Hydatinids have lightweight, external shells with a thin periostracum. The spire elevation varies from somewhat extended to slightly sunken. Gizzard plates are lacking, as is an operculum. There are about a dozen species worldwide in tropical and subtropical seas. Hydatinids feed primarily on polychaete worms.

References: Cernohorsky (1972), Boss (1982).

. . . .

Philine aperta

Hydatina albocincta

Superfamily: Philinacea Gray, 1850
Family: PHILINIDAE Gray, 1850
Species: *Philine aperta* (Linné, 1767)
Common Name: Open Paper-bubble
Size: 1 inch (25 mm)
Distribution: Norway to South Africa to the Philippines

The body of *Philine aperta* is more than twice the length of the shell. The shell is caplike, with a greatly expanded body whorl; it is fragile and white, with no sculpture except for curved growth lines. The animal can secrete sulfuric acid from glands in its skin as a defensive mechanism. It burrows through sand offshore, feeding on mollusks and polychaete worms. The species ranges from the Eastern Atlantic to the Indo-Pacific, but is found in much deeper water in tropical areas.

Philinids have reduced, internal shells that are entirely covered by the mantle in most species. The apex is hidden within the shell. There is no operculum. The internal gizzard plates, if present, are three in number, and corneous or calcareous. Besides *Philine, Spiniphiline* is the only other genus recognized in the family.

References: Marcus (1974), Gosliner (1987, 1988), Thompson (1976, 1988).

. . . .

Family: CYLICHNIDAE Adams & Adams, 1854
Species: *Scaphander lignarius* (Linné, 1758)
Common Name: Woody Canoe-bubble
Size: 2.5 inches (60 mm)
Distribution: Iceland to the Canary Islands, Mediterranean

The shell of *Scaphander lignarius* is relatively sturdy and opaque and ranges from tan to brownish orange in color. It has numerous finely incised spiral grooves. The spire is hidden and there is a parietal callus. The animal burrows to depths of 2 inches (50 millimeters) or more in sand seeking worms and bivalves on which it preys. As in most cylichnids, the animal is too large to retract completely into the shell and there is no operculum. Cylichnids have small parapodia and three calcareous internal gizzard plates. They live in soft muddy or sandy bottoms intertidally and to depths beyond 6,500 feet (2000 meters), feeding on foraminiferans and small invertebrates. Scaphandridae Sars, 1878 and Acteocinidae Pilsbry, 1921 are synonyms of Cylichnidae, although the name Scaphandridae is more often used. Some workers give all three familial status.

References: Marcus (1974), Thompson (1976, 1988).

. . . .

Superfamily: Retusacea Thiele, 1926
Family: RETUSIDAE Thiele, 1926
Species: *Retusa obtusa* (Montagu, 1803)
Common Name: Truncate Barrel-bubble
Size: 0.4 inches (10 mm)
Distribution: Arctic Sea to England, Nova Scotia, and the Aleutians

Scaphander lignarius

Retusa obtusa

Retusa obtusa has a fragile, smooth, white shell, sometimes tinged with amber. The spire can be flattened or somewhat produced. The animal is a protandrous hermaphrodite with direct development. It has been observed on intertidal mudflats eating the small gastropod *Hydrobia ulvae,* which it swallows whole. It has been recorded in depths as great as 1,000 feet (300 meters). Retusids have a small, narrow foot and can retract completely into their shells, but an operculum is usually absent. The cephalic shield has posterior tentacular processes, rather than anterior ones as seen in diaphanids. Gizzard plates are present in *Retusa* and absent in *Rhizorus.* Retusids feed on foraminifera and small mollusks. They have been reported as Jurassic fossils.

References: Boss (1982), Thompson (1976, 1988).

. . . .

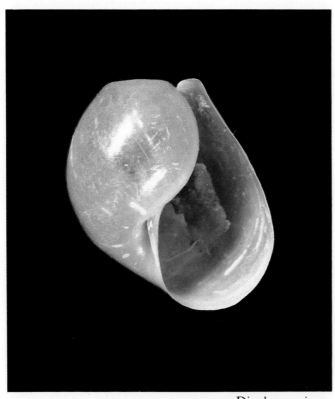

Diaphana minuta

Superfamily: Diaphanacea Odhner, 1914
Family: DIAPHANIDAE Odhner, 1914
Species: *Diaphana minuta* Brown, 1827
Common Name: Arctic Paper-bubble
Size: 0.2 inches (5 mm)
Distribution: New England, Arctic Sea, Mediterranean

The shell in *Diaphana minuta* is variable in proportions, but is always longer than it is broad and is somewhat expanded anteriorly. It is translucent white, has up to five whorls, a flattened spire, and a narrow umbilicus. The foot is forked at the rear. The animal lives from the low water mark of spring tides to depths of 1,150 feet (350 meters). Diaphanids have thin, fragile shells which can be external, as in *Diaphana,* or internal, as in *Colpodaspis.* The spire is low or sunken. An operculum is absent. The cephalic shield has anterior tentacular processes rather than posterior ones as seen in retusids. Diaphanids live mainly in the cold waters of the Arctic and Antarctic, in soft muddy or fine sandy bottoms from shallow water to depths of more than 3,300 feet (1,000 meters).

References: Boss (1982), Thompson (1976, 1988).

. . . .

Superfamily: Bullacea d'Orbigny, 1841
Family: BULLIDAE d'Orbigny, 1841
Species: *Bulla ampulla* Linné, 1758
Common Name: Ampulle Bubble
Size: 2.5 inches (60 mm)
Distribution: Tropical Indo-Pacific

Bulla ampulla has a solid, ovately globular shell that is unsculptured except for axial growth lines. Color varies from tan and pink through brown and greenish gray, with cream-colored spots and darker blotches. The aperture is white with a white parietal callus. The animals can be found intertidally in depths to 10 feet (3 meters), in sandy mud in beds of eel or turtle grass, enclosed in a cocoon of mucus and sand grains.

Bullids have sturdy, external, roundly ovate shells mottled with various shades of pink and brown. The spire is deeply sunken in a posterior umbilicus. The animal can

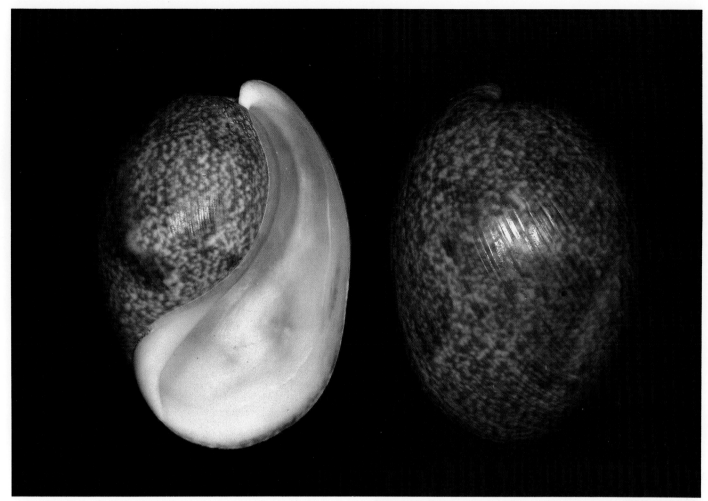

Bulla ampulla

withdraw completely into its shell, but has no operculum. Bullids are mainly herbivorous and usually nocturnal, living in shallow water in warm seas worldwide.

References: Boss (1982), Kilburn & Rippey (1982).

. . . .

Superfamily: Haminoeacea Pilsbry, 1895
Family: HAMINOEIDAE Pilsbry, 1895
Species: *Atys naucum* (Linné, 1758)
Common Name: White Pacific Atys
Size: 1.5 inches (40 mm)
Distribution: Tropical Indo-Pacific

In general, *Atys naucum* has a pure white, rather solid
shell, which is covered by yellowish brown periostracum,
but it sometimes has a pattern of wavy or jagged brown
axial lines. Sculpture consists of incised spiral grooves

Atys naucum

that become weaker toward the middle of the shell. The animal lives intertidally to depths of 65 feet (20 meters) in clean white sand.

Haminoeids occur worldwide in temperate and tropical seas. The shell is inflated and widest at the middle. It is external in most genera, including *Atys* and *Haminoea*, but internal in *Phanerophthalmus*. The spire is hidden within the shell. The animal, though large, can withdraw into the shell, except in the case of *Bullacta*, but there is no operculum. It has three large internal gizzard plates. Haminoeids have been reported to be herbivores, and to eat small bivalves. Some species are able to swim by flapping the well-developed parapodia of the foot. Atyididae and Atyidae are synonyms of Haminoeidae.

References: Boss (1982), Thompson (1976, 1988).

. . . .

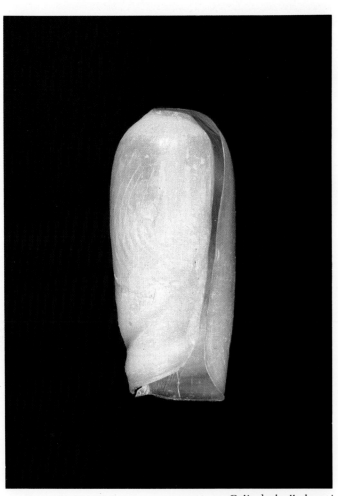

Cylindrobulla beaui

Superfamily: Cylindrobullacea Thiele, 1926
Family: CYLINDROBULLIDAE Thiele, 1926
Species: *Cylindrobulla beaui* Fischer, 1857
Common Name: Beau's Paper-bubble
Size: 0.6 inches (16 mm)
Distribution: Bermuda, Florida, Bahamas, Caribbean

Cylindrobulla beaui has a fragile, flexible, cylindrical shell with an anal sinus at the suture that extends half to two-thirds of a whorl back. The aperture is narrow along the body whorl, but opens broadly anteriorly. As in *Akera soluta,* the sunken spire and internal whorls can be seen from within the shell by looking up the shell axis. The animal lives in depths of 3 to 560 feet (1 to 170 meters), in sand often with sea grass. There are four species of cylindrobullids, three in the tropical Indo-Pacific and one in the Western Atlantic. They have thin external shells, usually less than 0.4 inches (10 millimeters) in length. The foot is narrow and lacks an operculum and parapodia. Jensen places the genus *Ascobulla* in the Volvatellidae and returns Cylindrobullidae to the Cephalaspidea from the Sacoglossa.

References: Boss (1982), Jensen (1989).

. . . .

Suborder: Anaspidea Fischer, 1883
Superfamily: Aplysiacea Rafinesque, 1815
Family: APLYSIIDAE Rafinesque, 1815
Species: *Aplysia dactylomela* Rang, 1828
Common Name: Spotted Seahare
Size: 16 inches (400 mm)
Distribution: Circumtropical

Aplysia dactylomela has a reduced, platelike internal shell. The living animal is pale yellow to light green in color with scattered, irregular, violet-black circles. It is common in shallow grass flats. Aplysiids have oral tentacles on the head; behind them are rhinophoral tentacles. They are called seahares because the rhinophores look like rabbit ears. They have internal, curved, flattened shells that in some species are calcified.

Seahares swim using undulating motions of the broad parapodia on either side of the large fleshy body. They occasionally wash ashore, which can prompt public concern about "livers" on the beach. *Aplysia vaccaria* Winkler, 1955 from California can reach lengths of 30 inches (76 centimeters) and weights of 35 pounds (16 kilograms), vying with *Syrinx aruanus* for the title of "world's largest gastropod." The animals are herbivorous and emit slimy purple ink if disturbed. Aplysiids are hermaphrodites and some species form mating chains, with each individual serving as a male for the one before it. The nervous system has giant nerve cell bodies that make seahares a primary research tool for neurophysiological studies of the cellular and biochemical bases of learning.

References: Abbott (1974), Kilburn & Rippey (1982), Wells (1986).

. . . .

Aplysia dactylomela

Family: AKERIDAE Pilsbry, 1895
Species: *Akera soluta* Gmelin, 1791
Common Name: Solute Paper-bubble
Size: 2 inches (50 mm)
Distribution: East Africa to the Marshall Islands

Akera soluta has a fragile, translucent shell with axial growth lines and more than 100 minutely incised spiral grooves. The spire is flat or slightly elevated. The whorls are straight-sided and curve only slightly toward the shell axis anteriorly. This allows the spire to be seen within the shell through the aperture by looking up the shell axis. The animal inhabits muddy sand flats intertidally and to depths of 30 feet (10 meters).

Akerids have lightweight, external, cylindrical shells. The shoulder has a sharp keel and a deep anal notch. The animal is unable to withdraw entirely into the shell and there is no operculum. It is able to swim by undulating its parapodia, which are flaplike extensions from the foot that wrap around the shell. Akerids have numerous internal gizzard plates; they have been reported as being both carnivorous and herbivorous.

References: Boss (1982), Coleman (1975), Gosliner (1987), Thompson (1988).

. . . .

Akera soluta

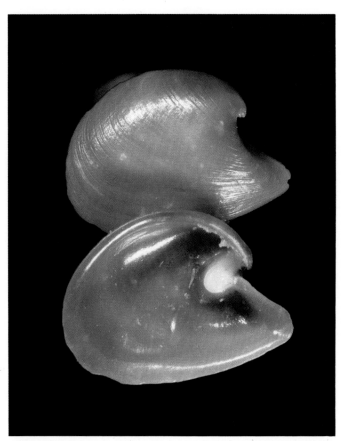

Julia exquisita

Suborder: Sacoglossa Ihering, 1876
Superfamily: Juliacea E. A. Smith, 1885
Family: JULIIDAE E. A. Smith, 1885
Species: *Julia exquisita* Gould, 1862
Common Name: Exquisite Julia
Size: 0.4 inches (10 mm)
Distribution: Tropical Indo-Pacific

Julia exquisita represents a bizarre group of animals, the bivalved gastropods. The sluglike animal has matched left and right valves that are connected by an adductor muscle, and which can enclose and protect the animal. There is a knoblike hinge tooth on the right valve and a corresponding socket on the left valve; the left valve bears the heterostrophic protoconch. *Julia borbonica* (Deshayes, 1863) and *J. japonica* Kuroda & Habe, 1951 are synonyms.

There are about a dozen species of juliids, most 0.4 inches (10 millimeters) or less in length. Species described before 1959 when the living animals were first discovered were named as bivalves. All are green in color and live on the green alga *Caulerpa.* Members of the genus *Berthelinia*

have more flattened shells and a weaker hinge than *Julia.* Juliids are found in the Indo-West Pacific, the eastern Pacific, and the Caribbean. The fossil record of the group extends to the Eocene. Strange as they may seem, juliids are not the only bivalved gastropods—some hipponicids form a basal attachment plate to which the shell muscles attach. Not to be outdone, some bivalves of the genera *Enigmonia* (Anomiidae) and *Ephippodonta* (Galeommatidae) can crawl like gastropods.

References: Kay (1968, 1979).

. . . .

Oxynoe antillarum

Superfamily: Oxynoacea Adams & Adams, 1854
Family: Oxynoidae Bergh, 1878
Species: *Oxynoe antillarum* Mörch, 1863
Common Name: Antillean Oxynoe
Size: 0.4 inches (10 mm)
Distribution: Florida, Bahamas, and Caribbean

The crawling animal of *Oxynoe antillarum* is about 2.5 times longer than its shell, reaching lengths of 1 inch (25 millimeters). It is light brown to green, with white spots; the tail and parapodia have tiny white papillae. The shell is white, thin, and glossy, with loosely coiled whorls, and a broad aperture which is constricted posteriorly. The animal lives on the green alga *Caulerpa.*

Oxynoids have fragile, reduced, partially internal shells that are too small to allow the animal to completely retract. The retractor muscle is reduced and there is no operculum. The animals do not swim with their parapodia, which can be autotomized (shed) to distract attacking predators. Oxynoids occur worldwide in warm water seas. The family Lobigeridae is a synonym of Oxynoidae.

References: Abbott (1974), Boss (1982).

. . . .

Volvatella cincta

Family: VOLVATELLIDAE Pilsbry, 1895
Species: *Volvatella cincta* (Nevill & Nevill, 1869)
Common Name: Girdled Volvatella
Size: 0.7 inches (18 mm)
Distribution: Tropical Indo-Pacific

Volvatella cincta has a strangely shaped shell that resembles a cape wrapped around a beheaded mannequin. The aperture is slitlike along the body whorl, leading to a spoutlike posterior excurrent pallial siphon. Anteriorly the aperture is broadly open, and the internal whorls can be seen by looking up the shell axis. Some *Volvatella* are known to burrow in sand to depths of 2 inches (50 millimeters) in beds of the green alga *Caulerpa.*

There are about twenty species of volvatellids, most in the tropical Indo-Pacific. They have fragile external shells with narrow apertures that open broadly anteriorly. The animal can retract completely into the shell, but there is no operculum. The foot is short and lacks parapodia. Arthessidae is a synonym of Volvatellidae. The genus *Ascobulla* was recently transferred to this family from Cylindrobullidae, which differs in radular characters.

References: Jensen (1989), Thompson (1979).

. . . .

Suborder: Notaspidea Fischer, 1883
Superfamily: Umbraculacea Dall, 1889
Family: UMBRACULIDAE Dall, 1889
Species: *Umbraculum umbraculum* (Lightfoot, 1786)
Common Name: Common Umbrella Shell
Size: 4 inches (100 mm)
Distribution: Circumtropical

Umbraculum umbraculum has a flat, platelike external shell that resembles that of some of the patellid limpets. The only remaining trace of coiling is in the apical, single-whorled protoconch, which is often eroded away in adult specimens. The apex is somewhat off-center; from it radiates the yellowish brown periostracum. The shell is white to cream externally, light yellow internally, sometimes with the central area orange or brown. There is a closed, circular muscle scar. The animal lives intertidally and in depths to 260 feet (80 meters); it feeds

Umbraculum
umbraculum

on sponges. The head has a pair of tentacles, and a pair of sensory rhinophores. The eyes are at the bases of the tentacles. The body is much larger than the shell; the massive foot is orange or yellow with paler bumps. There are two species of *Umbraculum*, *U. mediterranea* (Lamarck, 1812) and *U. umbraculum*, the latter with synonyms *U. sinicum* (Gmelin, 1791) and *U. indicum* (Lamarck, 1819).

References: Boss (1982), Coleman (1975), Kilburn & Rippey (1982).

. . . .

Family: TYLODINIDAE Gray, 1847
Species: *Tylodina fungina* Gabb, 1865
Common Name: Yellow Umbrella Shell
Size: 0.8 inches (20 mm)
Distribution: Southern California to Costa Rica

Tylodina fungina has a shell shaped and colored like a mushroom cap. It has a brown periostracum that in some cases extends beyond the edge of the shell. The animal is bright yellow, and often feeds on a sponge of the same color, as is true of the Australian species, *Tylodina corticalis* (Tate, 1889). It can be found intertidally under rocks and in depths to 80 feet (25 meters).

Tylodinids differ from umbraculids in having an open circular or horseshoe-shaped muscle scar rather than a closed one. The animal is smaller in proportion to the shell than it is in umbraculids, and in some species can retract entirely underneath. Tylodinids have two-whorled

protoconchs. Some species lack the central radular tooth. There are two genera, *Tylodina* and *Tylodinella*.

References: Boss (1982), Coleman (1975), Keen (1971), Thompson (1970).

. . . .

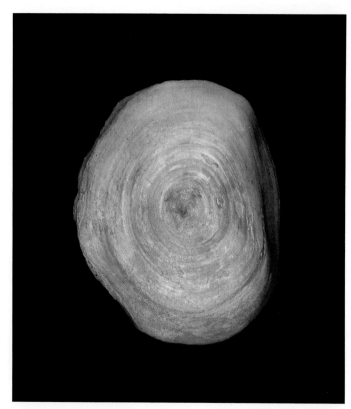

Tylodina fungina

Suborder: Thecosomata Blainville, 1824
Infraorder: Euthecosomata Meisenheimer, 1905
Superfamily: Limacinacea Férussac, 1822
Family: CAVOLINIIDAE d'Orbigny, 1842
Species: *Cavolinia tridentata* (Niebuhr, 1775)
Common Name: Three-toothed Cavoline
Size: 0.8 inches (20 mm)
Distribution: Worldwide

Cavolinia tridentata has a golden brown shell with three posterior spines, a projecting dorsal lip, and a globular ventral surface. Like all pteropods, it is pelagic, spending its entire life floating and swimming in the ocean. The animal has paired wings derived from the foot (hence the name pteropod) that extend through the aperture and are used for swimming. Flowery mantle lobes extend through lateral slits in the shell. It can swim at rates of about a third of a mile per hour (14 centimeters per second).

There are about thirty species of cavoliniids; all have bilaterally symmetric shells with no trace of spiral coiling. Shell shape can be needlelike *(Creseis)*, bottle-shaped *(Cuvierina)*, pyramidal *(Clio)*, or inflated *(Cavolinia)*. Like all thecosomatous pteropods, cavoliniids use an external spherical web of mucus to catch planktonic food. There are three subfamilies of Cavoliniidae: Cavoliniinae, Cuvierininae, and Cliinae, which is usually misspelled as "Clionae" or "Clioinae." It should not be confused with Clioninae, a group of gymnosomatous (without shells) pteropods. The oldest undoubted fossil cavoliniids are from the Eocene.

References: Lalli & Gilmer (1989), Spoel (1967).

. . . .

Family: LIMACINIDAE Férussac, 1822
Species: *Limacina retroversa* (Fleming, 1823)
Common Name: Retrovert Pteropod
Size: 0.1 inches (3 mm)
Distribution: North Atlantic

Limacina retroversa has a golden brown, left-handed shell of six to seven whorls. The surface is covered with fine spiral lines, particularly on the last whorl, and the shell has a deep, narrow umbilicus. Like other thecosome pteropods, it is pelagic, floating and swimming in the ocean for its entire life, and feeding on plankton by means of a mucous net. The species has been implicated in fish kills. It sometimes feeds on the minute planktonic organism *Gonyaulax excavata*, which produces the toxin that causes paralytic shellfish poisoning in humans. Fish that eat large quantities of *Limacina* that have fed on *Gonyaulax* might die as a result.

There are seven species of limacinids worldwide; they differ from cavoliniids in having the osphradium on the left side of the mantle cavity instead of the right, in having coiled, left-handed rather than bilaterally symmetric shells, and in having an operculum. The animals, like all thecosomes, are sequential hermaphrodites, starting life as males, and maturing as females. The fossil record of the family extends to the Eocene. Spiratellidae is a synonym of Limacinidae.

References: Lalli & Gilmer (1989), Spoel (1967).

. . . .

Cavolinia tridentata

Limacina retroversa

Infraorder: Pseudothecosomata Meisenheimer, 1905
Superfamily: Cymbuliacea Gray, 1840
Family: PERACLIDAE Tesch, 1913
Species: *Peracle reticulata* (d'Orbigny, 1836)
Common Name: Reticulate Pteropod
Size: 0.15 inches (4 mm)
Distribution: Worldwide

Peracle reticulata has a shell with a raised reticulate sculpture of small hexagons. The sculpture is non-calcareous and is often worn off in dead specimens. The shell is yellowish brown in color and left-handed; an operculum is present. The shell differs from that of *Limacina* in having the columella extended and spirally twisted, and in its reticulate sculpture.

There are seven species of peraclids; like other thecosomes they are pelagic, swimming and feeding in the open ocean, where they catch planktonic organisms in a mucous net. The wings differ from those of cavoliniids and limacinids in being fused into a single swimming plate rather than being paired. "Peraclis" and "Peraclididae" are common misspellings. The family is not known to have a fossil record.

References: Lalli & Gilmer (1989), Spoel (1967).

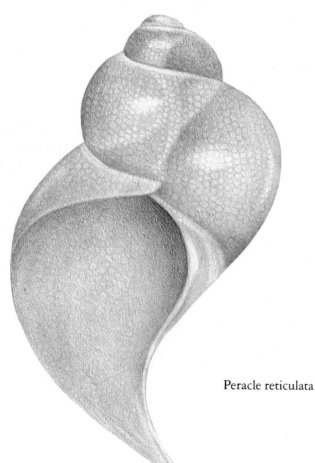

Peracle reticulata

Melampus bidentatus

Order: Pulmonata Cuvier, 1817
Suborder: Archaepulmonata Morton, 1955
Superfamily: Ellobiacea Adams & Adams, 1855
Family: ELLOBIIDAE Adams & Adams, 1855
Species: *Melampus bidentatus* Say, 1822
Common Name: Eastern Melampus
Size: 0.6 inches (15 mm)
Distribution: Southern Quebec to Caribbean

Melampus bidentatus is an abundant snail in salt marshes. It resembles a small cone shell, but lacks the anterior siphonal notch and has parietal and columellar folds and apertural lirations. The shell is uniform tan or brown, or spirally banded alternately with those colors. It has fine axial growth lines, and minute, incised spiral grooves on the shoulder. The animals lay their eggs on marsh grasses; emergence of the planktonic larvae occurs when the grasses are submerged at high tide.

Ellobiids live worldwide on temperate and tropical shores, in mangrove swamps, salt marshes, and under cast-up vegetation in the intertidal zone. Being pulmonates, they use the mantle cavity as a lung and have lost the gill. Most are right-handed, but *Blauneria* are left-handed. There is no operculum. The shells have parietal and columellar folds. The animals are sequential hermaphrodites, being male first, then becoming female. Ellobiidae is a replacement name for Auriculidae Férussac, 1821 and so has priority over Melampidae Stimpson, 1851.

References: Abbott (1974), Boss (1982).

· · · · · · · · · · · · · ·

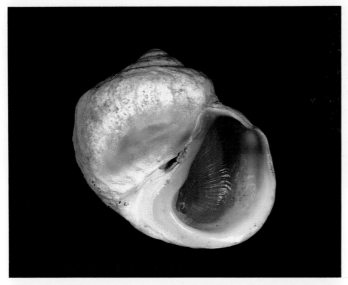

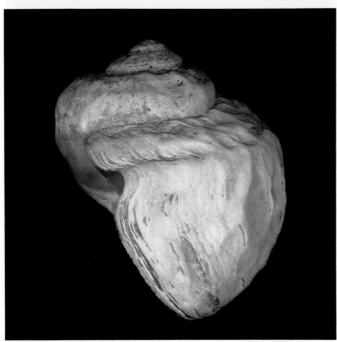

Amphibola avellana

Suborder: Basommatophora Schmidt, 1855
Superfamily: Amphibolacea Gray, 1840
Family: AMPHIBOLIDAE Gray, 1840
Species: *Amphibola avellana* (Bruguière, 1789)
Common Name: New Zealand Titiko
Size: 1.2 inches (30 mm)
Distribution: New Zealand

Amphibola avellana has a somewhat globular, yellowish gray shell with an irregularly wrinkled surface. The spiral cord at the shoulder leads to the apertural pulmonary sinus. The columella has a slight swelling and the shell is narrowly umbilicate. The animal inhabits high tidal mud flats; it feeds by digesting organic matter in ingested mud. *Amphibola crentata* (Gmelin, 1791) is a synonym. Amphibolids are the only pulmonates that have an operculum as adults. There are fewer than ten species in the family, all restricted to the Indo-Pacific; *Salinator* and *Amphibola* are the only genera.

References: Boss (1982), Powell (1979).

· · · · · · · · · · · · · ·

Superfamily: Siphonariacea Gray, 1840
Family: SIPHONARIIDAE Gray, 1840
Species: *Siphonaria gigas* Sowerby, 1825
Common Name: Giant False Limpet
Size: 3 inches (75 mm)
Distribution: Mexico to Peru

The largest of the siphonariid limpets, *Siphonaria gigas* has a heavy, grayish brown shell with strong radial ribs. The interior of the shell is dark brown at the edge and lighter tan to cream in the center. The exterior is often eroded, and sometimes bears stellate scars marking where a juvenile limpet had lived on the back of the adult. These scars indicate the ability to home; the animals move about on intertidal rocks, browsing on vegetation, but return to the same spot that they have molded to fit the contours of their shells.

There are about seventy species of siphonariids worldwide; they resemble patellid and lottiid limpets, but are easily distinguished by the large, oval muscle scar that is open on the right side, marking the pulmonary

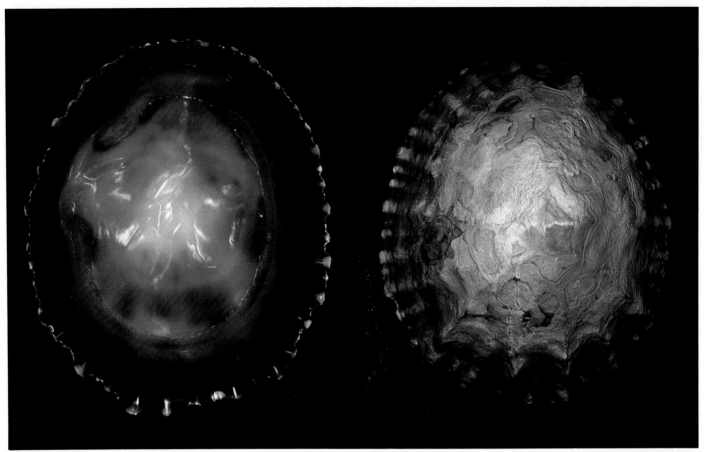

Siphonaria gigas

furrow. In patellids and acmaeids, the horseshoe-shaped muscle scar opens anteriorly. Siphonariids have a gill and an osphradium. The fossil record of siphonariids extends to the Cretaceous.

References: Boss (1982), Keen (1971).

. . . .

Trimusculus peruvianus

Family: TRIMUSCULIDAE Habe, 1958
Species: *Trimusculus peruvianus* (Sowerby, 1835)
Common Name: Peruvian False Limpet
Size: 1 inch (25 mm)
Distribution: Central America to Chile

Trimusculus peruvianus has an almost circular shell with fine radial ribs that are sometimes removed by erosion. The shell is white inside and out and has a circular muscle scar. The pulmonary furrow can be deep and is directed anteriorly to the right. The animal lives deep in rock crevices in the middle intertidal zone.

About seven species of trimusculids are known worldwide, on tropical and subtropical coasts. They resemble siphonariids but lack osphradium and gill. The shell in trimusculids tends to be regular, nearly circular, and white, whereas that in siphonariids is irregularly ovate with at least some dark pigmentation. The openings in the muscle scars are oriented differently—in siphonariids they are almost 90 degrees to the right of anterior, and in trimusculids, they are only 10 or 20 degrees to the right.

References: Boss (1982), Marincovich (1973), Yonge (1958).

. . . .

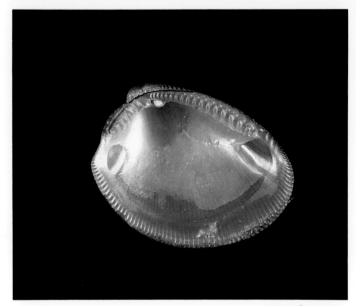

Nucula rugosa

Class: Bivalvia Linné, 1758
Subclass: Paleotaxodonta Korobkov, 1954
Order: Nuculoida Dall, 1889
Superfamily: Nuculacea Gray, 1824
Family: NUCULIDAE Gray, 1824
Species: *Nucula rugosa* Odhner, 1919
Common Name: Rugose Nut Clam
Size: 0.6 inches (15 mm)
Distribution: Madagascar

Nucula rugosa has a trigonally ovate, grayish brown shell with up to thirty-five ribs. A few of the ribs on each valve bifurcate or fuse; there are fine grooves crossing the ribs on their ventral sides and continuing into the areas between the ribs. The hinge has twenty-one to twenty-four anterior teeth and about nine posterior ones. The inner margin of the shell is denticulate. The species has been dredged in depths of 30 to 100 feet (10 to 30 meters).

There are about 150 living species of nuculids (nut clams); they occur worldwide, most commonly in the deep sea. In nuculids, the part of the shell anterior to the beaks is longer than the part posterior. The beaks point backward, and there is no external ligament. The hinge is taxodont, meaning it has numerous sharp, triangular teeth. The teeth lie on either side of a small ligament pit below the beak. The interior of the shell is nacreous with a regular pallial line and no pallial sinus. The adductor muscle scars are approximately of equal size. The gills are used for respiration only; the animals are deposit feeders, using the labial palps to collect detritus. The fossil record of nuculids extends to the Ordovician.

References: Boss (1982), Kilburn & Rippey (1982).

. . . .

Nuculana crassa

Superfamily: Nuculanacea Adams & Adams, 1858
Family: NUCULANIDAE Adams & Adams, 1858
Species: *Nuculana crassa* (Hinds, 1843)
Common Name: Stout Nut Clam
Size: 1 inch (25 mm)
Distribution: Victoria to Tasmania and South Australia

Nuculana crassa has a shiny, olive-yellow periostracum; the shell is rounded anteriorly and pointed posteriorly. A pronounced furrow runs from the umbo to the ventral margin. There is a small posterior gape dorsal to the furrow. Each valve has up to fifty concentric ribs. The species has been dredged in depths of 50 to 200 feet

(15 to 60 meters) on sandy bottoms.

There are about 250 species of nuculanids world-wide, most living in deep water. They resemble nuculids in being rounded anteriorly, having beaks pointing to the rear, and having a taxodont hinge with a ligament pit below the beak. In nuculanids the shell is more elongate posteriorly than in nuculids, and the interior is non-nacreous. There is usually a pallial sinus on the pallial line. The anterior adductor muscle is often larger than the posterior one. The oldest known fossil nuculanids are from the Devonian.

References: Boss (1982), Macpherson & Gabriel (1962).

. . . .

Neilo australis

Family: MALLETIIDAE Adams & Adams, 1858
Species: *Neilo australis* (Quoy & Gaimard, 1835)
Common Name: Southern Neilo
Size: 1.5 inches (40 mm)
Distribution: New Zealand

Neilo australis has more than forty lamellar concentric ribs on each valve. The shell is chalky white under an olive to brown periostracum and has a slight ridge running from the umbo to the posterior ventral margin. Inside, the shell is white, with a strong pallial sinus. The hinge has about thirty posterior teeth and twenty anterior. The animal burrows in mud in depths from 30 to 2,000 feet (10 to 600 meters).

Malletiids have ovate to elongate shells, often gaping both anteriorly and posteriorly. The hinge is taxodont, but differs from that of nuculids and nuculanids in lacking a ligament pit. The ligament is predominantly external and a pallial sinus is usually present. The beaks can point to the rear or front, or medially. The adductor muscles are approximately equal in size. The foot is modified for burrowing; most malletiids live in muddy bottoms in the deep sea. The earliest fossil malletiids are from the Ordovician.

References: Boss (1982), Powell (1979).

. . . .

Family: TINDARIIDAE Verrill & Bush, 1897
Species: *Tindaria striata* (King, 1831)
Common Name: Striate Tindaria
Size: 0.6 inches (15 mm)
Distribution: Southern Brazil to Straits of Magellan

Tindaria striata has an anteriorly rounded, posteriorly beaked shell with an olive-green periostracum. Sculpture is strong, consisting of more than forty concentric ribs. The escutcheon is well developed, running from the beaks to the posterior margin. There are eleven anterior and sixteen posterior hinge teeth. The animal lives in sandy mud bottoms in depths from 200 to 500 feet (60 to 150 meters).

Tindariids have solid, ovate to rostrate shells with beaks in front of the midline. The ligament is external and behind the beaks. Tindariids differ from nuculids and nuculanids in having the hinge teeth continuous beneath the beak and in having the beaks facing somewhat forward rather than backward. They differ from malletiids in that the pallial sinus is weak or absent. *Tindaria* is the only genus in the family, members of which occur primarily in the deep sea. The fossil record of tindariids extends at least to the Pliocene.

References: Rios (1985), Sanders & Allen (1977).

. . . .

Subclass: Cryptodonta Neumayr, 1844
Order: Solemyoida Dall, 1889
Superfamily: Solemyacea Carpenter, 1851
Family: SOLEMYIDAE Carpenter, 1851
Species: *Solemya velum* Say, 1822
Common Name: Atlantic Awning Clam
Size: 1 inch (25 mm)
Distribution: Nova Scotia to Florida

Solemya velum has an elongate, fragile shell that often cracks if dried. The shell is entirely covered by a shiny, olive-brown periostracum that extends in a fringe beyond the calcareous part of the valves ventrally and anteriorly. There are often lighter colored rays radiating from the umbo to the periostracal margin. The animal lives in shallow water in sulfur-containing muddy bottoms.

There are about twenty-five species of solemyids worldwide, some of which are gutless wonders, having reduced or absent alimentary canals. Nutrition is derived in part or entirely from symbiotic bacteria living in the gill. These bacteria oxidize sulfur, using the resulting energy to capture carbon from carbon dioxide. (Animals are unable to use carbon dioxide directly and must obtain carbon compounds in their diets or from symbionts. Plants, on the other hand, use energy from sunlight to break down carbon dioxide, capturing carbon and giving off oxygen.)

Solemyids have thin, elongate shells with rounded gaping ends and the periostracum extending beyond the valves (except dorsally). The beaks are toward the posterior end of the shell, and the hinge is weak and toothless.

The anterior adductor muscle scar is larger than the posterior one and has a line running from its ventral side obliquely to the dorsal margin, marking the attachment of muscles of the visceral integument and foot. The posterior muscle scar is bordered by a low radial rib running from the chondrophore. The pallial line is weak but complete; there is no pallial sinus. The fossil record of the family begins in the Devonian.

References: Abbott (1974), Moore (1969), Reid & Brand (1987).

. . . .

Tindaria striata

Solemya velum

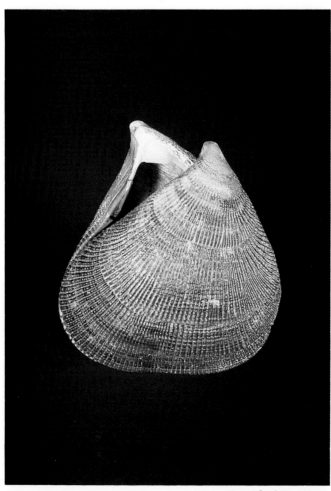

Septifer bilocularis

Subclass: Pteriomorphia Beurlen, 1944
Suborder: Isofilibranchia Iredale, 1939
Order: Mytiloida Férussac, 1822
Superfamily: Mytilacea Rafinesque, 1815
Family: MYTILIDAE Rafinesque, 1815
Species: *Septifer bilocularis* (Linné, 1758)
Common Name: Box Mussel
Size: 2 inches (50 mm)
Distribution: Tropical Indo-Pacific

Shell color in *Septifer bilocularis* varies from yellowish brown to red and bluish black. The shell is covered by a green or brown periostracum that is often eroded, revealing the underlying color. Each valve can have more than 100 radial ribs, with new ribs arising toward the margins between existing ribs. The beaks lie at the most anterior part of the shell. The anterior adductor muscle attaches to a shelflike septum below the beaks. The inner margin of the shell is denticulate. The animal lives

byssally attached intertidally and to depths of 100 feet (30 meters).

There are about 250 species of mytilids (mussels) worldwide, some of which are harvested commercially as food for humans. Mytilids have highly asymmetric shells with the beaks at or near the anterior end and pointing anteriorly. A half-cylinder of ligament posterior to the beaks connects the valves; the hinge is mostly toothless. The interior of the shell has a nacreous layer. The pallial line is simple or rarely has a small posterior concavity. The periostracum can be smooth or hairy. Most mytilids are byssate surface-dwellers, but some, such as *Lithophaga,* burrow in coral. Fossil mytilids are known from the Devonian.

References: Boss (1982), Moore (1969), Soot-Ryen (1955).

. . . .

Arca zebra

Superorder: Prionodonta MacNeil, 1937
Order: Arcoida Stoliczka, 1871
Superfamily: Arcacea Lamarck, 1809
Family: ARCIDAE Lamarck, 1809
Species: *Arca zebra* (Swainson, 1833)
Common Name: Atlantic Turkey Wing
Size: 3.5 inches (90 mm)
Distribution: North Carolina to Brazil

Cucullaea labiata

Arca zebra characteristically has a pattern of brown zig-zags on a white to tan background. The periostracum is yellowish brown, coarse, and fibrous. The hinge is long and straight, and can have more than 110 teeth in an uninterrupted row. The shell is broadest posteriorly and gapes ventrally, allowing the byssus to pass through. The animal lives intertidally and to depths of 80 feet (25 meters).

There are about 150 species of arcids worldwide. They have subtrapezoidal or ovate shells, often with the beaks toward the anterior end. Sculpture is usually radial, with concentric sculpture equal or weaker in strength. The hinge is taxodont with numerous teeth increasing gradually in size away from the beaks. The interior of the shell is porcelaneous, and has no pallial sinus. The animals live byssally attached to hard substrata. As do other arcoidans, they have eyes on the mantle edge that respond to changes in light intensity, allowing them to react to moving shadows. The eyes differ structurally from those of pectinids and probably evolved independently. The oldest undoubted arcid fossils are from the Jurassic.

References: Moore (1969), Waller (1980).

. . . .

Family: CUCULLAEIDAE Stewart, 1930
Species: *Cucullaea labiata* (Lightfoot, 1786)
Common Name: Hooded Ark
Size: 3.5 inches (90 mm)
Distribution: East Africa to Japan and Australia

Cucullaea labiata is the only living member of its family. It has a strongly inflated tan to brown shell, with a heavy, brown, felty periostracum. There are more than 100 fine axial and concentric ribs, about equal in strength. The interior of the shell is white to purple, has a weakly denticulate margin, and lacks a pallial sinus. The hinge is straight, with small teeth crossing it centrally and larger horizontal teeth laterally. There is a strong, projecting rib in each valve that serves as an attachment point for part of the posterior adductor muscle. The left valve is slightly larger than the right one, overlapping its rear ventral margin. There is no byssal gape. The animal lives in sand with the anterior end down, occurring in depths of 25 to 180 feet (8 to 55 meters). The oldest known fossil cucullaeids are from the Lower Jurassic.

References: Boss (1982), Morton (1981).

. . . .

Noetia ponderosa

Porterius dalli

Family: NOETIIDAE Stewart, 1930
Species: *Noetia ponderosa* (Say, 1822)
Common Name: Ponderous Ark
Size: 2.5 inches (60 mm)
Distribution: Virginia to Yucatan

Noetia ponderosa has a heavy, white shell with a black periostracum and twenty-seven to thirty-one medially grooved radial ribs. Concentric sculpture is in the form of numerous, fine ridges which are more apparent between the ribs. The shell has a strongly denticulate inner margin and lacks a pallial sinus. The beaks are almost medial and there is a strong posterior ridge. Juve-

niles attach byssally to hard surfaces, whereas adults live partially buried in sand in depths to at least 30 feet (10 meters). Subfossil specimens are found on beaches as far north as Massachusetts, indicating the warmer climate several thousand years ago. Noetiids can be distinguished from arcids in having raised ridges along the inner margin of one or both adductor muscle scars, and in having vertical rather than oblique ligamental grooves between the beaks and hinge. The family first appears in the fossil record in the Lower Cretaceous.

References: Abbott (1974), Boss (1982), Lyons (1989).

. . . .

Family: PARALLELODONTIDAE Dall, 1898
Species: *Porterius dalli* (E. A. Smith, 1885)
Common Name: Dall's Ark
Size: 0.8 inches (20 mm)
Distribution: Japan and Korea

Porterius dalli has an ovate shell that is posteriorly elongate. The shell is off-white with a yellowish brown adherent periostracum that forms raised, frilly concentric lamellae. There are more than eighty radial ribs, some of which bifurcate toward the posteroventral margin. Internally, the shell is white with a smooth margin. The hinge teeth have fine, irregular grooves and the ligament is posterior to the beaks. The animals live byssally attached to rocks and gravel from the low-tide mark to depths of 650 feet (200 meters), but lack a byssal gape.

There are only a few living species of parallelodontids, which can be distinguished from arcids and noetiids in having some of the hinge teeth horizontal, running parallel to the hinge rather than across it. The hinge is long and straight and the beaks are orthogyrous, meaning that they point medially rather than forward or backward. The ventral margin is not denticulate and there is no pallial sinus. The fossil record of parallelodontids extends to the Lower Ordovician.

References: Kuroda, Habe & Oyama (1971), Moore (1969).

. . . .

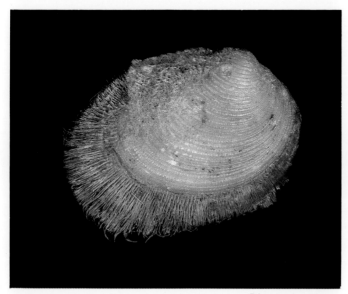

Limopsis sulcata

Superfamily: Limopsacea Dall, 1895
Family: LIMOPSIDAE Dall, 1895
Species: *Limopsis sulcata* Verrill & Bush, 1898
Common Name: Sulcate Limopsis
Size: 0.8 inches (20 mm)
Distribution: Massachusetts to Caribbean

Limopsis sulcata has an obliquely ovate, grayish white shell with numerous concentric ribs with fine radial grooves. The periostracum is thick around the shell margins and extends in a bearded fringe beyond them. The inner margins of the valves are smooth. The animal has been dredged in depths of 400 to 2,100 feet (120 to 640 meters).

There are about fifty species of limopsids worldwide, most living in the deep sea. They have a taxodont hinge similar to that of some arcaceans, but the shell is typically more ovate, less inflated, and lacks the posterior ridge of many arcaceans. The shell is usually monochromatic, lacking a color pattern. The ligament is short and confined mostly to a central triangular pit below the beaks. Hinge teeth curve in a series relatively symmetric about the ligament. The umbos are usually anterior to the midline. Internally, the shell is porcelaneous, not nacreous, and lacks a pallial sinus. The oldest known limopsids are from the Upper Triassic.

References: Boss (1982), Moore (1969), Oliver (1981).

. . . .

Glycymeris amboinensis

Family: GLYCYMERIDIDAE Newton, 1922
Species: *Glycymeris amboinensis* (Gmelin, 1791)
Common Name: Amboina Bittersweet
Size: 2 inches (50 mm)
Distribution: Thailand and Japan to Australia

Glycymeris amboinensis has a thick white shell mottled with various shades of brown. There are about twenty-four radial ribs on each valve, with hundreds of very fine, closely spaced, irregular concentric lamellae crossing them. The ribs are much broader than the spaces between them. The shell is subcircular, with length and height being almost equal. The inner margin is crenulate.

Glycymeridids (bittersweets) occur worldwide in warm seas; there are more than fifty species. They have subtrigonal to subcircular shells. The young are byssate, but the adults are free-living burrowers in shallow water.

They differ from limopsids in that the ligament is broad, not being restricted to a ligamental pit, in having ligamental grooves in the area above the hinge teeth, and in sometimes developing a ridge on the inner side of the posterior adductor muscle. The shell is porcelaneous and lacks a pallial sinus. The fossil record of the family dates to the Lower Cretaceous.

References: Matsukuma (1980), Moore (1969), Nicol (1967).

. . . .

Family: PHILOBRYIDAE Bernard, 1897
Species: *Philobrya sublaevis* Pelseneer, 1903
Common Name: Pelseneer's Philobrya
Size: 0.25 inches (6 mm)
Distribution: Circum-Antarctic

Philobrya sublaevis has a lamellose, pale yellowish brown periostracum, with darker radial ribs. The periostracum extends past the valve margins. The shell is white with discontinuous radial ribs, and has a flattened, axially ribbed prodissoconch. The hinge is virtually toothless, but its anterior dorsal margins protrude, serving as interlocking teeth. The animal broods its eggs in the gill cavity and lives in depths of 360 to 1,800 feet (110 to 560 meters).

There are probably more than twenty species of philobryids worldwide, with highest diversity in the southern oceans. They have ovate or obliquely ovate shells with projecting umbos, or a flat cap formed by the prodissoconch. The shell is non-nacreous and lacks a pallial sinus. The byssus extends between the anterior margins of the valves. The fossil record of the group ranges to the Eocene.

References: Dell (1964), Moore (1969).

. . . .

Philobrya sublaevis

Pteria avicular

Superorder: Eupteriomorphia Boss, 1982
Order: Pterioida Newell, 1965
Superfamily: Pteriacea Gray, 1847
Family: PTERIIDAE Gray, 1847
Species: *Pteria avicular* (Holten, 1802)
Common Name: Golden Wing Oyster
Size: 3 inches (75 mm)
Distribution: East Africa to the Caroline Islands

Pteria avicular is variable in color, ranging from saffron to dark brown. It can be monochromatic, or have alternately light and dark stripes. Sculpture consists of hundreds of fine, concentric, incremental growth lines. The long hinge line is straight or slightly concave and its posterior auricle projects farther than the elongate, obliquely elliptical disc of the shell. The animal lives byssally attached to hard surfaces intertidally and to depths of 10 feet (3 meters). *Pteria crocea* (Lamarck, 1819) is a synonym of *P. avicular;* "avicula" is a misspelling.

The Pteriidae (pearl oysters) contains about forty species, distributed worldwide in warm seas. The shell is subcircular to obliquely ovate, with winglike anterior and posterior dorsal projections (auricles) of the straight hinge line. The anterior auricle is smaller than the posterior one and there is a byssal notch below it in the right valve. The left valve is usually more inflated than the right one. Hinge teeth, if present, are oblique near the beaks. The valves are nacreous inside and the pallial line is usually discontinuous. Members of the pteriid genus *Pinctada* are farmed commercially to produce pearls. The fossil record of the pteriids extends from the Triassic.

References: Boss (1982), Moore (1969).

. . . .

Family: MALLEIDAE Lamarck, 1819
Species: *Malleus albus* Lamarck, 1819
Common Name: White Hammer Oyster
Size: 10 inches (250 mm)
Distribution: East Africa to Japan and Australia

Malleus albus has a shell shaped like a pick-ax, with long winglike anterior and posterior extensions of the straight hinge line. The body of the shell is greatly elongate, with undulating valve margins and an irregularly lamellose, grayish white surface. Inside, the shell has a pearly, bluish black central area, which contains the posterior adductor muscle scar, and a low, submedian ridge running toward the ventral margin. The deep, triangular ligament pit is centered on the hinge. The byssal notch is in the anterior margin of the right valve. The animal lives byssally attached on grass and rock flats in depths from 6 to 50 feet (2 to 15 meters).

Malleids have irregularly shaped, usually dorsoventrally elongate shells. Adults are generally monomyarian, with the anterior adductor muscle reduced or lost. The ligament area is triangular and is partially or completely occupied by a triangular pit. There are fewer than fifteen species, which occur worldwide in tropical and subtropical areas. Malleids are known from the Jurassic.

References: Boss (1982), Moore (1969).

. . . .

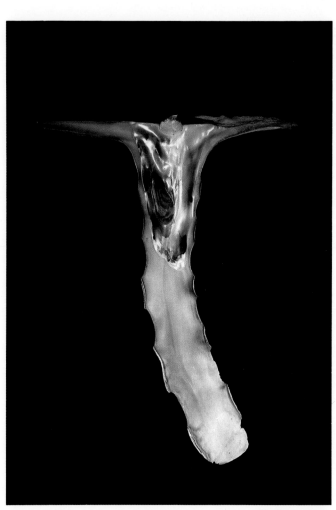

Malleus albus

Isognomon radiatus

Family: ISOGNOMONIDAE Woodring, 1925
Species: *Isognomon radiatus* (Anton, 1838)
Common Name: Lister's Tree Oyster
Size: 4 inches (100 mm)
Distribution: Florida to Brazil

Isognomon radiatus has an irregularly shaped, posteroventrally elongate shell that is often a light brownish yellow with purple stripes radiating from the anteriorly placed umbo. The exterior is flaky, with irregular lamellae; the interior is smooth and nacreous. The hinge is straight and has four to eight rectangular pits (sometimes as many as ten in large specimens). The animal lives byssally attached to hard objects intertidally and to depths of 10 feet (3 meters).

There are about twenty species of isognomonids worldwide in tropical and subtropical regions. The most distinctive feature of the shell is the vertical ligamental grooves at the hinge, which increase in number as the shell grows. Pteriids and malleids lack these grooves. The pallial line is usually discontinuous and there is no pallial sinus. The anterior adductor muscle is absent; the posterior adductor is large and curved. The fossil record of isognomonids dates to the Upper Permian.

References: Boss (1982), Moore (1969).

. . . .

Superfamily: Pinnacea Leach, 1819
Family: PINNIDAE Leach, 1819
Species: *Pinna nobilis* Linné, 1758
Common Name: Noble Pen Shell
Size: 36 inches (915 mm)
Distribution: Mediterranean

Pinna nobilis is one of the world's largest bivalves; only *Tridacna gigas* (Tridacnidae) and *Kuphus polythalamia* (Teredinidae) have been recorded larger (54 and 51 inches [137 and 130 centimeters], respectively). The largest known specimen is slightly more than 1 yard (0.9 meters) long, but specimens over 2 feet long (0.6 meters) are rare. The animals were harvested in ancient times and as recently as the nineteenth century to obtain the golden brown byssal threads, which were used to make gloves, stockings, and caps.

There are about twenty species of pen shells worldwide in tropical and subtropical seas. The shell is fan-shaped, with the beak at the narrow anterior end. The hinge is straight and toothless, extending the length of the shell. Most species live with the anterior end buried in muddy sand, anchored to buried stones or other hard objects by the byssus in depths of at least 330 feet (100 meters). Small commensal crabs live in the mantle cavities of some pen shells. The Lower Carboniferous marks the appearance of fossil pinnids.

References: Abbott (1972), Rosewater (1961), Wagner & Abbott (1990).

. . . .

Pinna nobilis

Ctenoides scabra

Order: Limoida Waller, 1978
Superfamily: Limacea Rafinesque, 1815
Family: LIMIDAE Rafinesque, 1815
Species: *Ctenoides scabra* (Born, 1778)
Common Name: Rough Lima
Size: 4 inches (100 mm)
Distribution: South Carolina to Brazil

Ctenoides scabra has numerous radial ribs with low, flattened spines along them that give the shell a somewhat shingled appearance. The periostracum is thin and tan to brown. The inside of the shell is a smooth, porcela-

neous white. There is an anterior byssal gape l ordered by a reflected shell margin. The living animal has hundreds of long, mobile tentacles protruding from the orange-red mantle. It lives from the low-tide mark to depths of 460 feet (140 meters).

There are about 125 species of limids (file shells) worldwide. The shell is ovate to subtrigonal in shape and typically has small dorsal auricles (as compared to those of pectinids). The hinge is usually toothless, but can have weak, pseudotaxodont teeth; there is a triangular ligamental pit. Some species can swim by flapping the valves, and some construct nests by entrapping debris with byssal threads. The fossil record of limids extends to the Lower Carboniferous.

References: Boss (1982), Merrill & Turner (1963), Waller (1978).

. . . .

Order: Ostreoida Férussac, 1822
Suborder: Ostreina Férussac, 1822
Superfamily: Ostreacea Rafinesque, 1815
Family: OSTREIDAE Rafinesque, 1815
Species: *Ostrea denselamellosa* Lischke, 1869
Common Name: Lamellose Oyster
Size: 5 inches (125 mm)
Distribution: Japan and Korea

Ostrea denselamellosa typically is ovate, although some individuals can be elongate. The shell is covered with irregular, flaky, concentric lamellae on the upper valve and radial ribs on the lower valve. It is mottled with slaty blue, gray, and brown. Inside, the shell is a glossy, but non-nacreous, white. The animal cements its shell to pebbles and broken shells in shallow bays to depths of 65 feet (20 meters). The species is harvested commercially in Japan and Korea, where it is considered a great delicacy.

There are about fifty species of ostreids (true oysters) worldwide in tropical and temperate seas. They lie on the left valve, either cemented to the substratum or free-living. The left valve is usually convex, the right (upper) valve is often flat. The anterior adductor muscle is absent, as are the foot and byssus in post-larval stages. The pallial line may be absent and there is no pallial sinus. There is a triangular ligament pit and the hinge is toothless in adults. Some species incubate their eggs in the mantle cavity. The family dates from the Upper Triassic.

References: Kira (1972), Stenzel (1971), Yoo (1976).

. . . .

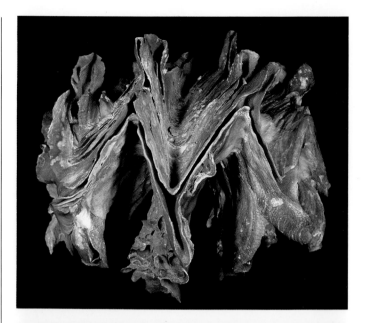

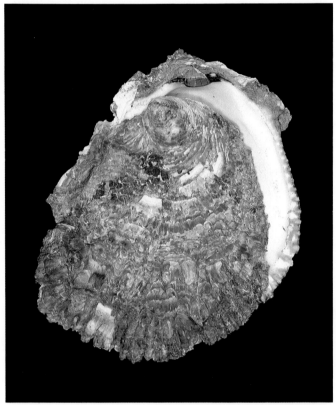

Ostrea denselamellosa

Hyotissa hyotis

Family: GRYPHAEIDAE Vyalov, 1936
Species: *Hyotissa hyotis* (Linné, 1758)
Common Name: Honeycomb Oyster
Size: 8 inches (200 mm)
Distribution: Circumtropical

Hyotissa hyotis has a subcircular shell, usually with a saw-toothed, sometimes jagged margin. It is similar to the ostreids of the genus *Lopha,* but is distinguished by the position of the muscle scars as described below, and by the spongy shell structure, which can often be seen in eroded areas at the margin of the shell. The animal lives subtidally, cemented to hard substrata.

Gryphaeids closely resemble ostreids in form and habit, but are distinguished from them by the hinge structure of the larval shell, the path of the intestine in relation to the heart, and the shape and position of the posterior adductor muscle scar. The muscle scar in gryphaeids is relatively circular, and is closer to the hinge than to the opposite margin of the valve. In ostreids it is kidney-shaped or crescentic, and farther from the hinge than from the opposite margin. There are five living species of gryphaeids, in the genera *Hyotissa* and *Neopycnodonte.* The family appeared in the Upper Triassic.

References: Abbott (1974), Stenzel (1971).

. . . .

Dimya tigrina

Superfamily: Dimyacea Fischer, 1886
Family: DIMYIDAE Fischer, 1886
Species: *Dimya tigrina* Bayer, 1971
Common Name: Tigrine Dimya
Size: 0.4 inches (10 mm)
Distribution: Bahamas to Colombia

Dimya tigrina has a subcircular, irregular, flaky, white shell with orange-brown radial stripes and hints of iridescence. The hinge is straight with an external ligament; a pit beneath the umbos holds the internal ligament. The species lives in depths of 80 to 1,000 feet (25 to 300 meters).

There are about a dozen species of dimyids worldwide in tropical and subtropical seas, mainly in deeper water. They resemble juvenile oysters, but can be recognized by the small anterior adductor muscle scar and a bilobed posterior scar. Ostreids and gryphaeids have only a posterior muscle scar, which is crescentic or circular, but not bilobed. Dimyids also differ from oysters in cementing on the right, rather than the left valve. The pallial line is sometimes broken into a series of dots; there is no pallial sinus. The foot and byssus are absent in post-larval stages. Fossil dimyids are known from the mid-Jurassic.

References: Bayer (1971), Yonge (1975, 1978).

. . . .

Superfamily: Plicatulacea Watson, 1930
Family: PLICATULIDAE Watson, 1930
Species: *Plicatula gibbosa* Lamarck, 1801
Common Name: Atlantic Kitten's Paw
Size: 1.5 inches (40 mm)
Distribution: North Carolina to Argentina

The shell of *Plicatula gibbosa* has five to twelve triangular radial ribs which produce a saw-toothed valve margin. Color is dull white to tan with short, reddish brown

Plicatula gibbosa

stripes on the ribs. The interior of the shell is white, and the posterior adductor muscle scar is sometimes raised. The animal cements to rocks intertidally and to depths of 300 feet (90 meters).

There are about ten species of plicatulids worldwide in warm seas. They live cemented on the right valve and have a tooth-and-socket hinge convergent on the ball-and-socket hinge of spondylids. In the upper valve, the sockets are next to the central ligament pit with the teeth outside. On the lower valve, sockets are outside, teeth inside. The valves are porcelaneous inside and lack a pallial sinus. The anterior adductor muscle is lost, and foot and byssus are absent in adults. Fossil plicatulids are known from the middle Triassic.

References: Boss (1982), Yonge (1975).

. . . .

Enigmonia aenigmatica

Suborder: Pectinina Waller, 1978
Superfamily: Anomiacea Rafinesque, 1815
Family: ANOMIIDAE Rafinesque, 1815
Species: *Enigmonia aenigmatica* (Holten, 1802)
Common Name: Mangrove Jingle Shell
Size: 2 inches (50 mm)
Distribution: Southeast Asia, Philippines

Enigmonia aenigmatica is unique among bivalves in being able to climb trees. The animal lives in high intertidal areas of mangrove forests and crawls about on the leaves and trunks of the trees by means of a ribbonlike foot extended through the byssal sinus, a hole in the bottom

valve. The shells of animals living on the mangrove leaves are gold, those on all other surfaces are reddish purple. If the animal is transplanted from leaf to bark, or vice versa, the shell gradually changes color accordingly.

There are about fifteen species of anomiids (jingle shells) worldwide. They have rounded to elliptical shells with the beaks usually set back from the margin. The byssal notch develops into a hole in the bottom (right) valve, through which the animal attaches its byssus. The byssus is calcified except in *Enigmonia*. The anterior adductor muscle is absent and there is no pallial sinus. There is often a branchial eye on the first gill filament, and *Enigmonia* also has pallial eyes that detect light through the left valve. The oldest anomiid fossils are from the Cretaceous.

References: Yonge (1977), Sigurdsson & Sundari (1990).

. . . .

Family: PLACUNIDAE Rafinesque, 1815
Species: *Placuna placenta* (Linné, 1758)
Common Name: Windowpane Oyster
Size: 8 inches (200 mm)
Distribution: India, Southeast Asia, Philippines

Because of its large, thin, transparent valves, *Placuna placenta* has been harvested for hundreds of years, originally as a substitute for glass and today for making trays, lampshades, and curios. It lives lying unattached on either valve on the surface of mudflats intertidally and to depths of 65 feet (20 meters). The right valve is slightly concave, the left valve slightly more convex, hardly leaving room for the crèpelike animal, which is one of the most flattened of all bivalves.

There are about five species of placunids, all in the Indo- and Eastern Pacific. The shell is thin, circular, and compressed, with beaks at the margin or nearly so. The anterior adductor muscle is absent and the shell has a weak or absent pallial line; there is no pallial sinus. The hinge is toothless; characteristic vee-shaped ligament and ridges radiate from the beaks. The fossil record of placunids extends to the Eocene.

References: Boss (1982), Yonge (1977).

. . . .

Superfamily: Pectinacea Rafinesque, 1815
Family: PECTINIDAE Rafinesque, 1815
Species: *Somalipecten cranmerorum* Waller, 1986
Common Name: Cranmers' Scallop
Size: 3 inches (70 mm)
Distribution: Somalia

Somalipecten cranmerorum is a recently discovered species, brought to light by the activities of Taiwanese trawlers in new fishing grounds off Somalia. The right valve has six ribs, the left five; the ribs decrease in strength toward the margins. The shell is red to orange in color, with fine mottles and bold oblique flammules of white or cream. The animal lives in depths of 500 to 1,000 feet (150 to 300 meters), probably on hard bottoms.

The family Pectinidae (true scallops) contains almost 400 species worldwide. The shell disc is circular to fan-shaped, with two auricles projecting along the straight hinge line. There is a triangular ligament pit below the umbos. The animal lies on the right valve, being byssally attached on hard surfaces as in *Chlamys,* free-living in sand as in *Pecten,* or, rarely, cemented as in *Hinnites.* The pectinids are united by having a ctenolium; a comblike structure along the byssal notch derived from the inner surface of the valve. It serves to spread the byssal threads into several bundles, making it more difficult to twist them. The ctenolium is present in all pectinids early in life, but is lost in adults of some species, particularly free-living forms. The anterior adductor muscle is lost; the posterior adductor muscle is what is served in restaurants as scallops. The mantle edge bears numerous eyes, which have lens, cornea, and retina. Most pectinids can swim by clapping the valves together and jetting backward; they can also move forward by keeping the mantle closed ventrally and ejecting water dorsolaterally. The fossil record of the group dates to the Triassic.

References: Waller (1972, 1978, 1984, 1986).

. . . .

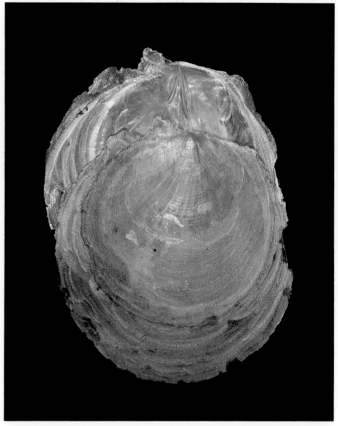

Placuna placenta

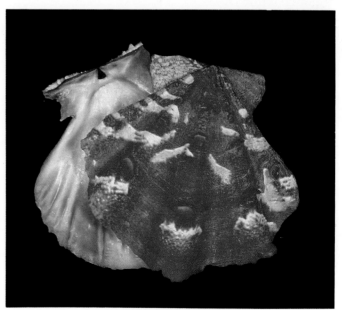

Somalipecten cranmerorum (paratype)

Parvamussium jeffreysii

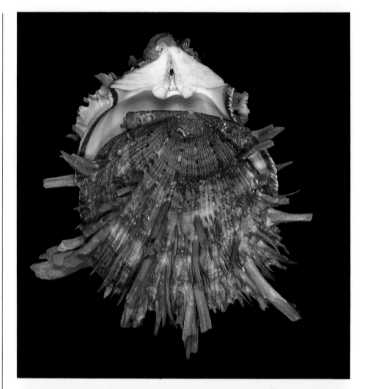

Spondylus americanus

Family: PROPEAMUSSIIDAE Abbott, 1954
Species: *Parvamussium jeffreysii* (E. A. Smith, 1885)
Common Name: Jeffrey's Glass Scallop
Size: 0.8 inches (20 mm)
Distribution: Japan to Indonesia

Parvamussium jeffreysii has unequal valves, with the left being larger than the right. Both valves have concentric sculpture and the right also has external radial ribs. Both valves have white, internal, radial ribs which can be seen through the translucent, light orange shell. A triangular ligament pit holds the resilium. The species has been recorded in depths of 330 to 1,800 feet (100 to 550 meters).

The propeamussiids comprise about thirty species, most in deep or polar waters. Like pectinids, propeamussiids have non-nacreous shells, lack the anterior adductor muscle and pallial sinus, and have mantle eyes with lens, cornea, and retina. They differ from pectinids in lacking the ctenolium and having different shell composition. The fossil record of propeamussiids extends to the Lower Jurassic.

References: Boss (1982), Habe (1968), Waller (1978).

. . . .

Family: SPONDYLIDAE Gray, 1826
Species: *Spondylus americanus* Hermann, 1781
Common Name: Atlantic Thorny Oyster
Size: 4 inches (100 mm)
Distribution: North Carolina to Brazil

Spondylus americanus, sometimes called the chrysanthemum shell, has numerous, erect, somewhat curved spines arrayed on the stronger of its radial ribs. The color varies from white to rose, with the juvenile shell often being yellow, orange, or red. The juveniles are much less spiny, and often have irregular lamellae on the bottom valve, thereby resembling some species of *Chama* (Chamidae).

There are about fifty living species of spondylids. They can easily be distinguished from other pectinaceans and chamids by the robust ball-and-socket hinge. Adult spondylids have heavy, spiny shells that are cemented to hard substrata on the right valve. Like pectinids, they have only the posterior adductor muscle, mantle eyes with lens, cornea, and retina, a triangular ligament pit, and a non-nacreous shell with no pallial sinus. They lack the ctenolium of pectinids. Fossil spondylids are known from the Jurassic.

References: Abbott (1974), Lamprell (1987), Waller (1978).

. . . .

Subclass: Paleoheterodonta Newell, 1965
Order: Trigonioida Dall, 1889
Superfamily: Trigoniacea Lamarck, 1819
Family: TRIGONIIDAE Lamarck, 1819
Species: *Neotrigonia margaritacea* (Lamarck, 1804)
Common Name: Common Brooch Clam
Size: 1.4 inches (35 mm)
Distribution: Southeastern Australia

Neotrigonia margaritacea has about twenty-four nodular radial ribs on each valve and numerous closely spaced concentric growth lines. The pattern of the ribs shows through on the inside of the valves, which are smooth centrally, crenulate at the margin, and have a white to pink nacre. The animal lives in sand or sandy mud in depths to 260 feet (80 meters).

Neotrigonia margaritacea

Trigoniids were extremely diverse during the Mesozoic, but most went extinct at the end of the Cretaceous, and only about five species survive today, all in Australia. The left valve of the shell has a strongly grooved tooth on either side of the beak that fits into a protruding, grooved socket on the other valve. The animals burrow using their large foot; the strong hinge keeps the valves aligned when gaping during burrowing. There is usually an anterior buttress supporting the hinge internally. The interior of the shell is nacreous. The adductor muscle scars are connected by the pallial line, which lacks a pallial sinus. The hinge is a short half-cylinder that connects the valves externally, posterior to the beaks.

References: Coleman (1975), Stanley (1977).

· · · · · · · · · · · · ·

Subclass: Heterodonta Neumayr, 1884
Order: Veneroida Adams & Adams, 1856
Superfamily: Lucinacea Fleming, 1828
Family: LUCINIDAE Fleming, 1828
Species: *Codakia tigerina* (Linné, 1758)
Common Name: Pacific Tiger Lucine
Size: 4 inches (100 mm)
Distribution: Tropical Indo-Pacific

Codakia tigerina has a subcircular shell which can have more than 100 radial ribs, and numerous concentric cords with about the same spacing as the ribs, with nodes where ribs and cords intersect. The valves gape somewhat dorsally around the ligament and the umbos point forward. The sunken lunule is larger in the right than in the left valve. Externally, the shell is off-white, internally, yellow with rose margins. The animal burrows intertidally in coral sand.

About 200 living species of lucinids are known. The valves are subcircular to ovate and the beaks point forward or medially. The anterior adductor muscle scar has a ventral, fingerlike extension inside the pallial line. There is no pallial sinus. The ligament is subinternal and situated posterior to the beaks. Lucinids construct an anterior incurrent mucous tube that allows them to filter feed while deeply buried. Both valves usually have two radial central (cardinal) teeth, and there are sometimes lateral teeth. Venerids are similar to lucinids in general shell shape, but lack the extension of the anterior adductor muscle, usually have a pallial sinus, and have three rather than two central hinge teeth. The family is known from the Silurian.

References: Allen (1958), Boss (1982).

· · · · · · · · · · · ·

Family: FIMBRIIDAE Nicol, 1950
Species: *Fimbria soverbii* (Reeve, 1842)
Common Name: Sowerby's Basket Lucine
Size: 4 inches (100 mm)
Distribution: Japan to Australia, Indonesia to Palau

During the 1800s, *Fimbria soverbii* was one of the few bivalve species avidly sought by collectors, and it is still difficult to obtain today. The transversely ovate shell can have more than forty strong, raised concentric lamellae and more than eighty radial ribs, which continue on the ventral faces of the lamellae, developing there as nodes anteriorly. Fimbriids are represented by only two living species, both in the Indo-Pacific. They differ from lucinids in lacking the fingerlike extension of the anterior adductor muscle and the anterior mucous tube. Fimbriids are shallow burrowers in coral sand. Their fossil record extends to the Carboniferous.

References: Allen & Turner (1970), Boss (1982), Dance (1969).

Family: THYASIRIDAE Dall, 1900
Species: *Thyasira dunbari* Lubinsky, 1976
Common Name: Dunbar's Cleft Clam
Size: 0.3 inches (8 mm)
Distribution: Arctic Canada

Thyasira dunbari was recently discovered on the northern islands of the Canadian Arctic. It has an elongate, anteriorly curving shell with projecting umbos. Shell color is buff, becoming darker toward the margins; the periostracum is brown. Sculpture consists of concentric growth

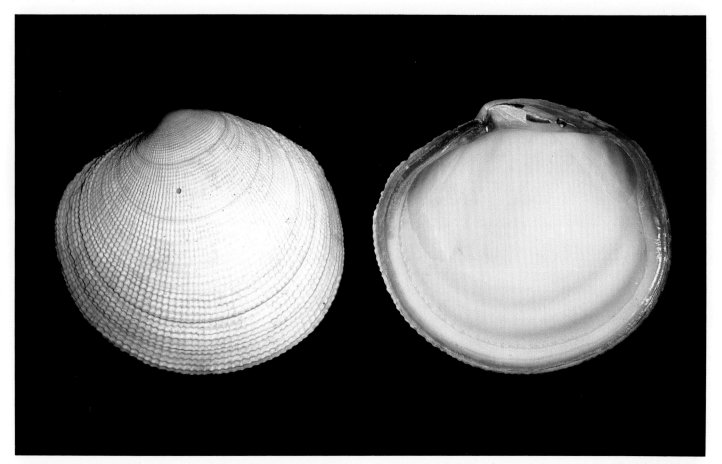

Codakia tigerina

Fimbria soverbii

Thyasira dunbari (paratype)

lines and shallow radial furrows. The animal lives in depths of 30 to 230 feet (10 to 70 meters) on muddy bottoms.

Thyasirids have rounded trigonal to subquadrangular shells, often with a marked posterior ridge. The umbos point anteriorly and the hinge is more or less toothless. The ligament is posterior to the beaks as in other lucinaceans. Like lucinids, thyasirids are filter-feeding burrowers that construct an anterior incurrent mucous tube. The adductor muscle scars are elongate; the anterior one lacks the ventral extension seen in that of the lucinids. There is no pallial sinus. The fossil record of thyasirids reaches the mid-Triassic.

References: Bernard (1972), Boss (1982), Moore (1969).

. . . .

Felaniella zelandica

Family: UNGULINIDAE Adams & Adams, 1857
Species: *Felaniella zelandica* (Gray, 1835)
Common Name: Zelandic Diplodon
Size: 1 inch (25 mm)
Distribution: New Zealand

The shell of *Felaniella zelandica* is subcircular and off-white to pink, with a thin, light yellowish brown periostracum. Sculpture consists of incised concentric growth lines of irregular strength. The animal lives from shallow water to depths of 300 feet (90 meters).

There are about fifty species of ungulinids worldwide. They resemble lucinids in shell form and in building an anterior incurrent mucus tube, but can be differentiated in having one of the two central hinge teeth split. The adductor muscle scars are elongate along the pallial line, whereas the extension of the anterior adductor scar in lucinids is inside the pallial line. There is no pallial sinus. The fossil record of ungulinids dates from the Upper Cretaceous.

References: Boss (1982), Powell (1979).

. . . .

Perrierina aucklandica

Superfamily: Cyamiacea Philippi, 1845
Family: CYAMIIDAE Philippi, 1845
Species: *Perrierina aucklandica* (Powell, 1933)
Common Name: Auckland Perrierina
Size: 0.08 inches (2 mm)
Distribution: New Zealand

Perrierina aucklandica has a minute but distinctive shell that is off-white and stained brown at the posterior end. Sculpture consists of fine concentric lines. The hinge has a series of taxodont-type teeth of either side. In cyamiids, the umbos are central or subcentral. The central hinge teeth are elongate and diverging and in some cases bilobed. The anterior and posterior muscle scars are connected by the pallial line, which does not have a sinus. The animal incubates eggs and larvae in the gills. The family occurs mainly in the southern hemisphere in circum-Antarctic waters. Cyamiids are not known as fossils before the Miocene.

References: Boss (1982), Powell (1979).

. . . .

Family: GAIMARDIIDAE Hedley, 1916
Species: *Gaimardia trapesina* (Lamarck, 1819)
Common Name: Trapeze Gaimardia
Size: 1 inch (25 mm)
Distribution: Tierra del Fuego to Kerguelen

Gaimardia trapesina has a plump shell with the umbos well to the anterior. An olive-green periostracum covers the smooth pink, purple, or brown shell, which is sculptured with irregularly spaced concentric growth lines. The animal lives on floating algae and to depths of 820 feet (250 meters).

There are probably fewer than twenty species of gaimardiids, mainly restricted to the southern hemisphere. Gaimardiids have inflated shells, often with the ventral margin straight or slightly concave anteriorly, constricting the shell and giving it a beaked appearance. The umbos are anterior and the hinge is weak, generally with one central tooth in the left valve, a bifid one in the right valve, an anterior lateral tooth in both valves, and a posterior lateral in the left valve. Both adductor muscles are present and a pallial sinus is lacking. Gaimardiids often live in floating seaweed. They incubate eggs and larvae in the gill. They are not known as fossils before the Miocene.

References: Boss (1982), Dell (1964).

. . . .

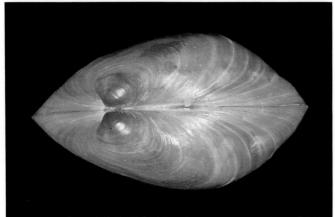

Gaimardia trapesina

Superfamily: Galeommatacea Gray, 1840
Family: GALEOMMATIDAE Gray, 1840
Species: *Ephippodonta macdougalli* Tate, 1888
Common Name: MacDougall's Ephippodonta
Size: 0.5 inches (12 mm)
Distribution: South Australia

Ephippodonta macdougalli is a bizarre bivalve that carries its half-moon valves flat above it while crawling around on its foot like a snail. It lives in the burrows of a type of shrimp under large, intertidal stones. About sixty ribs radiate from the umbos, many bearing papillose scales.

All galeommatids are able to crawl on the foot, and most have gaping valves, although the 180-degree gape of *Ephippodonta* is extreme. Many species live in association with other invertebrates. The hinge is usually toothless and the pallial line is simple, lacking a sinus. The adductor muscles are ovate and similar in size to each other.

References: Boss (1982), Cotton (1961), Mikkelsen & Bieler (1989).

. . . .

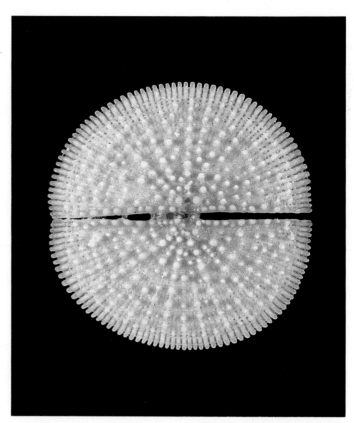

Ephippodonta macdougalli

Family: LASAEIDAE Gray, 1847

Species: *Pythina deshayesiana* (Hinds, 1845)

Common Name: Deshayes' Pythina

Size: 0.4 inches (10 mm)

Distribution: Tropical Western Pacific

Pythina deshayesiana has a white, wedge-shaped shell with strong chevrons of ribs and a straight ventral margin that is finely denticulate. The umbos are toward the anterior end. The valves are of equal size and close firmly, without a gape at the margin.

Lasaeids have the hinge plate indented under the beak. They differ from montacutids in having cardinal and lateral teeth on both valves; montacutids do not have true cardinals. The internal ligament is in a triangular pit. The fossil record of lasaeids extends to the Paleocene.

References: Moore (1969), Rosewater (1984).

. . . .

Family: MONTACUTIDAE Clark, 1855

Species: *Curvemysella paula* (A. Adams, 1856)

Common Name: Boomerang Clam

Size: 0.4 inches (10 mm)

Distribution: East Africa to Japan and New Guinea

Curvemysella paula lives symbiotically with hermit crabs; its bizarre, twisted boomeranglike shape allows it to fit along the crab's side within the shell. The ventral margin is strongly concave and the anterior end is narrower than the posterior end. Angled ridges run from the beaks to the ventral margins of both ends.

There are probably more than 100 species of montacutids worldwide, many of which live symbiotically with other invertebrates. They have a well-defined hollow under the beaks. The hinge lacks true cardinal teeth, but has thickened laterals, usually bent up at their umbonal end. Some authorities synonymize Montacutidae with Lasaeidae. The fossil record of montacutids dates from the Eocene.

Reference: Moore (1969).

. . . .

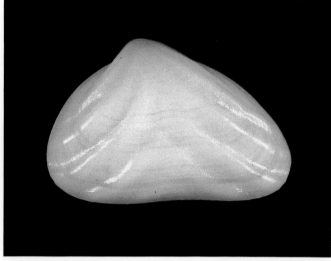

Pythina deshayesiana

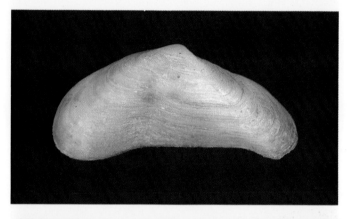

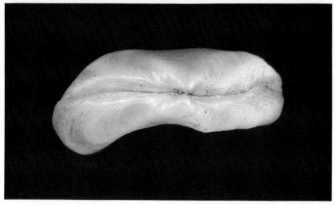

Curvemysella paula

Cardita crassicosta

Superfamily: Carditacea Fleming, 1820
Family: CARDITIDAE Fleming, 1820
Species: *Cardita crassicosta* Lamarck, 1819
Common Name: Thick-ribbed Cardita
Size: 3 inches (75 mm)
Distribution: Western Pacific

Cardita crassicosta has twelve or thirteen scaly radial ribs on each valve, with the strongest being posterior. The umbos are far forward and the ventral margin is concave anteriorly, giving the valves a beaked appearance. Color is highly variable, ranging from cream through yellow, orange, red, and slaty purple, often with brown markings between the ribs. Impressions of the ribs are seen on the interior of the valves, which are white to creamy yellow in color.

There are about fifty species of carditids worldwide. The animals live byssally attached; the shells are subcircular to subquadrangular, sculpted with radial ribs, usually solid, and have a small, deep lunule. The umbos usually point forward and the ligament is posterior to them and external. The anterior and posterior muscle scars are approximately equal in size and are connected by the pallial line; there is no pallial sinus. In most species, if not all, young are brooded in the gills. The known fossil record of carditids begins in the Devonian.

References: Boss (1982), Coan (1977), Moore (1969).

. . . .

Superfamily: Chamacea Lamarck, 1809
Family: CHAMIDAE Lamarck, 1809
Species: *Chama macerophylla* (Gmelin, 1791)
Common Name: Leafy Jewel Box
Size: 3.5 inches (90 mm)
Distribution: North Carolina to Brazil

The colors of *Chama macerophylla* span the spectrum from white and yellow to purple, with various combinations. The shell has leafy spines that can be quite long in specimens growing in quiet water. In the umbonal region the color sometimes differs from that of the rest of the shell. The interior is white, sometimes with areas of yellow or purple. The animal lives cemented to hard surfaces intertidally and to depths of 150 feet (45 meters).

There are about seventy species of chamids worldwide, mainly in tropical seas. They resemble oysters, but can be distinguished in having both anterior and posterior adductor muscle scars. They can be separated from *Spondylus* in their lack of the ball-and-socket hinge. The beaks in chamid point toward the anterior, and the ligament is posterior to them. Some chamids cement to hard substrates, *Chama* on the left valve and *Pseudochama* on the right valve. *Arcinella* is free-living as an adult. The oldest chamid fossils are from the Paleocene.

References: Abbott (1974), Bernard (1976), Boss (1982).

. . . .

Chama macerophylla

Superfamily: Crassatellacea Férussac, 1822
Family: CRASSATELLIDAE Férussac, 1822
Species: *Eucrassatella gibbosa* (Sowerby, 1832)
Common Name: Gibbous Crassatella
Size: 3 inches (75 mm)
Distribution: Baja California to Peru

The shell of *Eucrassatella gibbosa* is rather inflated, rounded anteriorly, and angled posteriorly. The beaks point medially or somewhat posteriorly. The lunule and escutcheon are relatively deep. Located in the umbonal region are concentric folds that end at the posterior ridge; the rest of the surface has irregular concentric growth lines. The periostracum is dark brown on a lighter brown shell, which sometimes has darker radial rays. The hinge teeth have fine transverse serrations. The animal lives in sand in depths from 16 to 360 feet (5 to 110 meters).

There are about thirty species of crassatellids worldwide, mainly tropical and subtropical in distribution. They have sturdy trigonal to subquadrate shells that are rounded anteriorly and often truncated posteriorly. The shells are smooth or have concentric ribs; radial sculpture is lacking. The ligament is internal in a pit below the beak; it often obliterates the upper part of the hinge tooth anterior to it. The adductor muscle scars are approximately equal in size and there is no pallial sinus. The fossil record of the group extends to the Devonian.

References: Coan (1984), Moore (1969).

. . . .

Eucrassatella gibbosa

Astarte undata

Family: ASTARTIDAE d'Orbigny, 1844
Species: *Astarte undata* Gould, 1841
Common Name: Wavy Astarte
Size: 1.3 inches (34 mm)
Distribution: Northwest Atlantic and northeast Pacific

Astarte undata has a sturdy shell with up to sixteen strong concentric ribs. The shell has a thick brown periostracum and a white, porcelaneous interior. It is commonly dredged in depths of 30 to 650 feet (10 to 200 meters). There are about thirty species of Astartidae, which are mainly northern in distribution in cold water. The shells are similar to those of crassatellids, but do not have a well-defined triangular ligament pit. The beaks are usually central and point forward. The oldest astartid fossils are from the Devonian.

References: Bernard (1983), Moore (1969).

. . . .

Superfamily: Cardiacea Lamarck, 1809
Family: CARDIIDAE Lamarck, 1809
Species: *Trachycardium isocardia* (Linné, 1758)
Common Name: Even Prickly Cockle
Size: 3 inches (75 mm)
Distribution: Gulf of Mexico and Caribbean

Trachycardium isocardia has a thick shell with thirty-two to thirty-seven rows of scaly ribs and a strongly denticulate margin. The scales are sharp posteriorly and blunt anteriorly. Color is a creamy light yellow with reddish brown

markings. The interior is salmon with a yellow margin. The animal lives in sand to depths of at least 65 feet (20 meters).

Cardiids (cockle shells) are represented by more than 200 species worldwide. They have a huge variety of shapes, from transversely elongate (as in *Papyridea*) to compressed and strongly keeled (as in *Corculum*). Most have radial sculpture and almost touching umbos. The short, external ligament is behind the beak. The hinge has two conical central teeth, usually with the anterior one larger in the left valve, and with some degree of fusion of centrals in the right valve. The lateral teeth are some distance from the centrals; sometimes only posterior laterals are present. The adductor muscle scars are usually approximately equal in size and there is no pallial sinus. Cardiids have a large foot and are good burrowers. The fossil record of the group extends to the Upper Triassic.

References: Keen (1980), Wilson & Stevenson (1977).

. . . .

Family: HEMIDONACIDAE Iredale & McMichael, 1962
Species: *Hemidonax donaciformis* (Schröter, 1786)
Common Name: Common False Donax
Size: 1.4 inches (35 mm)
Distribution: Philippines and Indonesia

Hemidonax donaciformis has a subtrigonal shell with a strong posterior ridge and tall umbos. It is sculptured with radial ribs and fine concentric growth lines. The shell is white or mottled with brown, and usually has at least a trace of brown on the inner posterior margin.

There are five known living species of *Hemidonax,* the only member of its family. *Hemidonax* has been placed in the Donacidae because of its similarity in shell shape to *Donax,* but has many anatomical differences that seem to preclude this placement. Most importantly, it lacks siphons, and consequently a pallial sinus and cruciform muscles. Recent workers have allied it instead with the cardiaceans. The fossil record of hemidonacids extends to the Oligocene.

Reference: Ponder et al. (1981).

. . . .

Trachycardium isocardia

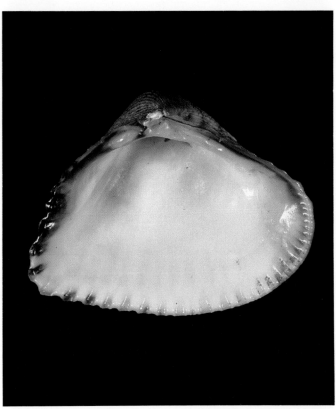

Hemidonax donaciformis

Family: TRIDACNIDAE Lamarck, 1819
Species: *Tridacna squamosa* Lamarck, 1819
Common Name: Fluted Giant Clam
Size: 16 inches (400 mm)
Distribution: East Africa to Japan and Samoa

Shells of *Tridacna squamosa* vary in color from white to pastel shades of yellow and orange. They have five or six strong ribs with large, erect, leaflike scales. There are sometimes smaller ribs at the dorsal margins, and, except on the scales, there are radial grooves throughout, which are more closely spaced on the ribs than in their interspaces. Both the scales and the body of the shell have low concentric ridges. The umbos are central and there is a dorsal gape where the byssus protrudes.

Tridacnids (giant clams) include the largest living shelled mollusk, *Tridacna gigas* (Linné, 1758), with a maximum recorded length of 54 inches (1.37 meters) and weights approaching 600 pounds (270 kilograms). There are seven living species of giant clams: five of *Tridacna* and two of *Hippopus*. The anterior adductor muscle is absent in adults and there is no pallial sinus. Tridacnids live in shallow water in coral reef areas with the hinge downward and valves gaping to expose the mantle to sunlight. The mantle contains symbiotic algae (zooxanthellae), which make food for the clam in return for a safe place to live. *Tridacna* have been called man-eating clams, but while it might be possible for an unwary diver to get a limb trapped when a clam closes its valves, there are no reliable reports of this happening. The oldest undoubted tridacnid fossils are from the Eocene.

References: Rosewater (1965, 1982).

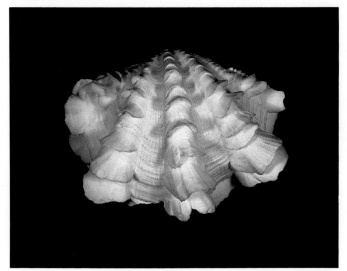

Tridacna squamosa

Superfamily: Mactracea Lamarck, 1809
Family: MACTRIDAE Lamarck, 1809
Species: *Mactra achatina* Holten, 1802
Common Name: Agate Mactra
Size: 2 inches (50 mm)
Distribution: East Africa to Japan

Mactra achatina has a light orange to brown shell with pink or purple near the beaks. It is speckled with white and often has alternating light and dark radial rays. The periostracum is yellow-brown, adherent near the margins, and arranged concentrically. The animal lives in depths of 10 to 130 feet (3 to 40 meters) in sand.

There are about 150 species of mactrids (surf clams)

worldwide. They are usually thin-shelled, although some, such as *Rangia* have thick shells. The shells are similar to those of mesodesmatids, as discussed below. The beaks point anteriorly and the valves often gape slightly at one or both ends. There is an inverted vee-shaped central tooth in the left valve, which fits between the two central teeth in the right valve, which are sometimes joined dorsally. The resilium is brown and triangular, fitting into a pit posterior to the central teeth. The lateral teeth can be quite long on both sides of the beak. Both adductor muscles are present and there is a pallial sinus. Fossil mactrids are known from the Upper Cretaceous.

References: Boss (1982), Moore (1969).

· · · · · · · · · · · · ·

Mactra achatina

Family: MESODESMATIDAE Gray, 1840
Species: *Atactodea glabrata* (Linné, 1767)
Common Name: Pacific Beach Clam
Size: 1.3 inches (34 mm)
Distribution: Tropical Indo-Pacific

Atactodea glabrata

Atactodea glabrata is an abundant species that lives at high population densities intertidally and in shallow water subtidally on sandy shores. The shell is smooth or has concentric ridges and a yellowish brown periostracum. The valves are white inside and have a shallow pallial sinus. *Atactodea striata* (Gmelin, 1791) is a synonym.

The forty or so species of mesodesmatids can be difficult to separate from mactrids. In general, if the shell is elongate anteriorly it is a mesodesmatid, if posteriorly, it is a mactrid. A few mactrids are longer anteriorly, but they have the beaks pointing forward, as do most mactrids, whereas mesodesmatids have the beaks pointing backward or medially. If the shell is very thin for its size it is a mactrid; mesodesmatids usually have thick shells. An easy anatomical distinction is that mesodesmatids have separated siphons whereas mactrids have united siphons. Fossil mesodesmatids are known from the Eocene.

References: Beu (1971), Boss (1982), Moore (1969).

· · · · · · · · · · · · · ·

Family: CARDILIIDAE Fischer, 1887
Species: *Cardilia semisulcata* (Lamarck, 1819)
Common Name: Half-ribbed Cardilia
Size: 0.8 inches (20 mm)
Distribution: Southeast Asia and Japan to Australia

Cardilia semisulcata has about a dozen radial grooves on the posterior half of the shell, bordered on the posterior margin by a zone with weak irregular ribs. The anterior half of the shell has only fine concentric growth lines. The thin, white shell has been dredged in depths from 16 to 300 feet (5 to 90 meters).

There are six known living species of cardiliids, five in the Western Indo-Pacific and one in West Africa. The shells are thin, white, and inflated, with beaks strongly curved forward and inward. Both adductor muscles are present; the posterior one inserts on a strong, shelf-like radial ridge. A pallial sinus is absent. There is an inverted vee-shaped central tooth in the left valve and a triangular one in the right valve. Lateral teeth are absent and there is a resilial pit. The oldest undoubted cardiliid fossils are from the Oligocene.

References: Boss (1982), Moore (1969).

. . . .

Cardilia semisulcata

Family: ANATINELLIDAE Gray, 1853
Species: *Anatinella nicobarica* (Gmelin, 1791)
Common Name: Nicobar Anatinella
Size: 1.5 inches (40 mm)
Distribution: India to Japan and Australia

Anatinella nicobarica is a rare species, and the only known member of its family, living or fossil. The shell is white and the beaks are slightly anterior. The posterior end is obliquely truncate. Sculpture consists of irregular concentric growth lines and almost microscopic radial threads. The anterior adductor muscle scar is narrow

and elongate, the posterior one has a thickened anterior margin. The shell resembles that of myids in being thin and white with a chondrophore projecting from the hinge, but anatinellids have a chondrophore in each valve, whereas myids have one only in the left valve. Also, anatinellids lack, and myids have, a pallial sinus.

References: Boss (1982), Moore (1969).

. . . .

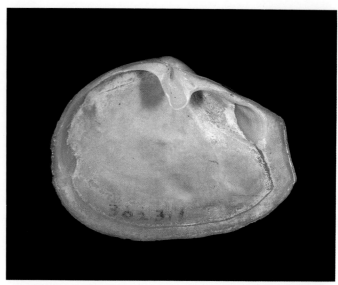

Anatinella nicobarica

Superfamily: Solenacea Lamarck, 1809
Family: SOLENIDAE Lamarck, 1809
Species: *Solen truncatus* Wood, 1815
Common Name: Truncate Jackknife Clam
Size: 6 inches (150 mm)
Distribution: East Africa to Thailand

Solen truncatus has a posteriorly elongate, straight-sided shell shaped like a quarter-cylinder. The shell is white, with pink or brown stripes paralleling the growth lines. There is a thin, shiny, yellowish brown periostracum, which is adherent at the ventral and posterior margins. The interior of the shell is white, with the external color pattern showing through. The animal is a rapid burrower in sandy mud flats.

Solenids have posteriorly elongate shells with the umbos at the anterior end. The valves are gaping and usually truncate at both ends. The adductor muscle scars are elongate and placed dorsally. There is a pallial sinus. Each valve has a single tooth below the umbo. The shells of solenids resemble those of cultellids, as discussed below. The fossil record of solenids dates to the Lower Eocene.

References: Boss (1982), Cosel (1989), Owen (1959).

. . . .

Solen truncatus

Siliqua radiata

Family: CULTELLIDAE Davies, 1935
Species: *Siliqua radiata* (Linné, 1758)
Common Name: Purple Razor Clam
Size: 4 inches (100 mm)
Distribution: India to Indonesia

Siliqua radiata has a smooth purple shell with white rays emanating from the beaks. The ray closest to the anterior is a brighter white than the others and corresponds in position to an internal rib. There are often two low ridges along the posterior dorsal margin.

Cultellids have shells resembling those of solenids, but they usually do not have the beaks as far forward, are not as elongate, and have rounded rather than truncate ends.

An exception is *Ensis,* which has two vertical and one horizontal tooth in the left valve below the umbo, whereas solenids have only one vertical tooth. Most solenids have an internally thickened anterior margin, whereas cultellids do not. Fossil cultellids are known from the Lower Cretaceous.

References: Boss (1982), Moore (1969), Owen (1959).

. . . .

Tellina radiata

Superfamily: Tellinacea Blainville, 1814
Family: TELLINIDAE Blainville, 1814
Species: *Tellina radiata* Linné, 1758
Common Name: Sunrise Tellin
Size: 4 inches (100 mm)
Distribution: South Carolina to Caribbean

Tellina radiata has a smooth, shiny shell, with some fine, low, irregular concentric growth marks. The ground color is white or cream with rays of yellow, orange, or pink. The shell has a deep pallial sinus that almost reaches the anterior adductor muscle scar. The animal lives in sand to depths of 50 feet (15 meters).

There are about 350 species of tellinids worldwide. They have laterally compressed shells, usually rounded anteriorly, and beaked or elongate posteriorly. There is a posterior bend, with the left valve curving toward the right valve. The shells are smooth or have concentric sculpture. The hinge has two cardinal teeth in each valve, at least one of them bifid, and may have lateral teeth. The ligament is external. Both adductor muscles are present and there is a large pallial sinus. Tellinids have two cruciform muscles that insert just below the posterior end of the pallial line. The small, roundish scars left by these muscles are more easily detected in tellinids than in other tellinaceans. Most tellinids are deposit feeders, lying on the right valve buried in sandy or muddy bottoms and using the incurrent siphon to vacuum up surficial debris. The fossil record of tellinids extends to the Lower Cretaceous.

References: Boss (1966, 1968, 1982).

. . . .

Donax variabilis

Family: DONACIDAE Fleming, 1828
Species: *Donax variabilis* Say, 1822
Common Name: Coquina
Size: 1 inch (25 mm)
Distribution: New York to Texas

Donax variabilis is an abundant species that can be collected by the handful on many beaches in Florida. That handful often contains a dazzling array of hues, as the shells can be any color of the spectrum except green and often have concentric and radial stripes. The species lives intertidally on sandy ocean beaches. The diversity of colors might serve to make it more difficult for predatory shore birds or fish to form a search image, and therefore harder for them to recognize their prey.

About fifty species of donacids live in shallow, warm seas worldwide. They have wedge-shaped, subtrigonal shells with the anterior end usually longer than the posterior, and the beaks pointing posteriorly. There are two cardinal teeth and well-developed laterals. Both adductor muscles are present and there is a pallial sinus. Some mesodesmatids resemble donacids but differ in having a resilium and resilial pit in the hinge and in lacking cruciform muscles. Fossil donacids are known from the Upper Cretaceous.

References: Boss (1982), Coan (1983).

. . . .

Gari squamosa

Family: PSAMMOBIIDAE Fleming, 1828
Species: *Gari squamosa* (Lamarck, 1818)
Common Name: Scaly Gari
Size: 1.2 inches (30 mm)
Distribution: Southeast Asia, Japan, Indonesia

Gari squamosa ranges in color from white to purple and has an elongate shell with anterior beaks and an obliquely truncate posterior end. There are oblique ridges running from the anterior dorsal margin to the posterior ventral margin, which merge with the nine to eleven prickly radial ribs on the posterior slope. The animals live in sand in depths to 65 feet (20 meters).

There are about 100 species of psammobiids worldwide; most are deposit feeders like the tellinids. They have elongate, rounded to subquadrate shells that gape, especially posteriorly. The hinge has one to three cardinal teeth; lateral teeth are reduced or absent. Both adductor muscles are present, as is the pallial sinus. They usually lack the posterior bend of tellinids. The family Solecurtidae is probably synonymous with Psammobiidae. The fossil record of psammobiids extends to the Upper Cretaceous.

References: Coan (1973), Matsukuma (1989).

. . . .

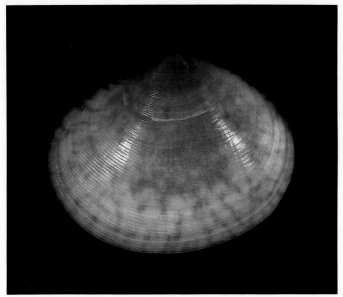

Semele purpurascens

Family: SEMELIDAE Stoliczka, 1870

Species: *Semele purpurascens* (Gmelin, 1791)

Common Name: Purplish Semele

Size: 1.4 inches (35 mm)

Distribution: Mexico to Ecuador; North Carolina to Uruguay

Semele purpurascens occurs in both the Western Atlantic and Eastern Pacific, and although these populations presumably have been separated for about three million years (since the uplift of the Isthmus of Panama), there are no consistent morphological features that separate them. Biochemical studies might help determine if these populations are of the same species. Shell color ranges from white to orange and purple with darker macula-

tions. Sculpture consists of small concentric growth lines and fine oblique threads.

There are about sixty species of semelids worldwide, almost half of them in the Eastern Pacific. The shells resemble those of tellinids but have a sunken resilial pit in the hinge. Lateral teeth and posterior flexure of the valves may be present or absent. Semelidae is a replacement name for Amphidesmatidae Deshayes, 1850, and so has priority over the synonymous Scrobiculariidae Adams & Adams, 1856. The fossil record of semelids extends to the Eocene.

References: Boss (1972), Coan (1988).

. . . .

Arctica islandica

Superfamily: Arcticacea Newton, 1891

Family: ARCTICIDAE Newton, 1891

Species: *Arctica islandica* (Linné, 1767)

Common Name: Ocean Quahog

Size: 4 inches (100 mm)

Distribution: Labrador to North Carolina; Iceland to France

Arctica islandica is the only living member of its family. It has a thick, subcircular shell with heavy brown or black periostracum and numerous fine concentric growth lines. Underneath the periostracum the shell is chalky

Trapezium oblongum

Meiocardia moltkiana

white. The animal lives on firm sand and sandy mud bottoms in depths to 300 feet (90 meters). The shell resembles that of *Mercenaria* (Veneridae), but can be distinguished in lacking a pallial sinus, lunule, and escutcheon, and in having a smooth rather than denticulate inner margin. Although only one species survives today, the Arcticidae were formerly a diverse group, with a fossil record reaching the Upper Triassic.

References: Moore (1969), Tebble (1976).

. . . .

Family: TRAPEZIIDAE Lamy, 1920
Species: *Trapezium oblongum* (Linné, 1758)
Common Name: Oblong Trapezium
Size: 2.5 inches (60 mm)
Distribution: Tropical Indo-Pacific

Trapezium oblongum has a sturdy, off-white shell, occasionally found with the umbos tinted pink. Internal coloration ranges from pure white to deep rose. Numerous radial ribs crossing the fine concentric growth lines give the external surface a beaded appearance. The animal lives on and under coral blocks in shallow water.

There are about ten species of trapeziids worldwide. They have elongate to subquadrate shells with the beaks near the anterior margin. Some species have a weak pallial sinus. There are three teeth near the beak and one elongate posterior lateral tooth. In some species the shell is distorted from growing in crevices. The fossil record of trapeziids extends to the Upper Cretaceous.

References: Kay (1979), Solem (1954).

. . . .

Superfamily: Glossacea Gray, 1847
Family: GLOSSIDAE Gray, 1847
Species: *Meiocardia moltkiana* (Gmelin, 1791)
Common Name: Moltke's Heart Clam
Size: 1.2 inches (30 mm)
Distribution: East Africa to Japan

Meiocardia moltkiana has a distinctively shaped shell, with the umbos tightly coiled and facing forward, a pro-

Calyptogena magnifica (paratype)

nounced posterior ridge, a convex posterior ventral margin, and strong concentric sculpture. The shell is white or cream with brown or red maculations. The animal lives in sand in depths to 150 feet (45 meters).

There are probably fewer than ten living species of glossids. They have greatly inflated shells that are heart-shaped in anterior view, with coiled, forward-pointing umbos. The adductor muscles are approximately equal in size and there is no pallial sinus. Glossids are known as Paleocene fossils.

References: Boss (1982), Moore (1969).

· · · · · · · · · · · · ·

Family: VESICOMYIDAE Dall & Simpson, 1901
Species: *Calyptogena magnifica* Boss & Turner, 1980
Common Name: Magnificent Calypto Clam
Size: 10 inches (250 mm)
Distribution: Galapagos Rift and East Pacific Rise

Calyptogena magnifica was discovered in 1977 by scientists on the submersible research vessel ALVIN. The animals live in profusion at the thermal vents along the deep-sea spreading centers at the Galapagos rift, at depths around 8,000 feet (2,500 meters). The shell is white, brittle, chalky, and slightly gaping. Sculpture consists of irregular concentric growth lines. The color of the periostracum is straw to brown.

Vesicomyids comprise about thirty species worldwide, mainly in deep water. They have ovate to elongate shells with forward-pointing umbos. The pallial sinus is weak or absent. Many vesicomyids have large gills that harbor symbiotic, sulfur-oxidizing bacteria. They live in sulfur-rich water around deep-sea thermal vents, or burrow in sulfur-rich sediment in non-vent areas. The alimentary tract is reduced as in the solemyids, which independently evolved a similar mode of life. The fossil record of vesicomyids extends to the Oligocene.

References: Boss & Turner (1980).

Polymesoda caroliniana

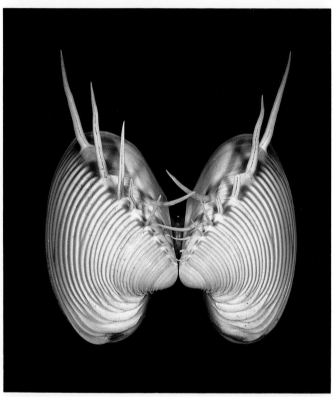

Pitar lupanaria

Superfamily: Corbiculacea Gray, 1847
Family: CORBICULIDAE Gray, 1847
Species: *Polymesoda caroliniana* (Bosc, 1801)
Common Name: Carolina Marsh Clam
Size: 2 inches (50 mm)
Distribution: Virginia to Texas

Polymesoda caroliniana has a sturdy, inflated shell with an olive-green to dark brown periostracum. The shell is usually eroded and chalky white at the umbos and in scattered patches elsewhere on the shell. Internally the valves are usually white, but sometimes have purple marginal markings and a peach-colored central dorsal area. The pallial sinus is small and triangular. The animal lives in mud in estuaries and brackish water within the influence of the tides.

There are about 100 species of corbiculids, most living in fresh water. They have rounded trigonal to ovate shells lacking lunule and escutcheon. The pallial sinus is small or absent. Corbiculids resemble some mactrids but lack the triangular resilium and resilial pit. The fossil record of corbiculids extends to the Jurassic and includes some marine forms.

References: Boss (1982), Emerson & Jacobson (1976).

. . . .

Superfamily: Veneracea Rafinesque, 1815
Family: VENERIDAE Rafinesque, 1815
Species: *Pitar lupanaria* (Lesson, 1830)
Common Name: Pacific Comb Venus
Size: 2.5 inches (60 mm)
Distribution: Baja California to Peru

Pitar lupanaria has some of the longest spines of any bivalve. The shell is white, with violet tints between the concentric lamellae. It has two posterior rows of spines; each spine has a purple spot at the base. The interior is white, with purple along the dorsal margins. The animal lives in sand intertidally and to depths of 100 feet (30 meters).

The venerids are the most diverse group of marine bivalves, with about 500 species worldwide, mainly in temperate and tropical seas. They usually have a distinct lunule and escutcheon and a pallial sinus of variable size and shape. There are three central teeth in each valve. The posterior lateral teeth are weak or absent and the anterior laterals may be present or absent. Lucinids are similar to venerids in general shell shape, but have an anteroventral extension of the anterior adductor muscle, lack a pallial sinus, and have only two central hinge teeth. Venerids are known as fossils from the Lower Cretaceous.

References: Boss (1982), Olsson (1961).

. . . .

lack lunule, escutcheon, and lateral hinge teeth. There is a well-developed pallial sinus. Some petricolids resemble pholadids, but are easily distinguished by their central hinge teeth, which pholadids lack. The fossil record of petricolids extends to the Paleocene.

References: Narchi (1975), Tebble (1976).

. . . .

Petricola pholadiformis

Cooperella subdiaphana

Family: PETRICOLIDAE Deshayes, 1839
Species: *Petricola pholadiformis* Lamarck, 1818
Common Name: False Angel Wing
Size: 2 inches (50 mm)
Distribution: Canada to Texas; Norway to Congo

Petricola pholadiformis has a posteriorly elongate, chalky white shell with about sixty radial ribs. Anteriorly, the ribs are more widely spaced and bear scales. The animal burrows in peat and clay. The species has been reported as far south as Uruguay, but records of it from there and Brazil refer to *Petricola stellae* Narchi, 1975.

There are about thirty species of petricolids worldwide, most of which bore into peat, clay, chalk, or limestone. They vary in shape from elongate to rounded and

Family: COOPERELLIDAE Dall, 1900
Species: *Cooperella subdiaphana* (Carpenter, 1864)
Common Name: Shiny Cooper's Clam
Size: 0.6 inches (16 mm)
Distribution: British Columbia to the Gulf of California

Cooperella subdiaphana has a fragile, shiny, white, ovate shell with fine concentric growth lines. The ligament is short and external, set immediately behind the beaks. The animal builds a nest of sand and mud in sheltered crevices intertidally and to depths of 150 feet (45 meters).

There are only three known living species of cooperellids, one in the Western Atlantic and two in the Eastern Pacific. The shells are thin, white, and ovate to subquadrate. The adductor muscle scars are small and oval, and there is a large pallial sinus. The shells resemble those of mactrids, but differ in their lack of lateral hinge teeth and a resilium and resilial pit. There are two central teeth in the right valve, three in the left; one tooth in each valve is bifid. The fossil record of cooperellids extends to the Miocene.

References: Boss (1982), Keen (1971).

· · · · · · · · · · · · · ·

Glauconome rugosa

Family: GLAUCONOMIDAE Gray, 1853
Species: *Glauconome rugosa* Reeve, 1844
Common Name: Wrinkled Glauconome
Size: 3 inches (75 mm)
Distribution: Southeast Asia and the Philippines

Glauconome rugosa has a white shell masked by a greenish brown periostracum with numerous minute, radial wrinkles. These wrinkles are also seen on the surface of the shell. The umbos are about one-third of the shell length from the anterior end and are usually eroded. The shell is white inside, with a narrow, deep pallial sinus that is half the length of the shell.

There are probably fewer than ten species of glauconomids, all in the Indo-Pacific, ranging from India to Japan to Australia. The shells have a green or brown periostracum. There are three central hinge teeth and no laterals. The pallial sinus is narrow and deep. Glauconomids live permanently buried deep in mud in estuaries and mudflats. They have a reduced foot and maintain contact with the surface through the siphons. In contrast, the venerids have a large foot and are active burrowers that are not deeply buried. Glaucomyidae is a synonym of Glauconomidae.

References: Boss (1982), Owen (1959).

· · · · · · · · · · · · · ·

Order: Myoida Stoliczka, 1870
Superfamily: Myacea Lamarck, 1809
Family: MYIDAE Lamarck, 1809
Species: *Mya arenaria* Linné, 1758
Common Name: Soft-shell Clam
Size: 6 inches (150 mm)
Distribution: North Atlantic and North Pacific

Mya arenaria is a common species often harvested commercially for food. The shell is white to light gray with a very thin periostracum. The species appears to have originated in Japan during the Miocene and spread to the northeastern Pacific and northwestern Atlantic. It became extinct in the northeastern Pacific in prehistoric times and was reintroduced sometime around 1870. The species was introduced to Europe during the 1500s. Its modern range is from the Bering Straits to Japan and California, Labrador to North Carolina, and Scandinavia to the Mediterranean. The animal lives buried in intertidal mudflats.

There are about twenty species of myids worldwide. They have chalky, white shells that gape at the rear, and a periostracum adherent at the margins. Both adductor muscles are present and there is a pallial sinus. The hinge lacks teeth and there is a projecting chondrophore in the left valve and a recessed area that holds the resilium below the beak in the right valve. The siphons are covered by a sheath and cannot be retracted entirely into the shell. The oldest known myids are from the Paleocene.

References: Bernard (1979), Boss (1982).

· · · · · · · · · · · · · ·

Mya arenaria

Corbula amethystina (holotype)

Spengleria rostrata

Family: CORBULIDAE Lamarck, 1818
Species: *Corbula amethystina* (Olsson, 1961)
Common Name: Amethyst Corbula
Size: 1 inch (25 mm)
Distribution: Panama to Ecuador

Corbula amethystina has a solid shell with a rounded anterior end and pointed posterior end. The beaks are nearly medial and point forward. The posteroventral margin of the right valve is curved, overlapping the left valve. Sculpture consists of relatively coarse concentric ribs. Color ranges from pink to violet; inside the valves are white, bordered with pink or brown. The animal lives in depths of 16 to 32 feet (5 to 10 meters).

The Corbulidae comprise about 100 species worldwide. Corbulids have sturdy shells with the right valve larger than the left; most are less than 1 inch (25 millimeters) in length. Both adductor muscles are present and the pallial sinus is weak or absent. The hinge has one central tooth in the right valve and a corresponding socket in the left valve. The fossil record of corbulids extends to the Upper Jurassic.

References: Boss (1982), Olsson (1961).

. . . .

Superfamily: Gastrochaenacea Gray, 1840
Family: GASTROCHAENIDAE Gray, 1840
Species: *Spengleria rostrata* (Spengler, 1793)
Common Name: Rostrate Gastrochaena
Size: 1.5 inches (40 mm)
Distribution: Florida to Brazil

Spengleria rostrata has an elongate shell with a widely gaping anterior end and a light yellowish brown periostracum. The posterior end is truncate. A triangular zone running from the beaks to the posterior margin is raised and covered with vertical folds. The portion of the shell anterior to this zone has fine, evenly spaced concentric ribs.

There are probably fewer than twenty species of gastrochaenids. They occur worldwide in tropical and subtropical seas, where they bore in soft rock, coral, and the shells of other mollusks. The shell, which is usually white, has a broad anterior gape that in some cases extends the length of the ventral margin. The anterior adductor muscle is reduced, the posterior one large, and there is a deep pallial sinus. The hinge lacks teeth or has a single weak central tooth. The ligament is external and behind the beaks. The fossil record of gastrochaenids extends to the Upper Jurassic.

References: Moore (1969), Morton (1983).

. . . .

Panopea abrupta

Superfamily: Hiatellacea Gray, 1824
Family: HIATELLIDAE Gray, 1824
Species: *Panopea abrupta* (Conrad, 1849)
Common Name: Pacific Geoduck
Size: 8 inches (200 mm)
Distribution: Alaska to the Gulf of California

Panopea abrupta inhabits mudflats intertidally and to depths of 230 feet (70 meters). It lives buried 2 to 3 feet (0.6 to 1 meter) deep in the mud, retaining contact with the surface through its enormous siphons, which can be three times the length of the shell. The species, known as the geoduck (pronounced "gooeyduck"), is harvested in the Pacific Northwest. Until recently the species was known as *Panopea generosa* Gould, 1850, a synonym.

There are about twenty-five species of hiatellids worldwide, some reaching sizes of almost 1 foot (0.3 meters), others being only an inch (25 millimeters) in length. Hiatellids have ovate to quadrangular shells, with valves gaping at both ends. The animal cannot entirely withdraw into the shell posteriorly. Both adductor muscles are present and the pallial line is discontinuous or irregular; there is usually a pallial sinus. The hinge has one or two weak central teeth; lateral teeth are lacking. Saxicavidae is a synonym of Hiatellidae. Hiatellid fossils have been reported from the Permian.

Reference: Yonge (1971).

. . . .

Superfamily: Pholadacea Lamarck, 1809
Family: PHOLADIDAE Lamarck, 1809
Species: *Cyrtopleura costata* (Linne, 1758)
Common Name: Angel Wing
Size: 7 inches (180 mm)
Distribution: Massachusetts to Brazil

Cyrtopleura costata has a lightweight, pure white shell with about thirty beaded, radial ribs per valve and fine concentric growth lines. The external sculpture is visible inside the valve, giving it a ribbed and pitted appearance. The beak is hidden by an umbonal reflection, which curves back from inside the valve. The foot muscles attach to a curved internal projection from the umbo in each valve. The animals can burrow to depths of 2 or more feet (0.6 meters) in mud, and can move up and down within their burrows.

There are almost 100 species of pholadids worldwide. Shell shape ranges from globular to posteriorly elongate. There is an anterior gape for the foot. In some species this gape is closed at maturity by a calcareous covering called the callum. The anterior adductor muscle attaches externally to the reflected umbonal region and so works in opposition to the posterior adductor muscle. Dorsal shelly plates called the protoplax and mesoplax protect the exposed adductor muscle. Pholadids use the shell to bore into various substrates, including clay, shale, limestone, gneiss, and wood. A few species are known to be bioluminescent. The fossil record of the group extends to the Jurassic.

References: Moore (1969), Turner (1954, 1955).

. . . .

Family: TEREDINIDAE Rafinesque, 1815
Species: *Teredo navalis* Linné, 1758
Common Name: Naval Shipworm
Size: 0.4 inches (10 mm)
Distribution: Worldwide

Teredo navalis is one of the most common of the seventy or so species of teredinids (shipworms). Most shipworms bore into wood, forming calcareous tubes, and cause large scale economic damage to wooden structures in marine environments. They have long, wormlike bodies with the shell valves covering only the anterior-most part of the body. The species are difficult or impossible to identify by the valves alone, which appear similar even between different genera. Distinctions are based primarily on the configuration of the pallets, which are stalked calcareous and periostracal structures that close the entrance of the burrow. *Kuphus,* which lives in mud in mangroves, forms a long, heavy calcareous tube, which can be longer than the valves of any living bivalve except *Tridacna gigas.* The fossil record of teredinids dates from the Cretaceous.

Reference: Turner (1966).

. . . .

Subclass: Anomalodesmata Dall, 1889
Order: Pholadomyoida Newell, 1965
Superfamily: Pholadomyacea Gray, 1847
Family: PHOLADOMYIDAE Gray, 1847
Species: *Pholadomya candida* Sowerby, 1823
Common Name: White Pholadomya
Size: 5 inches (130 mm)
Distribution: Caribbean

Pholadomya candida has long been considered one of the rarest of bivalves, and has even been reported to have

Cyrtopleura costata

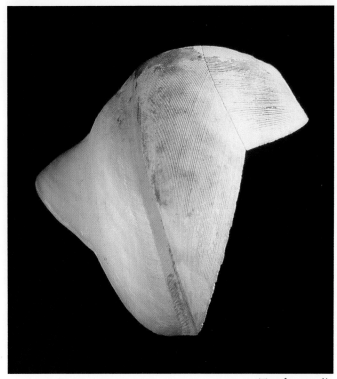

Teredo navalis

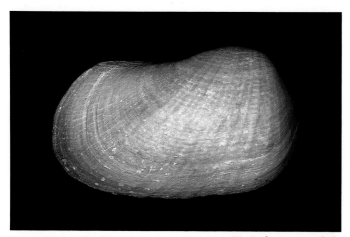

Pholadomya candida

gone extinct. No living specimens have been collected in this century, but freshly dead specimens with periostraca and ligaments still attached have been found in Venezuela. The shell is fragile, white, and posteriorly elongate. The interior of the valves appears slightly nacreous. The animal is apparently a deep burrower in relatively shallow water.

There are about ten living species of pholadomyids, all of them rare and some living in the deep sea. They have anterior beaks and generally have radial sculpture and a posterior gape. The hinge lacks teeth, or has a small denticle below the beak. The anterior adductor muscle scar is smaller and narrower than the posterior one. There is usually a pallial sinus. The group is highly diverse in the fossil record, and is known from the Mississippian.

References: Dance (1969), J. & W. Gibson-Smith (1981), Runnegar (1979).

· · · · · · · · · · · · · ·

Superfamily: Pandoracea Rafinesque, 1815
Family: PANDORIDAE Rafinesque, 1815
Species: *Pandora inaequivalvis* (Linné, 1758)
Common Name: Unequal Pandora
Size: 1.2 inches (30 mm)
Distribution: England to Mediterranean

Pandora inaequivalvis has a compressed shell with a flat right valve and a convex left one. The posterior dorsal margin of the right valve is strongly angled, and overlaps the margin of the left valve. The left valve overlaps the right one ventrally. Color is off-white to pale yellow with a nacreous interior. The exterior of the shell is often eroded, revealing the nacreous layer. There is a ligamental ridge (the lithodesma) extending internally from the beaks. The animal lives in sand and sandy mud intertidally and to depths of 16 feet (5 meters). *Pandora albida* Röding, 1798 is a synonym.

There are about twenty-five species of pandorids, most in the Northern Hemisphere. The beaks are anterior, and the shell has a nacreous interior. The right valve is flat or concave and smaller than the convex left valve, which overlaps it. There are no true hinge teeth, but instead low ridges on either side of the resilial notch at the beak. The pallial line is composed of a series of small, separate muscle scars; there is no pallial sinus. Pandorids are shallow burrowers that lie horizontally with the right valve up. The animals are hermaphrodites. The fossil record of pandorids extends to the Oligocene.

References: Tebble (1976), Yonge & Morton (1980).

· · · · · · · · · · · · · ·

Pandora inaequivalvis

Lyonsia hyalina

Family: LYONSIIDAE Fischer, 1887
Species: *Lyonsia hyalina* (Conrad, 1831)
Common Name: Glassy Lyonsia
Size: 1 inch (25 mm)
Distribution: Nova Scotia to South Carolina

Lyonsia hyalina has a lightweight, fragile shell, with a rounded, inflated anterior end and a long, tapering posterior end. The periostracum is thin, with numerous radial lines and is often covered with adherent sand grains. The interior of the shell is nacreous; the nacre can be seen externally if the umbos are eroded. The animals live from the low-tide mark to depths of 200 feet (60 meters).

There are fewer than two dozen species of lyonsiids. They typically have thin, subnacreous shells with beaks anterior and facing forward. Both adductor muscles are present, as is a shallow pallial sinus. The hinge lacks teeth, but there is a distinct ridge (lithodesma) running posteriorly from the beaks internally. The animals are hermaphrodites. The fossil record of lyonsiids extends to the Eocene.

References: Boss (1982), Moore (1969).

. . . .

Family: CLEIDOTHAERIDAE Hedley, 1918
Species: *Cleidothaerus albidus* (Lamarck, 1819)
Common Name: White False Oyster
Size: 3 inches (75 mm)
Distribution: Southern Australia and New Zealand

Although several names have been proposed for living cleidothaerids, it is likely that *Cleidothaerus albidus* is the only extant member of its family. The shells are irregular and oysterlike, being cemented to hard substrata by the right valve in depths of 3 to 130 feet (1 to 40 meters). Color ranges from white to olive-green, pink, and orange. The convex right valve is larger than the flattened left valve. The umbos are coiled and face forward. The hinge has a crescentic pit from which projects, in the right valve, a calcareous ridgelike structure, the lithodesma. The pit and lithodesma distinguish the shells from those of chamids, as does the lack of leafy sculpture. The anterior adductor muscle scar is longer than the posterior one. The pallial sinus is feeble or absent. The oldest known fossil cleidothaerids are from the Miocene.

References: Coleman (1975), Morton (1974), Powell (1979).

. . . .

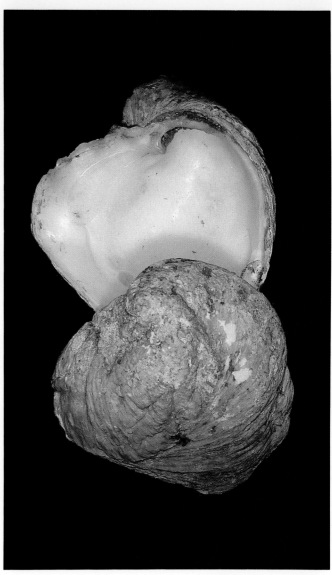

Cleidothaerus albidus

Myadora ovata

Poromya rostrata

Family: MYOCHAMIDAE Bronn, 1862
Species: *Myadora ovata* Reeve, 1844
Common Name: Ovate Myadora
Size: 1 inch (25 mm)
Distribution: Philippines to northern Australia

Myadora ovata has a solid shell with strong concentric ribs on both valves. The left valve is slightly concave and the right is strongly convex. The beaks hook posteriorly and are bordered by a depressed escutcheon that extends to the truncated posterior end. On the right valve, a ridge runs from the beak to the ventral margin of the truncation.

There are fewer than fifteen living species of myochamids, all in the Indo-West Pacific. There are two genera: *Myochama,* which lives cemented on the right valve and has a convex left valve, and *Myadora,* which has a concave left valve and convex right one. Some pandorids resemble *Myadora,* but have opposite valves concave and convex. Myochamids have a small pallial sinus, a toothless hinge, and a small lithodesma. The interior of the shell is subnacreous. The fossil record of myochamids extends to the Miocene.

References: Boss (1982), Moore (1969).

. . . .

Superfamily: Poromyacea Dall, 1886
Family: POROMYIDAE Dall, 1886
Species: *Poromya rostrata* Rehder, 1943
Common Name: Rostrate Poromya
Size: 0.3 inches (8 mm)
Distribution: North Carolina to Caribbean

Poromya rostrata is an uncommon species occasionally dredged in depths of 360 to 800 feet (110 to 240 meters). It resembles *P. granulata* (Nyst & Westendorp, 1839), but has a sturdier shell that is pinched posteriorly and has larger surficial granules. The interior of the shell is a nacreous silver-white.

Poromyids have smooth to granular shells that are subcircular to ovate in outline and nacreous or subnacreous internally; most are less than 1 inch (25 millimeters) in length. There are two living genera: *Poromya,* which has a single central hinge tooth in the right valve, and *Cetoconcha,* which lacks hinge teeth. The pallial sinus is small or obsolete. Most species live in muddy bottoms in the deep sea, and are carnivorous, feeding mainly on annelids taken in through the siphons. The fossil record of poromyids extends to the Cretaceous.

References: Abbott (1974), Allen & Morgan (1981), Bernard (1974).

. . . .

Cardiomya ornatissima

Family: CUSPIDARIIDAE Dall, 1886
Species: *Cardiomya ornatissima* (d'Orbigny, 1842)
Common Name: Ornate Cardiomya
Size: 0.4 inches (10 mm)
Distribution: North Carolina to Caribbean

Cardiomya ornatissima has a distinctive, heavily ribbed shell. There are at least three primary radial ribs, with a variable number of weaker ribs of secondary and tertiary strength between them. The species is commonly dredged in depths of 13 to 750 feet (4 to 230 meters). *Cardiomya costata* (Bush, 1885) and *C. glypta* Bush, 1898 are synonyms.

There are more than 100 species of cuspidariids worldwide, many of them occurring in the deep sea in depths greater than 3,300 feet (1,000 meters). The shells have a rounded anterior margin and a beaklike posterior margin

that is often extended into a long spout. The posterior dorsal margin is usually concave, and the beaks point to the rear. Sculpture can be smooth or ribbed. Both adductor muscles are present and the pallial sinus is weak or absent. Cuspidariids live buried in soft bottoms, with the tip of the siphons exposed at the surface. They eat small worms and crustaceans, sucking in prey detected by a ring of sensory tentacles on the siphons. The fossil record of cuspidariids extends to the Upper Cretaceous.

References: Allen & Morgan (1981), Bernard (1974).

. . . .

Euciroa galathea

Family: VERTICORDIIDAE Stoliczka, 1871
Species: *Euciroa galathea* (Dell, 1956)
Common Name: Galathean Euciroa
Size: 2 inches (50 mm)
Distribution: New Zealand

Euciroa galathea has a creamy white, inflated shell with a small posterior gape and a small, depressed lunule. The anterior end is rounded, the posterior somewhat constricted. Sculpture consists of numerous granular radial ribs and irregular concentric growth lines. The shell is brightly nacreous inside and has a minutely denticulate margin. There is an oblique ligamentous strip below the beaks internally. The species has been dredged in depths from 1,150 to 2,030 feet (475 to 620 meters).

Verticordiids comprise about fifty species worldwide; most live in the deep sea, many in depths beyond 3,300 feet (1,000 meters). They have roundly ovate, heart-shaped to subquadrangular shells, usually with radial ribs, and often with a small lunule. Both adductor muscles are present and the pallial sinus is weak or absent. The shell is nacreous internally and has one or two teeth in the right valve; the left valve is usually toothless. Verticordiids live buried in soft bottoms and use sticky tentacles around the siphons to capture small invertebrates. The fossil record of the family reaches the Paleocene.

References: Allen & Turner (1974), Bernard (1974), Powell (1979).

. . . .

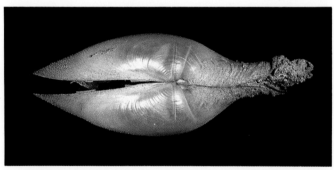

Laternula anatina

Superfamily: Thraciacea Stoliczka, 1870
Family: LATERNULIDAE Hedley, 1918
Species: *Laternula anatina* (Linné, 1758)
Common Name: Duck Lantern Clam
Size: 3 inches (75 mm)
Distribution: East Africa to Japan and Australia

Laternula anatina has a thin, fragile shell with a spoutlike, ventrally constricted, gaping posterior end and a rounded, gaping anterior. The surface of the shell

appears relatively smooth, but is sandpapery to the touch because of numerous tiny granules and minute spines. The pallial sinus is shallow, extending only half the distance from the posterior adductor muscle scar to the beak. The animals live in burrows in intertidal mudflats and to depths of 65 feet (20 meters).

There are about ten species of laternulids, all in the Indo-West Pacific with one in Pacific Antarctica. The shells are thin and fragile, rounded anteriorly and truncate or beaked posteriorly. The left valve is slightly larger than, and overlaps, the right one. The umbos are transversely split or fissured. There are no hinge teeth, but each valve has a protruding chondrophore which is supported by an internal buttresslike ridge. Both adductor muscles are present, as is the pallial sinus. The animals live in deep, permanent burrows in mud or muddy sand, and maintain contact with the surface through the siphons. Members of some species have siphonal eyes. Laternulids are known from the Upper Triassic.

References: Boss (1982), Morton (1976).

. . . .

Family: PERIPLOMATIDAE Dall, 1895
Species: *Periploma pentadactylus* Pilsbry & Olsson, 1935
Common Name: Five-fingered Periploma
Size: 0.8 inches (20 mm)
Distribution: Nicaragua to Panama (Pacific)

Periploma pentadactylus has a bizarre shell, with five radial ribs that project like claws at the margin. The second and fourth ribs are grooved along the top. The fifth, smallest rib borders the escutcheon. The species is placed in the subgenus *Albimanus,* which means "white hand"; "*pentadactylus*" means "five-fingered." The shell is atypical of periplomatids in having radial ribs and a scalloped margin.

There are fewer than thirty species of periplomatids. The right valve is larger than and overlaps the left one. The beaks are toward the posterior end of the shell and usually have a radial slit or fissure. The hinge is toothless and has two chondrophores that project ventrally toward the anterior end. The interior is subnacreous and the pallial sinus is usually wide but shallow. The animals are hermaphrodites and live buried horizontally in soft bottoms with the right valve up. The fossil record of the periplomatids extends to the Upper Cretaceous.

References: Olsson (1961), Boss (1982).

. . . .

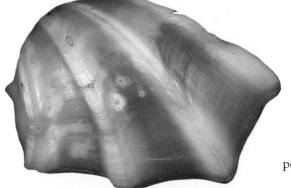

Periploma
pentadactylus
(syntype)

Thracia conradi

Family: THRACIIDAE Stoliczka, 1870
Species: *Thracia conradi* Couthouy, 1839
Common Name: Conrad's Thracia
Size: 3.5 inches (90 mm)
Distribution: Labrador to New York

Thracia conradi has an inflated, anteriorly rounded chalk white shell, with a light brown periostracum. The truncate posterior end is somewhat constricted and has a weak radial ridge. The left beak cuts into the right one. The animal lives with the larger right valve uppermost, buried 5 to 10 inches (130 to 250 millimeters) deep in muddy sand. It has two burrows, one for the incurrent siphon and one for the excurrent. The foot is small and the animal is probably sedentary, not relocating after establishing a burrow. It lives in depths of 13 to 650 feet (4 to 200 meters).

There are about thirty species of thraciids worldwide. Generally the right valve is larger and more convex than the left one and overlaps it. Sculpture often consists of concentric growth lines; sometimes the surface is granular. Both adductor muscles are present, as is the pallial sinus. The shell is not nacreous. The hinge lacks teeth and the resilium rests on an oblique chondrophore that in some cases lies along the posterior dorsal margin. A medial lithodesma is sometimes present below the umbo. The animals are hermaphrodites. Thraciids are known from the Jurassic.

References: Coan (1990), Thomas (1967).

. . . .

Superfamily: Clavagellacea d'Orbigny, 1844
Family: CLAVAGELLIDAE d'Orbigny, 1844
Species: *Brechites giganteus* Sowerby, 1888
Common Name: Giant Watering Pot
Size: 12 inches (300 mm)
Distribution: Southern Japan

Brechites giganteus is one of the largest of the clavagellids. Its valves are imbedded in the anterior chamber of the siphonal tube, and an irregular calcareous ridge extends between the valves, hiding the beaks. The siphonal tube has two to five sets of ruffles at its posterior end. Stones and shells are sometimes cemented to the tube. The animal lives in depths of 30 to 200 feet (9 to 64 meters). The name *Penicillus* is often used in place of *Brechites* in the mistaken belief that the latter name was not validly proposed.

There are about fifteen living species of clavagellids (watering pot clams), with two in the Mediterranean and the rest in the Indo-West Pacific. The young shell has free valves, one or both of which become imbedded in the sides of a long posterior siphonal tube as the animal grows. Anteriorly is a sievelike structure perforated by small holes or tubes, or there are tubes projecting around the anterior end or around the valves. The adductor muscles are usually reduced or absent in the adult. The animals live imbedded vertically in the bottom with the posterior end of the siphonal tube projecting. The fossil record of clavagellids extends to the Upper Cretaceous.

References: Smith (1976), Pojeta & Sohl (1987).

. . . .

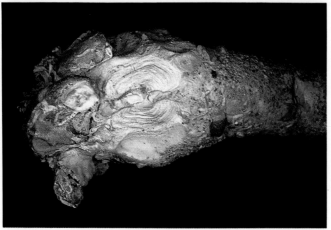

Brechites giganteus

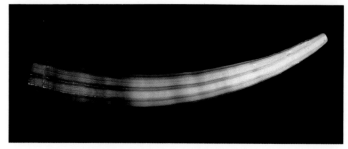

Dentalium elephantinum

Class: Scaphopoda Bronn, 1862
Order: Dentaliida Starobogatov, 1974
Family: DENTALIIDAE Rafinesque, 1815
Species: *Dentalium elephantinum* Linné, 1758
Common Name: Elephant Tusk
Size: 4 inches (100 mm)
Distribution: India to the Solomon Islands

Dentalium elephantinum has a solid, curved shell that is white posteriorly, gradually changing to dark green anteriorly. It has about ten primary longitudinal ribs and weak secondary ribs; the primary ribs are stronger on the concave side of the shell. The animal lives buried in sand in depths of 6 to 130 feet (2 to 40 meters).

Members of the order Dentaliida have a conical foot, whereas in the order Gadilida the foot is vermiform. They live buried in sandy bottoms with the narrow posterior (apical) end projecting from the substrate. They feed on foraminifera and other interstitial organisms captured with flexible filaments called captacula. Dentaliids have weakly to pronouncedly curved shells; some attain lengths of more than 6 inches (150 millimeters). They are smooth or sculptured with four to fifty or more longitudinal ribs, sometimes with secondary ribs in between. In cross-section, the shells are circular, oval, or polygonal. The apex is simple, sometimes with a small notch on the concave side and often with a deep slit on the convex side. Dentaliids occur worldwide from shallow to abyssal depths; living genera include *Antalis, Dentalium, Fissidentalium, Fustiaria, Graptacme,* and *Pictodentalium.* There are more than 200 species of dentaliids and more than 1,000 species of scaphopods. The fossil record of the family extends to the mid-Triassic.

References: Boss (1982), Palmer (1974).

. . . .

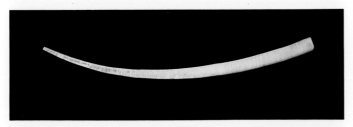

Gàdilina stapes

Family: GADILINIDAE Chistikov, 1975
Species: *Gadilina stapes* (Boissevain, 1906)
Common Name: Stirrup Tusk
Size: 2 inches (50 mm)
Distribution: Japan to Indonesia

Gadilina stapes is horseshoe-shaped in cross-section. There are two longitudinal angles on the concave side. The posterior end has fine longitudinal ribs, but most of the shell is smooth and shiny. Color is cream with transverse bands of grey. Specimens have been dredged in depths of 650 to 1,000 feet (200 to 300 meters).

The shell of gadilinids is usually less than 2 inches (50 millimeters) in length and is sometimes quite fragile. Curvature is weak to pronounced and the cross-section is subcircular to subtriangular. The shell is often smooth, but can be finely ribbed. The posterior end is typically truncate and usually has a small protruding pipe, which is sometimes broken off. The posterior aperture is quite small. Gadilinids occur in tropical and semitropical seas worldwide, in shallow to abyssal depths. The two main genera are *Gadilina* and *Episiphon*. The fossil record of the family reaches the Lower Jurassic.

References: Boss (1982), Habe (1968).

. . . .

Family: LAEVIDENTALIIDAE Palmer, 1974
Species: *Laevidentalium crocinum* (Dall, 1907)
Common Name: Orange Tusk
Size: 3 inches (75 mm)
Distribution: Japan

Laevidentalium crocinum ranges from white to saffron in color, and has a smooth, shiny shell. The shell is circular to slightly ovate in cross-section and has a small apical

notch. It has been dredged in depths of 160 to 1,300 feet (50 to 400 meters). Laevidentaliids can reach lengths greater than 4 inches (100 millimeters); they are circular to subcircular in cross-section, with weak to moderate curvature. The shell is generally shiny and without sculpture except for growth rings. The apex is simple or has a vee-shaped notch in the convex side. Laevidentaliids occur worldwide, from subtidal to bathyal depths; genera are *Laevidentalium* and *Rhabdus*. Their fossil record extends to the mid-Triassic.

References: Boss (1982), Habe (1968), Palmer (1974).

. . . .

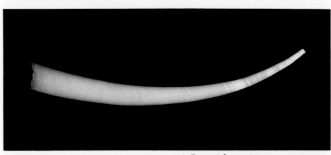

Laevidentalium crocinum

Family: OMNIGLYPTIDAE Chistikov, 1975
Species: *Omniglypta cerina* (Pilsbry, 1905)
Common Name: Waxen Tusk
Size: 3 inches (75 mm)
Distribution: Japan to Indonesia

Omniglypta cerina has a slender, elongate, relatively straight shell that ranges from white to light brownish orange in color. Sculpture consists of densely packed concentric growth rings, which can number more than 500 on a single shell. The animal lives in muddy bottoms in shallow water in bays in northern Japan, and in increasingly deep water to 6,200 feet (1,900 meters) farther south in its range.

Omniglyptids have rather fragile, thin shells that are up to 3 inches (75 millimeters) long. They are circular in cross-section and only slightly or moderately curved. The apex is simple or bears a weak slit on the convex side. The posterior end has numerous concentric rings,

Omniglypta cerina

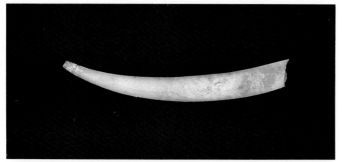

Gadila fusiformis

Bathoxiphus ensiculus

Pulsellum salishorum (paratype)

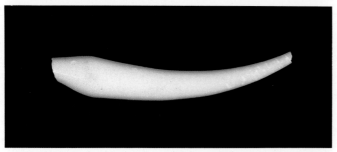

Polyschides spectabilis

which sometimes extend the length of the shell. The few species of *Omniglypta* are the only living members of the family.

References: Boss (1982), Kuroda, Habe & Oyama (1971).

· · · · · · · · · · · · ·

Order: Gadilida Starobogatov, 1974
Family: GADILIDAE Stoliczka, 1868
Species: *Gadila fusiformis* (Pilsbry & Sharp, 1898)
Common Name: Fusiform Toothshell
Size: 0.4 inches (10 mm)
Distribution: Monterey, California to Baja California

The shell of *Gadila fusiformis* is smooth and shiny, white to yellowish white, and about nine times longer than its greatest width. The posterior end sometimes has a few concentric rings. The apical aperture is circular and the anterior one nearly so. The animal has been dredged in depths of 20 to 1,200 feet (7 to 365 meters).

The order Gadilida is characterized by animals with relatively small shells and a wormlike foot with an expanded, distal, crenulated disc. Members of the family Gadilidae are generally less than 1 inch (25 millimeters) in length and have smooth, shiny shells. The shells are similar to those of siphonodentaliids but lack the posterior notches. Genera include *Cadulus* and *Gadila*. The fossil record of the group extends to the Cretaceous.

References: Boss (1982), Emerson (1962).

· · · · · · · · · · · · ·

Family: ENTALINIDAE Chistikov, 1979
Species: *Bathoxiphus ensiculus* (Jeffreys, 1877)
Common Name: Little Sword Tusk
Size: 1.2 inches (30 mm)
Distribution: Georges Banks to Caribbean; Western Europe

Bathoxiphus ensiculus has a laterally compressed shell, with an angular keel on both the convex and concave sides. Most of the curvature is in the posterior one-third.

The cross-section is a flattened oval. The shell is grayish white in color, with concentric growth lines of irregular strength. The apical notch on the convex side is wide and square-sided. The animal lives in muddy sediments in depths from 1,150 to 11,000 feet (350 to 3,400 meters).

Entalinids occur worldwide on the continental shelf and the abyssal plain. Shells are up to 2 inches (50 millimeters) in length, oval, or polygonal (rarely circular) in cross-section and moderately to strongly curved. There are two to thirteen primary longitudinal ribs. The apex is simple or notched on the convex side. The fossil record of entalinids extends to the Paleocene.

References: Boss (1982), Emerson (1962).

. . . .

Family: PULSELLIDAE Boss, 1982
Species: *Pulsellum salishorum* Marshall, 1980
Common Name: Salish Tooth Shell
Size: 0.4 inches (10 mm)
Distribution: British Columbia to Washington

Pulsellum salishorum has a white, moderately curved shell, with both apertures circular. Juvenile shells are glossy, but the surface of adults is usually dulled by erosion. The species has been collected in sandy or gelatinous mud at depths of 10 to 300 feet (3 to 91 meters).

Pulsellids are usually less than 1 inch (25 millimeters) in length, and are straight to moderately curved. They are round or dorsoventrally compressed in cross-section. The shell is smooth or has longitudinal striations or numerous concentric ribs. The apex is usually simple, but sometimes has two lateral notches. The described genera are *Pulsellum* and *Compressidens*. The fossil record of the pulsellids extends to the Paleocene.

References: Boss (1982), Marshall (1980).

. . . .

Family: SIPHONODENTALIIDAE Simroth, 1894
Species: *Polyschides spectabilis* (Verrill, 1885)
Common Name: Notable Toothshell
Size: 1 inch (25 mm)
Distribution: Georges Bank to Maryland

Polyschides spectabilis is one of the largest of the siphono-dentaliids. The shell is smooth, solid, and evenly curved, with a pronounced swelling immediately behind the constricted, oblique, anterior aperture. The apical aperture is cut by four slits, with the two lateral ones deeper and the dorsal and ventral ones shallow and inconspicuous. The slits are often lost due to injury of the shell. The animal has been dredged in depths of 8,800 to 11,000 feet (2,680 to 3,400 meters).

Siphonodentaliids have smooth, shiny shells, usually less than 1 inch (25 millimeters) in length, and are circular or ovate in cross-section. The apex has from two to ten slits or notches. They are similar to the gadilids, which lack the apical slits. The maximum diameter of the shell is at the anterior aperture (as in *Siphonodentalium*) or just posterior to it with the aperture constricted (as in *Polyschides*). Siphonodentaliids are known from the Paleocene.

References: Boss (1982), Palmer (1974).

. . . .

Class: Cephalopoda Schneider, 1784
Subclass: Nautiloida Lamarck, 1812
Order: Nautilida Agassiz, 1847
Family: NAUTILIDAE Rafinesque, 1815
Species: *Nautilus pompilius* Linné, 1758
Common Name: Chambered Nautilus
Size: 8 inches (200 mm)
Distribution: Eastern Indian Ocean to Fiji

Nautilus have long fascinated people because of their beautiful shells with internal chambers and their reputations as living fossils, slowly dwindling to extinction in the deep sea. In the past thirty years, knowledge of *Nautilus* has greatly increased as living animals have been studied in the laboratory and tracked in the field. *Nautilus* live in depths around 1,000 feet (300 meters) and dive deeper than that on occasion. At depths much below 2,500 feet (750 meters), the shells would be crushed by water pressure. They migrate upward at night to depths of 330 feet (100 meters). The chambers of *Nautilus* are connected by a thin tube called the siphuncle, which regulates buoyancy by controlling the amount of liquid in the chambers. *Nautilus* feed on crustaceans and scavenge dead animal material.

Authorities disagree on the number of species of *Nautilus,* arguing for four to six species. *Nautilus pompilius* is the most widespread of these. The most recently named species is *Nautilus belauensis* Saunders, 1981, from the Palau Islands in the western Pacific. It is possible that other isolated, distinctive populations will also be recognized as valid species. *Nautilus* might be speciating and radiating, rather than heading for an extinction that would end a lineage with roots in the Upper Cambrian. The family Nautilidae itself dates from the Upper Triassic.

References: Saunders & Landman (1987), Ward (1988).

. . . .

Nautilus pompilius

Argonauta argo

Subclass: Coleoida Bather, 1888
Order: Octopoda Leach, 1817
Family: ARGONAUTIDAE Lamarck, 1809
Species: *Argonauta argo* Linné, 1758
Common Name: Common Paper Nautilus
Size: 10 inches (250 mm)
Distribution: Warm seas worldwide

Argonauta argo is the largest of the half dozen species of paper nautilus, all of which are pelagic in the open ocean. The fragile shell, which serves as a cradle for the eggs, is secreted by the webs of the first pair of arms of the female. The female sits in the shell, with the webs extended around it. Small organisms such as fish, arthropods, and pteropods that brush against the web are caught with one of the tentacles and eaten. Male argonauts lack a shell and are much smaller than the females—the male of *A. argo* is only 0.5 inches (12 millimeters) long and is one of the smallest cephalopods. The function of the penis is fulfilled by the hectocotylus, the third left arm modified for carrying sperm. It is inserted in the mantle cavity of the female and detached. Early researchers thought this detached arm was a parasitic worm and it was named *Hectocotylus.* The fossil record of argonautids extends to the Miocene.

References: Nesis (1987), Young (1960).

. . . .

Order: Sepiida Naef, 1916
Family: SEPIIDAE Rafinesque, 1814
Species: *Sepia esculenta* Hoyle, 1885
Common Name: Edible Cuttlefish
Size: 7 inches (180 mm)
Distribution: Japan to the Philippines

The cuttlebone of *Sepia esculenta* is ovate in outline, with a sturdy, straight spine projecting from the posterior end. The anterior end is smoothly rounded. The ventral surface is transversely striate posteriorly and unsculptured anteriorly. The dorsal surface is pustulate. The species, which inhabits the continental shelf, is harvested commercially in Japan, South Korea, and China.

There are about 100 species of sepiids (cuttlefish). The family is not represented in the Americas, but is widespread in warm seas in the rest of the world. The internal cuttlebone serves as a buoyancy regulator in which the animal controls the proportion of liquid to gas. Cuttlefish are nocturnal predators; their tentacles can be retracted into special pockets and are shot out to capture prey. During the day they hide in sand or camouflage themselves by matching the color pattern of the substratum. Fossil species are known from the Jurassic.

References: Adam & Rees (1966), Nesis (1987).

. . . .

Family: SPIRULIDAE Rafinesque, 1815
Species: *Spirula spirula* (Linné, 1758)
Common Name: Common Spirula
Size: 1 inch (25 mm)
Distribution: Tropical Atlantic and Indo-West Pacific

Spirula spirula is the only known member of its family, living or fossil. The animal can reach 2.3 inches (58 millimeters) in length and is about 2.5 times the length of its internal shell. The spirally coiled shell has chambers connected by a siphuncle; the animal regulates its buoyancy by adjusting the liquid content of the chambers. The first of the chambers is spherical, the rest are cylindrical. The animal is pelagic, inhabiting depths of 1,600 to 3,300 feet (500 to 1,000 meters) during the day and 330 to 1,000 feet (100 to 300 meters) at night. It normally

swims with head down. The empty shells float and are often cast up on beaches far north or south of the natural range of the species.

Reference: Nesis (1987).

. . . .

Sepia esculenta

Spirula spirula

Class: Polyplacophora Blainville, 1816
Suborder: Lepidopleurina Thiele, 1910
Family: LEPIDOPLEURIDAE Pilsbry, 1892
Species: *Lepidopleurus cajetanus* (Poli, 1791)
Common Name: Cajetan Chiton
Size: 1 inch (25 mm)
Distribution: Mediterranean and Western Europe

Lepidopleurus cajetanus has an oblong, elevated, solid shell. The lateral areas of the valves are strongly raised and the sculpture consists of strong terraces, such that the front valve resembles a circular flight of rounded stairs. Color is dull white, buff, or dusty pink.

Lepidopleurids are relatively small chitons, usually less than 2 inches (50 millimeters) in length. The valves are well developed and generally sculptured with granules. Insertion plates of the valves are absent or weak and unslit. The girdle is narrow and minutely scaly or spiky. The gill is short and posterior. There are about fifty species, which live from shore to depths of more than 23,000 feet (7,000 meters). The fossil record of lepidopleurids extends to the Carboniferous.

References: Kaas & Van Belle (1980, 1985), Moore (1960).

. . . .

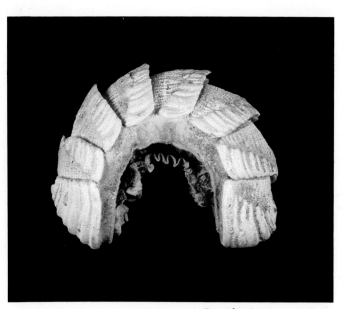

Lepidopleurus cajetanus

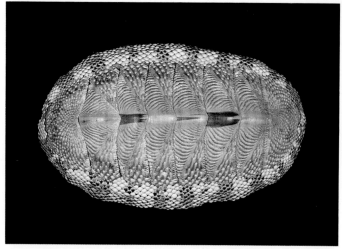

Chiton tuberculatus

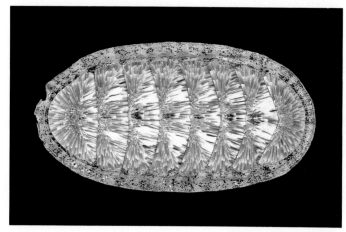

Ischnochiton wilsoni

Suborder: Ischnochitonina Bergenhayn, 1930
Family: CHITONIDAE Rafinesque, 1815
Species: *Chiton tuberculatus* Linné, 1758
Common Name: Common West Indian Chiton
Size: 3 inches (75 mm)
Distribution: Bermuda, Florida, Bahamas, Caribbean

Chiton tuberculatus is distinguished from all other species of chitons in having strong, flat, longitudinal ribs in the central area and a checkering of nodules, rather than radial ribs, on the terminal valves. The shell is grayish to brownish green, with the raised sculpture often lighter in color. The girdle is alternately banded with light and greenish black areas. The insides of the valves are greenish or bluish white. The animal lives on wave-swept shores in the intertidal zone.

Chitonids are distinguished from other polyplacophorans in having comblike teeth on the insertion plates on the valve margins. The girdle may be scaly, spiny, or nude and leathery. There are about 100 species of chitonids worldwide, some of which reach lengths of 4 to 5 inches (100 to 125 millimeters). The fossil record of the family extends to the Cretaceous.

References: Bullock (1988), Kaas & Van Belle (1980).

· · · · · · · · · · · · ·

Family: ISCHNOCHITONIDAE Dall, 1889
Species: *Ischnochiton wilsoni* Sykes, 1896
Common Name: Wilson's Chiton
Size: 1.3 inches (34 mm)
Distribution: South Australia and Victoria

Ischnochiton wilsoni has an elongate, oval shell with rounded ends. The base color is pinkish white to yellowish brown, with longitudinal grayish streaks on the central areas of the valves and radial streaks on the lateral areas and terminal valves. The girdle is light yellow or pink, often banded, and covered with numerous irregularly placed black dots. The animal lives under rocks in shallow water.

The ischnochitonids comprise some 200 species worldwide, and are found intertidally to depths of 2,000 feet (600 meters). Most are less than 2 inches (50 millimeters) in length. The exposed parts of valves two to seven are usually divided into central and lateral areas by a diagonal rib, with the lateral area elevated. The insertion plates are slitted and their teeth are grooved or buttressed exteriorly. The girdle does not overlap the valves and has scales, spicules, and tiny hairs. Some species are known to brood the young in the mantle cavity. Fossil ischnochitonids are known from the Eocene.

References: Kaas & Van Belle (1980, 1990).

· · · · · · · · · · · · ·

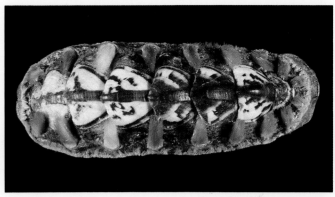

Acanthochitona astrigera

Suborder: Acanthochitonina Bergenhayn, 1930
Family: ACANTHOCHITONIDAE Pilsbry, 1893
Species: *Acanthochitona astrigera* (Reeve, 1847)
Common Name: Star-bearing Chiton
Size: 1 inch (25 mm)
Distribution: Bahamas and Caribbean

Acanthochitona astrigera has a slender, elongate shell with the girdle covering the anterolateral areas of the valves. The girdle bears eighteen tufts of more than 100 white to light amber spikes. The valves are dark blue-green to black, usually with white markings on the second and fifth valves and sometimes on others as well. The anterior insertion plate has five slits. The animal lives among brown algae in the intertidal zone of rocky shores subjected to heavy surf action.

There are more than 100 species of acanthochitonids worldwide, living intertidally and to depths of 2,000 feet (600 meters). They usually have the shell partially to completely buried in the girdle. The girdle is smooth or hairy but usually not scaly, and often has bundles of small, prickly spikes. The insertion plate of the tail valve has two or more slits. The fossil record of acanthochitonids extends to the Lower Oligocene.

References: Ferreira (1985), Lyons (1988).

· · · · · · · · · · · · ·

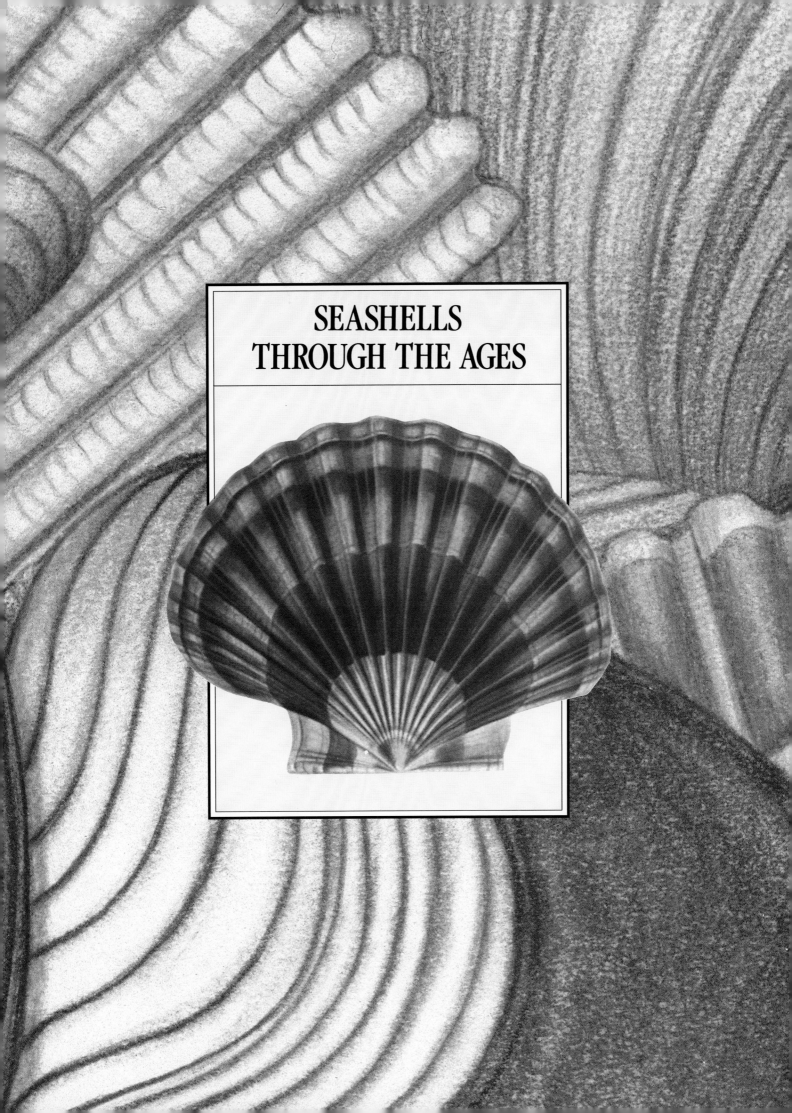

SEASHELLS
THROUGH THE AGES

CHAPTER ONE

SHELLS IN CULTURE AND COMMERCE

Mollusks have been used in many ways by various human cultures. Originally, they were harvested as food by primitive peoples, and their shells adapted as tools and utensils. The beautiful colors and patterns of shells inspired their use as jewelry and ornaments, and since ancient times, shells have been incorporated in artistic works, in both representational and abstract ways. Shells have been traded extensively throughout the world, both as commodities and currencies. A considerable amount of our knowledge of the cultures of primitive peoples comes from studying the shell remains in archeological sites.

SHELL MIDDENS

The earliest use of mollusks by humans was probably as food. Evidence of mollusks in the human diet has been found in a 300,000-year-old archaeological site at Nice, France. In addition to eating large game animals, the creators of the site also gathered mollusks including oysters, mussels, and limpets. In a cave at Gibraltar, heaps of discarded shells, known as "middens," reveal that the limpet *Patella vulgata* and the mussel *Mytilus edulis* formed a considerable part of the diet of the Neanderthals who occupied the site. At the Haua Fteah cave in Libya, starting about 70,000 years ago, the inhabitants discarded shells of *Patella* and *Trochus* species in the middens along with the bones of gazelles, sheep, zebra, and bovines. Shell middens in caves in South Africa from 70,000 to 120,000 years ago show that thirteen species of mollusks

were used as food, including *Patella, Diloma, Turbo,* and *Perna* (Meehan 1982).

Prehistoric shell middens have been found in many parts of the world, including Denmark, the Mediterranean coast, South Africa, Australia, the Philippines, Tasmania, Japan, Tierra del Fuego, and California. Middens have been recorded from many places on the eastern seaboard of the United States, including Boston and Cape Cod, Massachusetts; New Haven, Connecticut; Charleston, South Carolina; St. John's River, Florida; and Mobile Bay, Alabama (Christenson 1985). Most middens date from the period between 8,000 and 4,000 years ago, when sea levels reached heights similar to the current one. Most older middens have been lost because shorelines from times of lower sea levels are now underwater (Meehan 1982).

Shells in middens can inform the archaeologist about more than just the diet of a people. Carbon-14 dating and amino acid racemization techniques can establish the age of shells and thus the age of a site. Changes in midden composition can reflect changing food preferences or changes in the environment affecting the availability of some species. Oxygen isotope ratios in shells show the temperature of the water in which they were collected, and can thus reflect climate and seasonality. Analysis of growth rings in bivalve shells can show changes in salinity and temperature as revealed in the spacing, width, and coloration of the rings. Growth rings can help in determining the season in which shells were collected. A settled people might utilize a resource year-round, whereas nomadic ones might use it only at certain times of year. The size and rate of deposition of middens can help in inferring population sizes. The disposition of shells within a site can help determine

Detail of a drawing by Mathilde Duffy showing limpet shells from various parts of the world.

whether the site represents a dump, a food processing area, or a home base (Safer & Gill 1982, Meehan 1982).

Not until the 1970s did anthropologists investigate a modern hunter-gatherer society in which mollusks comprise a significant part of the diet. In 1972 and 1973, Betty Meehan and Rhys Jones spent twelve months with the Anbarra group of Gidjingali aborigines in Arnhem Land in the Northern Territory of Australia to learn about their culture and how it might be reflected in archaeological remains. Meehan accompanied groups of women and children gathering shellfish and food plants, while Jones went with men on hunting trips (men also gathered shellfish occasionally).

Meehan documented 106 Linnaean species of mollusks collected by the Gidjingali, including forty gastropods, sixty-four bivalves, one cephalopod, and one chiton. The Gidjingali recognized fifty-four taxa among these. Correspondence between native and Linnaean names ranged from a case where the Gidjingali had dif-

ferent names for two ecological forms of the oyster *Saccostrea cucullata* to a case where they lumped together six Linnaean species of arcacean bivalves under one name. There is also a term, *lugaluga,* for a group of at least eleven species of gastropods that are rarely found alive and are not used for food. In twenty-five cases there is a one-to-one correspondence between Gidjingali taxa and Linnaean species. These tend to be the species that are of greatest dietary and economic importance to the Gidjingali, and thus have been subject to the greatest attention. In an additional twenty-six cases, the Gidjingali taxon corresponds to two or three Linnaean species. As an example, the term "andjalabaikurda" includes *Pugilina wardiana* and *Syrinx aruanus;* the Gidjingali believe that the former is the young of the latter. The relatively

A modern-day midden on Bonaire, Netherlands Antilles, composed of shells of the conch, *Strombus gigas*.

high degree of coincidence between Linnaean and native taxa is encouraging evidence that the species we recognize in nature are real, not artificial constructs of the museum-bound scientist.

The Gidjingali exploit three main habitats when collecting mollusks: open-sea beaches of sand and mud flats, mangroves, and rocky coasts. Of the 334 days Meehan spent observing, mollusks were gathered on 194 (58 percent) of them. The proportion of time spent collecting mollusks, rather than in other foraging activities was influenced by the distance of the camp from shellfish beds, whether it was wet or dry season, and the ceremonial obligations of the men, which left more food-procuring duties to the women. The best time to collect mollusks on the sand and mud flats was at the lowest tides, when more species were available in greater amounts.

During the 1972–1973 season, the Anbarra community of Gidjingali, which averaged about thirty-four people, collected about 14,700 pounds (6,700 kilograms) of mollusks, or about 76 pounds (34.5 kilograms) per gathering day. About 98 percent of the mollusks collected were bivalves. Gastropods were collected incidentally to bivalves, except for *Syrinx aruanus* and *Melo amphora,* the shells of which were used as scoops or water containers. *Syrinx* and *Melo* could be collected only at extremely low tides. On almost half of the collecting days, only a single species was collected, even though the Anbarra could collect, on any given day, half of the species they eat during the year. Evidently, collecting expeditions were aimed at particular species. The greatest number of species were collected on days when storms had cast the mollusks onto the beach.

The most commonly collected species were the bivalves *Tapes hiantina* (on 65 percent of collecting days), *Mactra meretriciformis* (28 percent), *Anadara aliena* (15 percent), and *Modiolus micropterus* (14 percent), and the gastropod *Pugilina wardiana* (14 percent). The most important by weight were the bivalves *Tapes hiantina* (61 percent), *Batissa violacea* (18 percent), *Modiolus micropterus* (6 percent), *Anadara granosa* (5 percent), and *Mactra meretriciformis* (5 percent). The contribution of these five main species was about 95 percent of the total weight gathered.

All mollusks were cooked by baking or boiling before they were eaten; only rarely were any eaten raw. The radulae were removed from the larger gastropods before they were eaten. Some gastropods seemed to be eaten mainly to add a bit of variety to the diet as they were not staple foods. Mollusks were cooked in three different types of sites: dinnertime camps, processing sites, and home bases. Dinnertime camps were sites near collecting areas where the day's catch was cooked and eaten. Sometimes these camps were used only once; other times they were used repeatedly. At processing sites, heavy-shelled species of mollusks were cooked and the flesh transported to home base. At home bases, mollusks were cooked in open hearths. Debris from the hearths was cleaned up every week or two and deposited in heaps in unfrequented areas around the hearth complex. These heaps often developed into middens, sometimes incorporating the shell debris of earlier home bases.

Of the 14,700 pounds (6,700 kilograms) of mollusks collected, about 21 percent of the weight was flesh, the remainder was shell. One kilogram of steamed bivalve flesh yields about 800 kilocalories (1 kilocalorie equals the Calorie of dieters). The Anbarra diet averaged 0.3

The giant gastropod, *Syrinx aruanus,* on a mud flat at dawn.

pounds (0.13 kilograms) of mollusk flesh per person per day. This means that the typical person received 106 kilocalories and 1 ounce (30 grams) of protein per day from mollusks. Thus, about 5 percent of the Anbarra caloric intake came from mollusks in 1972–1973, with a range as high as 9 percent and as low as 2.5 percent in some months. Similarly, about 15 percent of total protein came from mollusks, with a monthly range of 8 to 26 percent. Other animal sources of food included ducks, geese, bustards, wallabies, kangaroos, cats, turtles, snakes, lizards, fish (including stingrays and sharks), crabs, and prawns. These accounted for 38 percent of calories and 65 percent of protein, with the rest of the diet composed of vegetable matter.

The mollusks consumed by the Anbarra in 1972–1973 would have produced about 500,000 valves, occupying about 280 cubic feet (8 cubic meters). Knowledge of the Anbarra's habits can aid in interpreting the middens left by their ancestors and by other peoples. In some of the ancient middens in the Anbarra area, there are dramatic differences in proportions of species. In one case, valves of *Tapes hiantina,* the most important species in 1972–1973, constituted only 2 percent of the midden. When Meehan returned to Anbarra in 1974, she found that the shellfish beds had been destroyed by freshwater flooding from heavy rains. The aborigines, who knew that the shellfish would recolonize, temporarily shifted their subsistence strategies, concentrating more heavily on other animal sources of protein. Thus, reading the record of the middens is tricky but rewarding, and can tell us much about the lifestyles of ancient peoples.

MOLLUSK FISHERIES

Ever since the days of hunter-gatherers, mollusks have been an important resource for humans. The fisheries in a dozen countries each harvested more than 100,000 metric tons of mollusks in 1988, according to the *FAO Yearbook of Fishery Statistics.* These dozen countries accounted for 80.6 percent of the world production of 17 billion pounds (7.8 million metric tons) in that year. The catch in the United States alone was worth $378,000,000. Not surprisingly, the Japanese have the most extensive mollusk fisheries, bringing in 20.2 percent of world production in 1988. China accounted for

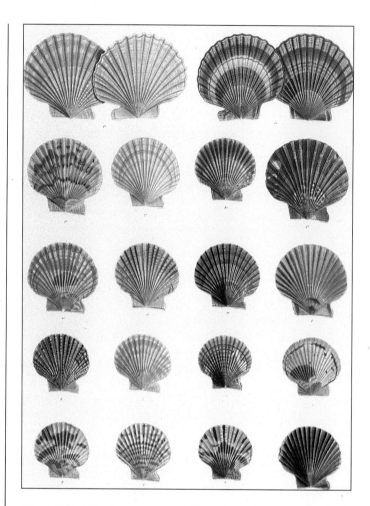

The edible Mediterranean scallop, *Aequipecten opercularis,* from J. C. Chenu's *Illustrations Conchyliologiques.*

18.5 percent, the United States 11.6 percent, and South Korea 10.7 percent of world production. No other country accounted for more than 5 percent.

Important gastropods produced at fisheries include *Turbo cornutus, Concholepas concholepas,* and *Buccinum undatum,* and *Haliotis, Busycon, Littorina,* and *Strombus* species. About a dozen species each of oysters, mussels, and scallops are harvested commercially worldwide, the most heavily exploited being *Crassostrea gigas, Mytilus edulis,* and *Patinopecten yessoensis.* In the eastern United States, two kinds of scallops are fished: bay scallops, *Argopecten gibbus,* and sea scallops, *Placopecten magellanicus.* Marine bivalves other than oysters, scallops, and mussels are included in fisheries' statistics as clams. A broad range of commercially harvested species fall in this category, including *Anadara granosa, Anadara subcrenata, Arctica islandica, Cerastoderma edule, Spisula solidissima, Mesodesma donacium, Chamalea gallina, Venerupis japonica, Protothaca*

thaca, Mercenaria mercenaria, and *Mya arenaria,* all of which were taken in quantities greater than 22 million pounds (10,000 metric tons) in 1988.

ROYAL PURPLE

Muricid snails have been used by people in many parts of the world to produce the dye known as Tyrian or royal purple. The earliest mention of the use of the dye is in one of the legends of Melkart, the Phoenician equivalent of Hercules. Melkart and the nymph Tyros came upon a dog playing among seashells along the shore. Tyros saw that its mouth was stained purple, and wanted a cloak of that color. Melkart gathered some of the shells and invented the industry that would later make Tyre famous (Gerhard 1964).

In the Mediterranean, three species of muricids were used as dye sources, *Stramonita haemastoma, Hexaplex trunculus,* and *Bolinus brandaris.* (The first was formerly placed in the genus *Thais,* the latter two in *Murex.*) The hypobranchial gland in the mantle cavity of these snails produces a clear mucous fluid that changes color on exposure to atmospheric oxygen in direct sunlight, turning white, then pale yellow, green, then blue, and finally purple. Little is known about the function of the fluid; it is thought to be a defensive secretion, or used for narcotizing prey. Similarly, little is known about the chemistry of the color changes, but the end of the series produces the chemical indigo or its brominated derivative dibromoindigo. Variation in the color of the dye results from variations in methods of processing, and from differing proportions of these chemicals in extracts from each species. Indigo from mollusks is the same substance as indigo from plant sources (Hoffmann 1990).

By 1600 B.C., the Phoenicians had learned how to extract the dye, crushing small shells whole and extracting the dye gland from larger ones. The accumulated soft tissues were mixed with seawater and simmered in covered lead vats for several days. Wool or cotton was dipped into the vats, with deeper colors resulting from re-dipping. Supposedly 12,000 specimens of *Bolinus brandaris* were needed to produce 0.08 ounces (1.5 grams) of the pure dye (Safer & Gill 1982). By 1000 B.C. dyeing was a thriving business for the Phoenicians in Tyre and Sidon in what is now Lebanon, and popula-

tions of dye-producing species must have been greatly reduced. The search for additional sources of these species might have been partially responsible for the long voyages and colonization of the Phoenicians throughout the Mediterranean (Gerhard 1964).

Perhaps because of the great amount of labor involved in producing the dye, its use was restricted to individuals of high rank, hence the name royal purple. Julius and Augustus Caesar allowed only themselves and their highest officials to wear purple. Under the Romans, the production of purple dye became a state monopoly. The Romans found that purple-dyed fabrics were one of the few goods that the Chinese would accept in return for silk.

Muricid gastropods were also used to produce purple dye in other parts of the world. In Ireland, *Nucella lapillus* was used as the source, and Irish shell middens consisting of *Nucella* have been dated as far back as 1000 B.C.

Concholepas concholepas from Kiener's *Coquilles Vivantes.*

Although mollusk dyes seem not to have been used in ancient Japan, in this century Japanese fishermen have used *Thais luteostoma*, and *Rapana venosa* to mark their clothes. The permanent dye allows for identification if they drown. In the Western Hemisphere, purple dye, probably from *Concholepas concholepas* has been identified on Peruvian fabrics more than 2,000 years old (Safer & Gill 1982). In modern times, and possibly in pre-Columbian times as well, *Plicopurpura patula* has been the most widely used source of molluscan purple in the Western Hemisphere. *Plicopurpura patula* discharges a fluid when disturbed that changes color on exposure to sunlight. Among the Mixtecs in West Mexico, the dyers carry hanks of cotton to the shore, pluck the snails from the rock and pour the fluid on the cotton. The snails are then replaced on the rocks for further "milking" in the future. This process preserves the populations, unlike the destructive methods in the Old World (Gerhard 1964).

SHELL MONEY

Shells have been used for money all over the world, with the exception of South America and Australia. The most famous of the shell moneys is the money cowrie, *Cypraea moneta*, which has circulated in more parts of the world than any modern currency, with the possible exception of the U.S. dollar, which is readily spent on the black market in many countries. Around 1800, cowries could be spent as money in Burma or Timbuktu, Benin or Bengal, on the Ganges or the Niger, and had even been introduced in North America.

Why should cowries have been so widely used? They are light in weight but very solid and durable, being almost impossible to break accidentally. They could be used as ballast in ships, making economic use of space usually wasted. They were cheaper to supply than the lowest denomination coins that could be minted, and were impossible to profitably counterfeit. Although the money cowrie is widespread in the Indo-Pacific, ranging from East Africa to Hawaii and beyond, most of the cowries circulated as money came from the Maldive Islands. The species is abundant in the Maldives, and is smaller in size there than in many parts of its range, typically being three-quarters of an inch or less. The smaller shell

allowed more units per weight (typically 400 cowries per pound) and was thus cheaper to ship.

Cowries were in circulation in China as early as the seventh century B.C., and in Africa by the tenth century. But the heyday of the cowrie did not begin until the early 1500s when the Portuguese began shipping them to West Africa to finance the slave trade. The Dutch and English began shipping cowries in the 1600s. After 1845, European traders began flooding the market with cowries from East Africa and rampant inflation took hold. By the turn of the century cowries were falling from favor as a currency, although their use continued in some areas for several decades after that (Hogendorn & Johnson 1986).

In North America, currencies based on tusk shells and clam shells were used by the native peoples. The Nootka on Vancouver Island in British Columbia collected the tusk shell, *Antalis pretiosum*, ate the flesh, and traded the shells to neighbors to the south. Strings of the

In addition to their use as currency, cowrie shells have been used as decorative elements in masks and costumes.

The money cowrie, *Cypraea moneta (upper left)*, and other common Indo-Pacific cowries.

tusk shells were used as money by the Yurok of northern California. The strings were each 27.5 inches (70 centimeters) long, and all the shells on a string were the same length. The larger the shells, the fewer it took to complete the string, and the greater the string's value. A string of only eleven shells was considered extremely rare. A nearby group, the Tolowa, always had ten shells to the string, and the length of the string determined its value. Farther south, on the coast of central California, the Pomo Indians used strings of shell beads made from the Pismo clam, *Tivela stultorum,* as currency. Cylindrical beads made from the thickest part of the shell were worth much more than the standard disc-shaped beads. On the east coast of North America, belts of beads made from the quahog, *Mercenaria mercenaria,* were used for ceremonial exchanges, but under colonial influence came into use as a currency in the Dutch and English colonies. Purple beads were more valuable than white ones, because only a small part of the quahog shell is purple (Safer & Gill 1982).

TRADE ROUTES

Shells that are used as currency often are found in areas far removed from the native habitats of the species. Likewise, species used for tools and ornaments are often transported long distances. The occurrence of such species in archeological sites can often be of great assistance in establishing the trade routes of ancient peoples.

In the American Southwest, more than ninety species of mollusks have been found at archeological sites of the Pueblo Indians. The shells come from three geographical areas, and many of the species are restricted to those areas. Species from the Pacific coast of California and northern Baja California include *Olivella biplicata* and *O. baetica* and five kinds of *Haliotis.* Species from the Gulf of California include *Glycymeris gigantea, Oliva incrassata, Conus princeps,* and *Melongena patula.* Representatives from the Gulf of Mexico include *Fasciolaria distans, Strombus gigas,* and *Oliva sayana.* Shells from the Gulf of Mexico are found almost exclusively at sites east of the continental divide. Trade is thought to have proceeded up the Rio Grande to the Pecos River into New Mexico. *Haliotis* from California have been found as far north as southwest Colorado and east to the Texas panhandle.

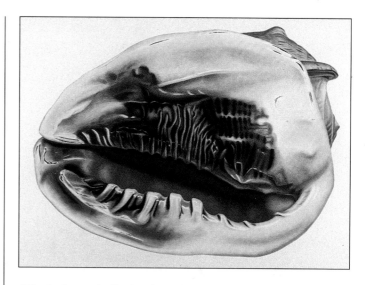

The helmet shell, *Cassis madagascariensis,* is from the Western Atlantic, not Madagascar, despite its name.

The main trade route was from San Diego to the Gila River into Arizona. Trade from the Gulf of California went up the Sonora and Yaqui Rivers into Arizona and New Mexico. Some shells from the Gulf of California were processed at the coast, to reduce the weight to be transported. For example, the central area of *Glycymeris* shells was discarded when bracelets were made. Shells in the southwest were not used for food or money, and rarely as tools. They were used primarily for making ornaments, and were also carved, painted, and inlaid as mosaics with turquoise and other minerals (Tower 1945, Kean 1965). Many of the shells had symbolic meanings, for example, *Olivella biplicata* was associated with war, whereas the green abalone, *Haliotis fulgens,* was associated with sacred water and rain (Safer & Gill 1982).

Trade routes have also been traced in other parts of the Americas. A large variety of marine shells have been recovered from Indian sites in Illinois. A few shells have been found in sites more than 4,000 years old, but they did not appear in great quantity until the establishment of efficient trade routes between A.D. 1200 and 1500. Species that have been recovered include *Cassis madagascariensis, Prunum apicinum, Oliva sayana, Olivella jaspidea,* and most abundantly, *Busycon contrarium. Busycon* was used as a dipper and made into ornaments, beads, and other objects (Parmalee 1958). At sites in Oklahoma, elaborately carved *Busycon* shells have been recovered in large numbers (Phillips & Brown 1978). *Busycon* is one of

the largest common shallow water gastropods in the Gulf of Mexico and the eastern United States, which accounts for its extensive use by native Americans.

In southern coastal Ecuador, between 2800 B.C. and A.D. 1500, *Spondylus* and *Strombus* were harvested for inland trade. Until 1100 B.C., trade was restricted to the Ecuadorian sierra. From 1100 B.C. to 100 B.C., it expanded south into Peru, with *Spondylus* and *Strombus* becoming entrenched in the culture of the central Andes, where they were symbolically associated with the deities. From 100 B.C. to A.D. 1500, trade spanned the region from Quito to Lake Titicaca. After A.D. 200, highland obsidian and copper were exchanged for the shells (Paulsen 1974). In Ecuador and Peru, as in many parts of the world, study of shell artifacts at archeological sites allows documentation of the spread and evolution of economic systems.

Above: The shell of the abalone *Haliotis kamtschatkana* was used by native peoples in the Pacific Northwest. *Below:* The Green Abalone, *Haliotis fulgens.*

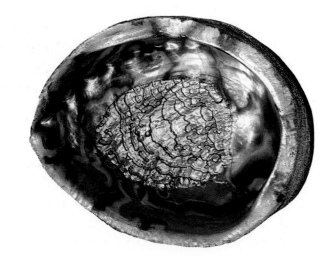

CHAPTER TWO

SACRED SHELLS: MOLLUSKS IN RELIGION, FOLKLORE, AND MYTHOLOGY

Eric P. Kjellgren

To many people, shells are simply things of beauty—objects to be picked up on the beach or purchased at a shell shop and displayed at home as examples of the fascinating designs of nature. But in many cultures, both past and present, shells and the mollusks that make them have played important roles in religion, folklore, and mythology, and have given rise to a wide variety of superstitions and folk remedies. Tales and traditions about mollusks span the globe from New England to New Guinea and are found in religious texts from the Bible to the Bhagavat Gita. In the mythic traditions of the world, mollusks in one form or another have created the earth, sheltered demons, cured warts, given birth to gods, brought the dead back to life, and even become vampires. Since it would be impossible to include all of these traditions in a single chapter, this essay is only an introduction; a highlight tour of the "supernatural history" of mollusks around the world.

Snails are the most common mollusks in religious and folk traditions. The only direct references to mollusks in the Bible—Leviticus 11:30 and Psalms 58:8—mention snails and speak of them as slow and vile creatures. Many non-Western religious traditions, however, give snails a more positive and prominent role. In the Hindu mythology of India, for instance, a sacred chank shell (*Turbinella pyrum*) is carried as a trumpet by the god Krishna as a symbol of his victory over the evil demon Panchajana. According to the story, Panchajana lived inside a chank shell at the bottom of the sea and performed deeds so evil that Krishna sought to destroy him.

When Krishna finally found the demon, the two fought to the death and, after a long battle, Krishna emerged the winner, taking Panchajana's shell as a token of his victory. Because of this mythical battle, the chank in India was closely associated with warfare and in former times was blown ceremonially before combat. The most famous sounding of the chank in Indian legend occurs in the Bhagavat Gita, a lengthy philosophical and sacred epic, in which the warrior king Arjuna debates the ethics of duty and warfare with Krishna (who is disguised as his chariot driver). Arjuna argues that he cannot attack the enemy armies because he has many relatives on the opposing side, while Krishna strives to convince him that, as a member of the warrior caste, it is his duty to fight. Krishna wins the argument and Arjuna agrees to go to war. With a blast of his chank trumpet, Krishna then sounds the call to the great battle (Hornell 1914).

Shell trumpets appear in the myths of cultures as widely separated as Greece and Hawaii. In classical Greek mythology, several different gods are described carrying conch trumpets, but the figure most closely associated with the conch (probably *Charonia lampas*) is the god Triton. Triton was one of the gods of the sea and was said to ride in a chariot drawn by two horselike sea monsters. He always carried his conch trumpet at his side and, when he sounded it, it was said that it could be heard to the far ends of the earth. Greek shepherds of old used a similar, though less deafening, trumpet to summon home their flocks when they were scattered at the end of the day (Locard 1884).

In Hawaii and other cultures throughout the Pacific, conch trumpets often play a role in the exploits of the mythic heros and gods. One legend recorded on the island of Oahu tells of a chief named Kapuni and his

Detail of a drawing by Mathilde Duffy showing colorful bivalve shells from various parts of the world.

The Triton's Trumpet, *Charonia tritonis,* is found throughout the Indian and Western Pacific Oceans.

adventures in pursuit of a sacred conch shell (in this case *Charonia tritonis*). Traveling in the company of two gods, Kapuni hears a mysterious conch being blown and decides that he must have it. The conch, however, is owned by a race of dwarfs, known as e'epa, and is well guarded in their sacred temple. Kapuni sneaks into the temple at night and steals the shell, which he then takes to the island of Hawaii. Unfortunately, on Hawaii, another chief named Kiha steals the conch from Kapuni by sending a clever dog as the thief. After this second theft, the conch became known as the "Kiha-pu" ("conch of Kiha") and was said to have been passed down within the Hawaiian royal family until the early twentieth century (Westervelt 1915). References to conch trumpets occur in many myths throughout the islands of the Pacific, because the use of shell trumpets both by people and their gods is common almost everywhere that large gastropods are found.

Another group of snails that are almost universally distributed in folklore and mythology are the cowries (genus *Cypraea*). Because of the resemblance of their ventral sides to the female reproductive organs, cowries are often used as symbols of fertility. In ancient Rome, the cowrie was associated with the goddess Venus and became known as the "Concha veneris." During certain festivals, cowries were carried around on poles accompanied by phallic symbols, the union of the two assuring the continued fertility of the people and the land (Locard 1884). Similar uses of the cowrie as a symbol of female fertility occur throughout the world.

Cowries are also used in other ritual practices. Among the peoples of southern India, the money cowrie *(Cypraea moneta),* more famous for its use as a currency, is used in divination and fortune telling. In one ritual, the diviner, or *kanisan,* draws a special diagram on the floor onto which he pours a bag of cowries. The kanisan uses special incantations that give the cowries supernatural powers; the cowries then tell him where he should place them on the diagram and how he should interpret the results. Women in southern India also act as diviners, using a wicker tray full of cow dung and turmeric in which a series of money cowries have been embedded. Here, again, the cowries are thought to have supernatural powers. During the ritual, rice and certain leaves are placed on the cowries and then the client's hand is held over the tray. As the client's hand is moved about over the cowries, magical hymns are sung and the client's fortune is interpreted by the diviner (Thurston 1912).

Another fascinating use of the money cowrie is found among the Ojibwa Indians, who lived in the western Great Lakes area of the United States and Canada. The money cowrie is not native to North America, having been introduced by Europeans as a trade good. Ojibwa legend, however, says that the cowries, known as *megis,* were brought to the people by a mythical bear spirit who swam a great ocean and emerged covered with megis shells when he hauled himself out to rest. The most interesting use of megis among the Ojibwa came during the initiation rites of the Midewewin society, an important religious group. At this ceremony, a man who was being

Money cowries have been used in various ritual objects, such as this enigmatic African doll.

initiated into one of the eight levels of the society, was "shot" with powerful magic by the initiators who pointed special otter skin bags at him. Once shot with this magic, the man was "dead" and could only be revived by a second shot from the sacred otter skins. After being shot the second time, the initiate coughed up a megis shell, which was thought to be the physical form of the magic that had been shot into him. After the initiate had been shot twice, shells were then shot at random into the surrounding crowd, resulting in a general free-for-all of people coughing up the small cowries (Dewdney 1975). This unique ceremony, often referred to as "shell shooting," and the preceding examples represent only a few of the many ritual uses of cowrie shells found throughout the world. The cowries, more than any other shell, have inspired the mythic imagination on subjects as diverse as fertility and fortune telling.

Although most myths and legends about snails focus on marine species, there are also a large number of stories that feature land snails as the central characters. Many of these stories come from Africa, where some of the larger species of land snails were an important source of food. One comic tale from the Ashanti people of West Africa tells of the snail, Nwa, who decides that he is going to conquer all of the lands around him, and therefore, sends word to his neighbors to prepare for war. His neighbors, however, laugh at his threats. Despite their derision, Nwa proceeds to attack, and eventually vanquish, all of his enemies. Growing arrogant and hungry for new challenges, he then decides to make war on the gods. This angers the supreme god, Wulbari, who slaps Nwa a tremendous blow across the face. Ever since Nwa was slapped, the Ashanti claim, a snail wears his face "sideways" and cannot travel in a straight line because of the force of the god's blow (Rattray 1927).

A more unusual tale comes from the Wachaga people, who tell of a village and its supernatural snail protector. In the story, two villages are at war. Each day there is a battle and a large number of people are killed. People from the first village gather up their dead and take them to a place where there is a giant land snail. This snail crawls over the dead, covering them with its slime which restores them to life. The next day the same warriors who died the day before go out again to fight. The chief of the second village, finding that his enemies are undiminished, sets out to find the cause of their miraculous recovery. He eventually learns the secret of the snail's power and sends out a group of his warriors who spear the snail to death, thereby ending the unfair advantage of the other village (Werner 1925). Thus, in some African traditions, land snails have been credited with almost godlike supernatural powers.

A fascinating molluscan parallel to Aesop's fable, "The Tortoise and the Hare," comes from Burma but involves a snail and a horse. The horse makes insulting remarks to the snail, because he moves so slowly. The indignant snail challenges the horse to a race the following day, to which the horse agrees. The snail then recruits his relatives, who position themselves at intervals along the race course. In return for their help, he promises them some of the horse's meat (which is valued as a medicine for sore muscles) if the trick works. The next day, the race begins. The horse charges ahead only to find that, no matter how fast he runs, the snail is always "ahead" of him, since each of the snail's relatives moves out onto the race course when the horse gets near. The horse eventually tries to run so fast that he drops dead from exhaustion. The snail then divides the meat among his relatives, who use it to cure their sore muscles. And that, according to the story, is why snails never have sore muscles (though how one can tell whether a snail has sore muscles is difficult to say) (Aung 1948).

Perhaps the strangest story told about snails concerns the land snail "vampires" of Perak, in Malaysia. According to legend, when cattle graze in the fields, land snails (probably from the genus *Alycaeus*) crawl out and drink the cattle's blood through their shadows. In areas where these snail "vampires" abound, people claim that their cattle will soon weaken and even die from loss of blood. It is further claimed that, if you step on one of the snails and crush it, you can see the blood the snail has drunk (Frazer 1925).

Tales about bivalves are less common than those involving snails, but there are still a wide variety of different myths and legends in which clams, scallops, and their kin play important roles. The story of the birth of Venus from a scallop shell (genus *Pecten*) is probably the best known. Although the story is usually associated with the famous painting by Botticelli, images of Venus and other gods and goddesses being born from scallop shells were widespread in classical times. There is even a depiction of the birth of Venus on a fresco from Pompeii, which was buried by a shower of ash when Mount Vesuvius erupted in A.D. 79. For all of the different artistic renditions it has inspired, however, the story behind this famous image is relatively simple. In the myth, Venus's father, Zephyr, decides that his daughter should be educated in Cypress, which can only be reached by an ocean voyage. When Venus is born, Zephyr places her on a scallop shell so that she can float away to receive her education. Aside from this incident, the scallop shell plays no further part in the story. More often in Roman times, Venus, as a goddess of fertility, was associated with cowries, as mentioned before.

In medieval times, scallop shells were associated with St. James of Compostela. Devotees making a pilgrimmage to his shrine in Spain would wear a scallop shell on their hats as a sign that they were going to this holy site. Inside the shell was an image of the Crucifixion or the Virgin Mary. When the pilgrims reached the shrine, a priest would bless the scallop shells, which were then carried as tokens of the pilgrimmage. The association of the scallop with St. James continued well into the modern era, and, even today, the shell is still known as the "Pilgrim's scallop" *(Pecten jacobaeus)*.

A remarkable instance of mythical bivalves occurs in a legend recorded among the Micmac Indians, who lived in what is today northern Maine and New Brunswick, Canada. The story tells of Glooskap, a mythical creator and hero figure, and his battle with the evil sorcerer Win-pe who kidnaps several members of Glooskap's family and then escapes in a canoe. After considering the matter for several years, Glooskap decides to pursue Win-pe and summons a whale to carry him across the ocean. Glooskap climbs onto the whale's back and sets out after his enemy. As the two near the far shore of the ocean, a group of clams (who for undisclosed reasons are Glooskap's enemies) begin to sing to the whale from underneath the sand. In some versions of the story the larger clams sing in resonant bass voices, while the smaller ones sing in falsetto. In their song, they tell the whale to throw Glooskap into the sea and drown him. The whale, however, does not understand the clam language, so Glooskap has to translate. He tells the whale that the clams are urging her to swim faster, so he can

reach the shore sooner and be on his way. Thus, Glooskap, through his knowledge of "clam," avoids disaster and reaches shore despite the malevolent intentions of the singing mollusks. Once on land, he eventually finds and kills Win-pe (Leland 1884).

There are a large number of American Indian stories in which bivalves figure prominently. Many center on the large freshwater mussels (family Unionidae) that occur throughout the great river drainages of the United States. Among the Omaha on the Great Plains, for example, certain freshwater mussels were considered so sacred they were kept hidden from sight and never allowed to touch the ground. Because of mussels' importance to ceremonial life, a number of interesting legends have sprung up about their origin and character. The Pawnee tell a story that explains why freshwater clams have a lustrous, pearly interior while their exteriors are a

The most famous representation of a scallop shell is in Botticelli's *Birth of Venus*. Scallops and other shells prominent in mythology are favored subjects of artists, as seen in Bernini's *Fontana del Tritone*.

dull and unattractive brown. According to this tale, freshwater clams first came into being because of a woman named Young Duck. Young Duck was a young and beautiful woman, who was married to a hawk that had been transformed into a handsome youth. An evil old woman, jealous of Young Duck's beauty, attacks her, steals the top half of her skin, and replaces it with her own shrivelled hide. Young Duck then goes off to live alone in shame and the old woman goes back to Young Duck's husband. The husband, however, soon discovers the switch and begins to search for his bride. When he finds her, Young Duck is still wearing the old woman's skin. Young Duck tells her husband to change back into a hawk and carry her up into the sky. When the couple reaches a great height, she tells him to drop her and she falls to earth. When she hits the ground, she is turned into a freshwater clam which, as one can plainly see, has the "old woman's" skin on the outside but is still young and beautiful on the inside (Dorsey 1906).

The giant clam *(Tridacna gigas)* is another bivalve that looms large in both fact and mythology. Traditions surrounding this largest of bivalves are found mostly on the islands of the southwest Pacific where the clams live in greatest abundance. As in the familiar B-grade science fiction movies of our own culture, giant clams in Pacific mythology often appear as monstrous figures, who devour a wide variety of mythical villains, heros, and heroines. One such story involves a snake named Inuri, a member of a large family, who falls in love with one of his own sisters and asks her to marry him. The sister, of course, refuses, so Inuri turns himself into a man and continues to court her. Not recognizing him as her brother, the sister marries Inuri in his human form. Inuri's brothers learn of the deception and plot to kill Inuri as punishment for his heinous act. The brothers invite Inuri to go with them to gather shellfish. During their search, Inuri sees a giant clam and wishes to take it home. Seeing their chance for revenge, the brothers tell Inuri that the only way to kill the clam is to bite the large muscle that the clam uses to close its shell. Inuri sticks his head into the clam and bites down on the muscle. The clam quickly closes on Inuri's head, and his brothers, in their rage, cut him to pieces with their knives. The pieces of Inuri then become all of the hazards of the ocean including thunder, heavy surf, and saltwater croc-

odiles (Kamma 1975). Tricking someone into sticking his or her head into a giant clam is a theme found in many Pacific myths, and is usually considered a source of comic relief in stories that address otherwise serious topics such as incest.

Whereas most traditions about giant clams center on their supposed appetites, a few myths give them a far more important role. In one tale from Vanuatu (formerly the New Hebrides), a huge giant clam lives far out at sea and emits an eerie light. The clam is seen by a mythical hero named Ambat, who lives on an island with his brothers. Not wishing to overexert himself, Ambat sends each of his brothers out in turn to investigate the mollusk and its strange light. However, the brothers are too afraid to approach the clam, so Ambat finally makes the reconnaissance himself. When Ambat reaches the clam, it

Above: Giant clams from J. C. Chenu's *Illustrations Conchyliologiques.* *Right:* A giant clam alive in the reef, showing its colorful mantle.

attacks him, and they fight a great battle. Ambat succeeds in killing the clam, which is so large it rises out of the sea and becomes an island (Deacon 1934). Thus, in some myths, giant clams are invoked in shaping the geography of the Pacific.

In the creation myth from the island of Nauru in Micronesia, a giant clam forms not merely a single island but the entire world. At the beginning of the universe, Ancient Spider, the Nauruan creator being, floats freely in the cosmic void. One day, he finds a giant clam shell and, after some effort, succeeds in squeezing inside. Groping about in the darkness in the tiny space between its valves, Ancient Spider comes upon a snail shell, which he turns into the moon to give him light. The light from the moon proves inadequate, however, so he searches until he finds a second snail shell that later becomes the sun. The world is now lighted, but the space between the shells is still too small for comfort. Ancient Spider decides that the upper shell must be raised higher

to provide more room. He lets the "moon" snail try to lift the upper shell, but the snail succeeds in raising it only a small amount. Ancient Spider than engages the services of a large worm who, after great exertion, raises the upper shell so high that it becomes the sky. The lower shell, in turn, becomes the earth, and the sweat generated by the worm during his efforts becomes the ocean in which the island of Nauru now sits (Dixon 1916).

Other groups of mollusks appear in mythology, although not as often as snails and bivalves. Among the cephalopods, octopuses have long been important figures in the mythology of the Pacific Islands, while giant squids are thought to be the inspiration for many mythical sea monsters, including the fearsome Scylla of *The Odyssey* and the ship-destroying Kraken of Norway.

Unusual traditions also surround scaphopods or "tusk shells." Among various American Indian tribes of California and the Pacific Northwest, scaphopod shells of the genus *Antalis* (formerly placed in *Dentalium*) were

Despite legends of voracity, octopuses are harmless to humans, except for a few poisonous species in Australia.

used as a form of money, and consequently play a prominent role in the native folklore and mythology. Mythical figures in "dentalium" tales spend a great deal of time seeking, finding, stringing, losing, and gambling away their dentalia shells, and often go to extreme lengths to get even a small supply. One Washington state tale tells of an old miser visited by the god Moos-Moos. Moos-Moos tells the old man that there is a great store of dentalia hidden under a large stone high on the slopes of Tacoma (Mt. Rainier). Driven by his insatiable greed, the miser makes the arduous journey up the mountain and finds the dentalia. He becomes so overjoyed with the possession of such a vast wealth of shells that he forgets to thank the gods for their generosity. To punish him for his forgetfulness, the angry gods send a terrible storm, in which the miser loses all of his dentalia and falls asleep

for thirty years. When the old man finally awakes, he finds himself cured of his greed, and he lives out the rest of his life in peace (Judson 1910).

Among the Karok Indians of California, dentalia shells play their most important role in native cosmology. In Karok myth, the creator being is a large dentalium shell named Pisava, who comes to life in a mythical body of water called the Upriver Ocean. Pisava's first act is to create more dentalia shells of various shapes and sizes, so that people, when they are eventually created, will have plenty of money. Pisava journeys downriver from the ocean creating villages where he places hairs from his head, which, in turn, become people and still more dentalia. He also creates purses in which these dentalia can be kept without breaking. Only after he has created all the paraphernalia associated with dentalia does Pisava concern himself with creating the other things on which the people depend for survival (Kroeber and Gifford 1980). To the Karok, then, dentalium money not only had a central place in society, but was responsible for the creation of the world, as well.

Mollusks have also spawned an intriguing variety of lesser superstitions and folk remedies. Most of these center around land snails. In rural Kentucky, for instance, it was believed that if a young woman found a snail on the first day of May and put it on a plank in the hot sun, the snail would trace the first letter of her future husband's name in its slime trail. Similar beliefs are recorded in England, where this superstition undoubtedly began. Likewise, on May first, if a young woman found a snail that had pulled back inside of its shell, it was a sign that she would marry a man who owned a house. If the snail was out of its shell and crawling around, she would marry a man who did not own a house (Thomas and Thomas 1920). In the north of England, it was said that if you seized a black land snail by its "horns" and threw it over your left shoulder, you would have good luck. This was especially true if you caught the snail within three days of becoming engaged, because it meant that the marriage would go well.

Many types of marine snails were seen as harbingers of good luck. In Scotland, large periwinkles were hung over the hearth in a fisherman's home to bring him luck at sea. Children on the Atlantic coast of France wore necklaces of limpet shells as talismans and, in Brittany, snail shells were often placed in the cradles of newborn babies to ward off evil. In some African-American folk traditions it was believed that if you cooked nine snails and rubbed yourself with the grease, you would be protected from any spells your enemies might try to cast on you (Hyatt 1970). Land snails, however, could also be bad omens. In Cornwall, any miner who encountered a snail on his way to work had to appease it with a few drips of tallow from his candle, or he would have bad luck. Similarly, there are a number of African-American spells that "put the snail" on your enemies to make them slow and easily tired.

Mollusks also play a part in folk medicine. A widely held belief is that land snails can cure warts. One snail wart remedy used in South Glamorgan and West Pembrokeshire, England, requires rubbing a black land snail

The common periwinkle, *Littorina littorea*.

back and forth over each wart while reciting a magical phrase. After each wart has been treated, the snail is pinned to the branch of a tree with as many thorns as the patient has warts. As the snail dies and shrivels up, the warts disappear (Frazer 1925).

Snails were also used in treating more serious ailments. In Cornwall it was believed that a child's cough could be cured by making the child drink a mixture of two or three boiled snails in tea or barley water. The cure for ague was to sew up a garden snail in a small pouch, which was worn around the neck for nine days, and then thrown into a fire. While the snail was being consumed by the flames, it would shiver and shake with "ague." When the snail was burned up, the patient's ague would be cured. In a Kentucky superstition a toothache could be cured by rubbing a snail or slug on your gums. It was also believed that eating a snail each morning for nine days would cure tuberculosis. Belief in snail cures has been widespread. Perhaps some of the less outrageous ones had some sound medical basis, although this has yet to be investigated. We have seen how mollusks inspired the mythic imagination; perhaps they can inspire the imaginations of medical researchers, too.

CHAPTER THREE

COLLECTING SHELLS

Many people, when they think of collecting shells, picture doing so on beautiful, white, sandy beaches with the waves rolling in. However, sandy beaches, especially those with heavy surf, are not productive habitats for mollusks. Only a few agile burrowers such as *Donax, Hastula,* and *Bullia* can survive in the shifting sands of the surf zone. When a sandy beach has large numbers of shells cast up in the drift line, this indicates the presence of more productive habitats nearby.

The stable substrata of intertidal mud and sand flats have much more diverse communities of mollusks. They are home to various surface-living bivalves such as ostreids and placunids and burrowing bivalves such as myids, solenids, mactrids, venerids, cardiids, glauconomids, lucinids, tellinids, semelids, psammobiids, pholadids, and laternulids. These are preyed upon by carnivorous gastropods, including naticids, muricids, buccinids, and turbinellids. Other inhabitants of mud and sand flats include herbivorous strombids, scavenging nassariids, and deposit-feeding cerithiaceans. Mangroves on mud flats are populated by isognomonid and ostreid bivalves and littorinid, ellobiid, truncatellid, batillariid, potamidid, and cerithideid gastropods.

Many of the inhabitants of intertidal sand and mud flats also occur subtidally, where they are joined by scaphopods, solemyid, glycymeridid, pinnid, crassatellid, and astartid bivalves; and gastropods such as tonnids, cassids, harpids, olivids, volutids, conids, and terebrids. Sandy areas can have varying amounts of rubble mixed in, and often grade into reef flats. Many of the

Detail of the drawing *Lonely Heart Shell* by Mathilde Duffy.

mollusks found on sand flats also occur in sandy pockets within the reef, along with mitrid, costellariid, and cerithiid gastropods.

Within reefs and rocky areas live many mollusks that prefer hard substrata. Only a few kinds of mollusks, such as ovulids and coralliophilines, live in direct association with corals, but the coral rubble around living reefs is rich in mollusks, because it supports luxuriant growth of algae and encrusting invertebrates on which many gastropods and polyplacophorans feed. Typical reef-dwelling gastropods include members of Conidae, Buccinidae, Bursidae, Ranellidae, Cypraeidae, Triviidae, Fasciolariidae, Haliotidae, Muricidae, Columbellidae, Trochacea, and Turridae. Bivalves include arcids, chamids, limids, mytilids, pectinids, spondylids, and tridacnids.

Rocky intertidal areas typically support a rich molluscan fauna. A variety of limpets are usually present, such as patellids, lottiids, fissurellids, and siphonariids. These, along with chitons, neritids, trochaceans, and littorinids, feed on vegetation and sessile invertebrates encrusting the substratum. Muricids often occur on intertidal rocks, where they feed on mytilids and barnacles.

A well-equipped field collector makes use of many different tools depending on the habitat being investigated. Screens are good for sorting shells out of sand and mud. The size of the screen and its mesh depend on the size of the mollusks the collector is interested in finding. Nested sets of brass-frame screens with graduated mesh sizes are available from geology supply houses. Collectors can also make their own screens with wooden or plexiglass frames. Promising areas for screening on sand and mud flats sometimes can be recognized by the presence of snail trails and bivalve burrows. When snorkeling or scuba diving, some collectors use a sieve to sift

Intertidal rocks on the Washington coast harbor many kinds of mollusks.

shell valves are at the anterior end, and the calcareous pallets, which are essential for identification, are at the posterior end.

In reef areas, the best collecting is found in areas of dead coral rubble. When overturning dead coral slabs, prudent collectors grab the far side and lift it toward them, to allow lurking eels and other creatures to escape. Before examining the underside of the slab, take a quick look at the substrate below for mollusks attempting to crawl away or bury themselves. Next, scan the bottom of the slab for movement—some gastropods, such as *Stomatella,* avoid light and will start crawling to seek shelter. Many mollusks are well camouflaged. Careful searching often reveals cryptic shells such as chitons and byssally attached bivalves overlooked at first. Small shells hiding in crevices can be removed with tweezers. To reach more inaccessible specimens, some collectors carry mechanical fingers, which are used by mechanics to retrieve parts dropped into engines. Make sure to always return rocks and coral slabs to their original positions, otherwise sessile organisms growing on them will die.

Algal washing is an excellent way of obtaining live specimens of small species that otherwise are found only as worn specimens in the drift-line or when screening sand. Handfuls of marine algae or grass are pulled apart in a bucket to which fresh water (not sea water) is then added. Most mollusks, except for byssally attached clams, will drop to the bottom. The algae is then rinsed and removed piece by piece, leaving a residue for sorting. By washing only one species of algae at a time, the persistent collector can accumulate valuable data on habitat preferences of micromollusks. Mollusks that can be collected in this manner include trochids, turbinids, scissurellids, skeneopsids, cingulopsids, eatoniellids, rissoaceans, cerithiaceans, columbellids, marginellids, rissoellids, omalogyrids, orbitestellids, opisthobranchs, mytilids, and lasaeids.

Some shell collectors maintain a notebook in which they record ecological data in the field while it is still fresh in their minds. A station number keys information about each locality to the specimens collected there. The notebook should be written in pencil or indelible ink as it is likely to get wet in the field. A plastic station number label is made with a hand-held label maker (available at most hardware stores) and stored with the specimens.

sand from under rocks and coral slabs and in sandy pockets on the reef. In grass flats and other areas where sediment cannot easily be scooped into a screen or sieve, it can be fanned in with the hand or a small board. Screening can be an excellent way of finding small specimens that would otherwise escape notice.

Rocks and coral blocks cast up on shore often show the telltale circular or oval openings of the burrows of boring bivalves such as gastrochaenids, mytilids, and pholadids. The shells can be collected by carefully excavating the burrows with hammer and chisel, although inevitably some specimens are smashed by an overenthusiastic blow or an ill-timed slip. Other bivalves, such as petricolids, can be found boring in peat; and the teredinids (shipworms) bore in wood. When collecting shipworms, be careful to dissect the whole animal, which can be quite long, from the wood, because the

One system for assigning station numbers is to use the collector's initials and the last two digits of the year, for example, GR91-13, GR91-14, GR91-15, and so on.

Before collecting in a given area, collectors should familiarize themselves with rules and regulations that might affect them. For example, some jurisdictions ban shell collecting, and others require permits or have restricted seasons. Collecting in some areas can be hazardous. People snorkeling in tropical waters for the first time can get sunburnt all the way to their fingertips, because the ultraviolet rays of the strong tropical sun can penetrate several feet underwater. Some methods of collecting are hazardous, for example, nocturnal collecting. People collect at night, using waterproof flashlights, because many mollusks that hide during the day crawl about actively at night. However, it is easy to lose one's bearings at night, so be sure to leave two lights on the shore to serve as landmarks. Keeping track of time and tides is also important for safety, as it is easy to become stranded on an offshore sandbar or reef by a returning

tide. Many other tips for shell collectors can be found in Jacobson (1974) and Coleman (1976), including information on cleaning and preserving specimens.

Increasingly, rather than collecting shells, hobbyists are photographing the living animals and documenting

Top: Bivalves can be collected by digging in tidal flats such as these on the Washington coast. *Bottom:* The Indo-Pacific *Nerita plicata* in an intertidal crevice.

Tide pools, such as these at Yaquina Head, Oregon, often support a rich molluscan fauna.

their habitats. Often it is necessary to collect a few specimens in order to confirm identifications, but with experience, field identification is possible for most species. Repeated collecting and observing in one area, in different seasons, over a period of years can lead to an intimate knowledge of a fauna, and can be an important way of monitoring environmental health. If the species composition changes and some species become locally extinct, that can be a sign of environmental degradation. This kind of baseline information is not available for most local faunas and represents a realm where the amateur can make an important contribution. If we don't know what the fauna of an area was before an oil spill, how can we assess faunal recovery in its aftermath? The dead shells found in an area can give some idea of its fauna, but dead shells can persist for hundreds of years,

and may not give an accurate indication of the species currently living in an area. Perhaps someday shellers will maintain life lists of species observed in the wild, as birders have done for many years, and will contribute to environmental monitoring as birders have done.

Although considerable concern has been expressed in recent years about the possibility of over-collecting shells, the main threat to populations of marine mollusks is habitat destruction. To date, no species of marine mollusk is known to have been driven extinct by human activities, although this is not true for land and freshwater species. A single storm can cast millions of mollusks to die on the beach, and in contrast the activities of shell collectors must be regarded as inconsequential. As long as humans are careful not to damage habitats, their activities are likely to be no more threatening to mollusk populations than those of other predators, providing they take only a few specimens of each species for their own use, and leave any juveniles and egg masses they might encounter to stock the next generation. In a few places that are subjected to heavy collecting pressures such as Sanibel Island, strict rules concerning collecting have been enacted to ensure maintenance of adequate population levels. In some parts of the world, such as the Philippines, commercial shell collecting has resulted in severe local environmental degradation and depletion of molluscan populations. This is cause for much greater concern than the activities of individual collectors.

Field activities are only a small part of the shell collector's world. Many people trade shells with other collectors around the world. Some have never picked up a shell on a beach, but have amassed huge collections from mail order shell dealers. There are shell clubs in most of the major cities in the world, many of which run shell shows that are open to the public. Rice (1991) provides information about shell clubs and shell dealers worldwide.

As a shell collection grows, it can become impossible to display all the shells. One solution is to house the collection in cabinets with shallow drawers. Each lot is placed in a cardboard tray or plastic box with its label. One lot consists of all the specimens of one species collected in one place at one time. Lots are kept in order by their classification, often alphabetized by genus and species within a family.

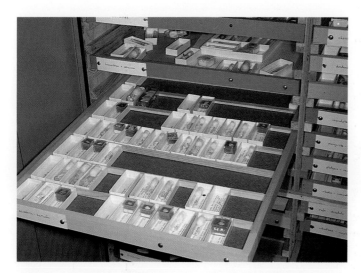

Above: **A museum cabinet at the Academy of Natural Sciences in Philadelphia.**

People with large collections often number their lots. Keeping a hand-written catalogue recording the information associated with each lot safeguards against misplacement of specimens and labels. Catalogue numbers are assigned in consecutive order (although they need not start from the number one). The number should be written in india or other indelible ink on the labels and the shells. Collectors reluctant to write on their shells should record the measurements of the specimens, especially if they have more than one example of a species. Specimens too small to be written on can be put in cotton-plugged vials or plastic boxes, along with the catalogue number on a slip of paper.

Today, shell collections can be easily computerized with a home computer and a database program. Computerization serves two functions: First, it allows information to be sorted in various ways, so that, for example, labels can be printed and lists of species from particular families or parts of the world can be generated. Second, it ensures that all the information about a specimen is recorded, by giving a more detailed list of items to be recorded than is possible in a hand-written catalogue. This enhances the value of the collection, particularly if the collector is planning eventually to donate it to a museum. (A computerized collection is also much easier to appraise.)

About two dozen fields of information are sufficient for the needs of most collectors. All the fields pertaining to a particular lot are called a record. Examples of types of information that a collector might want to include in a record are shown below. The number of alphabetic or numeric characters recommended for the length of the contents of each field is shown in parentheses. Field lengths should not be longer than needed because they affect the processing speed of database programs.

Catalogue number (6)	101237
Class (14)	Gastropoda
Order (20)	Caenogastropoda
Superfamily (20)	Tonnacea
Family (20)	Ranellidae
Genus (20)	Charonia
Subgenus (22)	(Charonia)
Species (22)	tritonis
Subspecies (22)	variegata
Author (31)	Lamarck
Year named (4)	1816
Continent (13)	North America
Ocean (16)	Western Atlantic
Country or Island Group (25)	United States
Subdivisions of above (80)	Florida Keys, Monroe County, Florida, Gulf of Mexico
Specific locality (80)	Bay at northeast end of Vaca Key by Marathon airport
Habitat (80)	Living at 3 meters in Thalassia bed
Station number (10)	BB80-114
Date collected (11)	19 SEP 1980
Collector(s) (30)	Bergeron, B.
Number of specimens (4)	1
Size (30)	267 × 149 mm
Source (30)	Novel Shell Shop
Cost (8)	$20.00
Date obtained (11)	15 NOV 1983
Date catalogued (11)	07 APR 1991
Remarks (255)	Collected by SCUBA With operculum

Catalogue number: Each lot receives a unique catalogue number, which ties together the specimens, labels, and record.

Classification: The most often used ranks are listed, and others, such as subfamilies and suborders, can be added as desired. The field lengths shown are a couple of characters longer than the longest name of each rank that I know of: order Systellommatophora; superfamily Architectonicacea; family Prochaetodermatidae; genus *Nipponocrassatella*; species *roseoprodissoconchus* (for a venerid in the genus *Pitar*) and *extracarinacostata* (for an omalogyrid snail less than 0.02 inches [0.5 millimeters] long in the genus *Ammonicera*).

Author and date: If the subspecies field is used, then author and date refer to the subspecies name. If not, they refer to the species name. The longest combination of authors likely to be encountered is Bucquoy, Dautzenberg & Dollfus. Author and date are sometimes combined as one field, as they are often cited together. Database programs usually allow sorting on the last word of a field, so it is still possible to sort by date even if it is combined in a field with author. Parentheses can be used around author and date in such a field as needed, although this will make it hard to sort the field, as Reeve, 1848 and (Reeve, 1848) would alphabetize differently. A collector who intends to routinely sort the author field might consider adding a yes/no field for parentheses to avoid this problem. The computer would then be programmed to print "(Author, Date)" with parentheses if the field said yes and "Author, Date" without parentheses otherwise.

Locality levels: Locality data are split into several fields to simplify computer searching and sorting. In addition to the fields listed here, the collector might want to specify fields for river or county if they anticipate sorting by that information. Note that the ocean field is left blank for land and freshwater species, except those on oceanic islands. Because political boundaries often do not correspond to natural geographic ones, it can sometimes be difficult to determine what information is appropriate for a particular locality field. For example, the Falkland Islands are currently a British possession, but are part of a different continent. Should United Kingdom be mentioned when a lot from the Falklands is catalogued? Similar questions arise with many island groups and territories. What is important is not whether the answer is yes or no, but that the answer be the same each time. For example, if you enter the Ryukyu Islands as a subdivision of Japan one time, do not enter them as an island group the next time, because you would then have to remember to search both the subdivision field and the country/island group field to find all the lots from the Ryukyus. Consistency is essential for a database system to work best.

Station number: If a collector maintains a field notebook, as discussed above, the station numbers used therein provide an easy way to generate lists of species collected at each location.

Size: This field is important primarily if the collector does not want to write catalogue numbers on specimens. The measurements of the specimen will help ensure that it is not accidentally separated from its data. Measurements are best made with calipers; models with dial and digital read-outs are available. If there are many specimens in a lot, their sizes are better recorded in the remarks field, to prevent the size field from growing too long. Collectors who exchange shells might use this field to record a range of sizes available for trade. They might also want a yes/no field that indicates if a given lot has specimens that they are willing to trade, and a field that tells the condition of specimens (Gem, Fine, Good, etc.).

Remarks: This field contains any information that does not readily fit in the other fields, such as collecting technique, or a list or previous owners of a specimen.

A GEOGRAPHICAL INDEX TO BOOKS
ON SHELLS

Worldwide

Abbott (1989), Abbott & Dance (1982), Dance (1976), Eisenberg (1981), Harasewych (1989), Horikoshi (1989), Lindner (1978)

Eastern Atlantic

Angola: Gofas et al. (1985)
Canary Islands: Nordsieck & Garcia-Talavera (1979)
Cape Verde Islands: Burnay & Monteiro (1977)
Cyprus: Tornaritis (1987)
Europe: Bouchet et al. (1979), Lozet & Dejean-Arrecgros (1977), Nordsieck (1969, 1972, 1982)
Gabon: Bernard (1984)
Greece: Tenekidis (1989)
Great Britain: Fretter & Graham (1962), Graham (1988), Jones & Baxter (1987), McMillan (1968), Tebble (1976), Thompson (1988)
Iceland: Thorson (1941)
Italy: Parenzan (1970–1976)
Madeira Islands: Norsieck & Garcia-Talavera (1979)
South Africa: Kilburn & Rippey (1982)
Spain: Aarsten (1984), Mosquera (1983)

Western Atlantic

Bermuda: Jensen & Clark (1986)
Brazil: Rios (1985)
Canada: Abbott (1968, 1974), Bousfield (1960), Emerson & Jacobson (1976), Macpherson (1971), Morris (1973), Rehder (1981), Turgeon et al. (1988)
Caribbean: Abbott (1958), Humfrey (1975), Jong & Coomans (1988), Lozet & Pétron (1977), Petuch (1987), Warmke & Abbott (1961)
Cayman Islands: Abbott (1958)
Florida: Lyons (1989), Vilas & Vilas (1970), Williams (1988)
French Guiana: Takeda & Okutani (1983)
Jamaica: Humfrey (1975)
Massachusetts: Zinn (1984)
Mexico: Vokes & Vokes (1983)
Netherlands Antilles: Jong & Coomans (1988)
New York: Jacobson & Emerson (1971), Long Island Shell Club (1988)
Puerto Rico: Warmke & Abbott (1961)
Surinam: Altena (1969–1975), Takeda & Okutani (1983)

Texas: Andrews (1977)
United States: Abbott (1968, 1974), Emerson & Jacobson (1976), Morris (1973), Rehder (1981), Turgeon et al. (1988)

Eastern Pacific

Alaska: Barr & Barr (1983)
California: McLean (1978)
Canada: Abbott (1968, 1974), Bernard (1983), Morris (1966), Quayle (1960), Rehder (1981), Turgeon et al. (1988)
Central America: Keen (1971), Olsson (1961)
Chile: Marincovich (1973)
South America: Bernard (1983), Keen (1971), Olsson (1961)
United States: Abbott (1968, 1974), Behrens (1980), Bernard (1983), Keen & Coan (1974), McLean (1978), Morris (1966), Rehder (1981), Rice (1973), Turgeon et al. (1988)

Indo-Pacific

Arabian Peninsula: Bosch & Bosch (1982, 1989), Sharabati (1981, 1984), Smythe (1982)
Australia: Coleman (1975), Cotton (1959, 1961, 1964), Ludbrook (1984), Macpherson & Gabriel (1962), Shepard & Thomas (1989), Short & Potter (1987), Wells & Bryce (1986), Wilson & Gillett (1971)
Christmas Island: Wells et al. (1990)
Cocos-Keeling Islands: Maes (1967)
Easter Island: Rehder (1980)
Hawaii: Kay (1979)
Korea: Yoo (1976)
Japan: Habe (1968, 1977), Kira (1972), Kuroda et al. (1971)
Marshall Islands: Brost & Coale (1971)
Mascarene Islands: Drivas & Jay (1988)
New Guinea: Hinton (1972)
New Zealand: Beu & Maxwell (1990), Powell (1979)
Pacific: Cernohorsky (1971, 1972, 1978)
Persian Gulf: Biggs (1973)
Philippines: Springsteen & Leobrera (1986)
Polynesia: Salvat & Rives (1975)
South Africa: Gosliner (1987), Kilburn & Rippey (1982), Liltved (1989), Richards (1987)
Sri Lanka: Kirtisinghe (1978)
Taiwan: Lan (1980)

Antarctic

Dell (1964), Hain (1990)

GLOSSARY

adductor muscle: a muscle in a bivalve attached inside the shell that contracts to close the valves.

aperture: the opening of a gastropod shell through which the head and foot protrude (apertural, *adj.*).

apex: the tip of the spire of a gastropod shell; the anterior end of a scaphopod shell (apical, *adj.*).

axial: parallel to the axis of coiling in a gastropod, usually corresponding to a line drawn from the apex to the anterior end of aperture or siphonal canal (compare *spiral*).

beak: the angle marking where growth of a bivalve shell started.

body whorl: the last whorl of a gastropod shell.

boreal: occurring in northern parts of the world.

buccal mass: a structure of cartilage and muscle that supports the center of the radula.

bursa copulatrix: a structure in females that digests excess sperm obtained during fertilization.

byssal gape: an opening in the margins of a bivalve shell for passage of the byssus.

byssus: a bundle of threads or fibers secreted by a bivalve's foot by which it attaches itself to solid objects (byssal, *adj.*).

calcareous: composed of calcium carbonate, often used in referring to opercula (compare *corneous*).

callus: a shelly, sometimes thickened layer spread over the inner side of the aperture or on the spire in some gastropods (callous, *adj.*).

cancellate: cross-hatched; having sculptural elements of equal strength intersecting at approximately right angles.

chondrophore: an internal projection from the hinge of a bivalve with a hollowed-out area for attachment of ligament.

ciliary feeder: an animal that captures food in mucus on the gill, and moves it to or near the mouth by means of cilia.

circumtropical: occurring worldwide in tropical areas.

columella: the central pillar of a spirally coiled gastropod shell, extending from the apex to the base, around which the whorls are built, and part of which can usually be seen on the inner side of the aperture.

columellar fold: a spiral ridge on the columella projecting into the interior of the shell.

columellar muscle: a muscle that attaches to the columella, which, when contracted, pulls the animal into its shell.

concentric: curving about a common center, said of features of sculpture and pattern in bivalves and limpets (compare *radial*).

corneous: of a hornlike material, typically used in referring to an operculum (compare *calcareous*).

crenulate: finely notched or corrugated at the edges.

ctenidium: gill; the typical respiratory organ in marine mollusks, also used for feeding in bivalves.

denticle: a small tooth or projecting point.

deposit feeder: an animal that eats sediment and digests organic material contained in it.

detritus: fine, loose debris containing organic material.

dextral: right-handed; of a gastropod shell, having the aperture opening on the right side when viewed with the spire up. The great majority of gastropods are dextral (compare *sinistral*).

direct development: hatching directly from the egg to life on the bottom without passing through a planktonic stage.

dorsal: situated near the back of an animal; near the hinge in bivalves, opposite the aperture in gastropods.

escutcheon: a usually smooth area extending posteriorly from the beaks in bivalves, and sometimes bordered by a ridge in each valve.

estuary: a brackish water area where a river enters the ocean.

excurrent: pertaining to or used for expulsion of water.

filter feeder: an animal that uses a filter (the gill in mollusks) to trap food floating in the water, such as planktonic organisms and organic debris.

foraminiferan: a marine protozoan with a calcareous shell.

free-living: not attached to a surface.

gizzard plates: corneous or calcareous structures in the stomach used to crush food; found in many opisthobranchs.

growth lines: lines on the surface of a shell indicating former positions of the shell edge at rest periods during growth.

heterostrophic: having the whorls of the protoconch coiling in a different direction than those of the teleoconch.

hinge: collective term for structures of the dorsal part of a bivalve shell, such as interlocking teeth, that function during opening and closing of the valves.

incurrent: pertaining to or used for intake of water.

intertidal zone: the area bounded by the high and low tides.

labial: pertaining to the lip (of a shell).

labial palps: fleshy appendages on either side of the mouth of a bivalve that are used in feeding.

lamella: a thin, often elongate, plate or scale (lamellae, plural).

lamellose: ornamented with thin plates.

larva: an early stage of an organism that must pass through a metamorphosis before assuming adult characteristics (larvae, plural).

lateral: pertaining to the side.

lateral peg: a peg projecting from the columellar side of an operculum.

lateral tooth: a tooth next to the central tooth of the radula (compare *marginal tooth*).

ligament: a horny elastic structure that joins the valves of a bivalve dorsally and acts as a spring causing them to open when the adductor muscles relax.

ligament pit: a depression in the central area of the hinge of a bivalve for attachment of the ligament.

lip: the outer or inner edge of the aperture of a gastropod.

lithodesma: a small calcareous plate reinforcing the ligament in some bivalves.

mangrove: a brackish water coastal swamp in the tropics or subtropics, dominated by mangrove trees; the tree itself.

mantle: a membranous covering of mollusks that secretes the shell and periostracum.

mantle cavity: a space between the mantle and the body of a mollusk that contains the respiratory organs.

marginal tooth: a tooth on the outside of a radular ribbon (compare *lateral tooth*).

multispiral: having many whorls.

muscle scar: a mark on a shell showing where muscles were attached.

nacreous: pearly or iridescent; a type of shell structure consisting of thin leaves of aragonite (a form of calcium carbonate) parallel to the inner surface of the shell (compare *porcelaneous*).

nucleus: the point at which growth of the operculum begins. The nucleus of an operculum can be lateral (on the columellar side), terminal (at the end), or at various places in the interior.

operculum: a horny or shelly plate that wholly or partially closes the aperture in some gastropods when the animal is retracted (opercula, plural).

osphradium: a sensory organ in the mantle cavity of some mollusks that detects chemical substances in water.

oviduct: a tube that carries eggs away from the ovary.

pallial: pertaining to the mantle (pallium).

pallial groove: the space between the foot and the mantle-lined shell in some limpets and chitons.

pallial line: a mark near the ventral margin in bivalves where the edge of the mantle was attached to the shell.

pallial sinus: a notch or embayment in the posterior part of the pallial line showing where the siphonal retractor muscles attached.

parapodia: lateral extensions of the foot in gastropods, often used in swimming (parapodium, singular).

parietal: of the inside wall of the aperture of a gastropod.

paucispiral: having few whorls.

pelagic: inhabiting the open ocean (compare *planktonic*).

periostracum: a horny covering or skin on the outside of many shells that protects them from erosion.

periphery: the greatest circumference (widest part) of a whorl of a spirally coiled gastropod.

planktonic: floating in water, usually of minute organisms with weak or no power of locomotion (compare *pelagic*).

porcelaneous: resembling porcelain, like an enameled surface (compare *nacreous*).

proboscis: a flexible, extensible, tubular snout.

prodissoconch: the embryonic shell of a bivalve (compare *protoconch*).

protoconch: the embryonic shell of a gastropod, which is often different in structure, sculpture, or color from the adult shell (compare *teleoconch, prodissoconch*).

radial: extending from the center in the manner of rays; said of features of the sculpture and pattern of bivalves and limpets, where the center corresponds to the beaks and the apex, respectively (compare *concentric*).

radula: a rasplike ribbon of teeth, used in feeding by most mollusks (except bivalves).

resilial pit: a depression in the central area of the hinge of the bivalve in which the resilium is seated.

resilium: a usually triangular ligamental structure on the inner hinge margin of bivalves that makes the valves open when the adductor muscles relax.

rhinophore: an olfactory tentacle found in opisthobranchs.

rostrate: extended into a beak shape, usually describing an end of a bivalve shell.

selenizone: a band of growth lines on the surface of a shell, marking the former positions of a notch or slit in the outer lip.

sinistral: lefthanded; of a gastropod shell, having the aperture opening on the left side when viewed with the spire up (compare *dextral*).

siphon: an elongation or fold of the mantle that brings water into or expels it from the mantle cavity in most mollusks.

siphonal canal: a tubular extension of the aperture in some gastropods for enclosing the siphon. Many species have a siphonal canal at the anterior end of the aperture, and some also have a posterior canal.

siphonal notch: a notch in the aperture of some gastropods through which a siphon protrudes.

spiral: winding outward from the center (like a watch spring); parallel to the direction of growth of the whorls of a coiled gastropod (compare *axial*).

spire: all of the whorls of a coiled gastropod shell except for the last one.

style sac: a digestive chamber at the anterior end of the stomach in some mollusks.

subcircular: almost circular in outline, said of a bivalve shell or operculum.

subquadrangular: somewhat four-cornered in shape.

subquadrate: somewhat four-sided in outline.

substratum: the surface on which an organism lives and feeds (substrata, plural).

subtidal: in shallow water below the low-tide mark.

subtrapezoidal: somewhat trapezoidal in outline.

subtrigonal: somewhat three-cornered in shape.

subtropical: nearly tropical; bordering the tropical zone.

suctorial: feeding by means of suction with the proboscis.

supratidal: above the high-tide line.

suspension feeder: an animal that feeds on organic material suspended in water.

suture: a continous spiral line marking the junction of the whorls in a gastropod shell.

symbiotic: living together in close association (said of two unrelated species).

symbiont: an organism involved in a symbiotic relationship.

taxodont: with numerous short hinge teeth, some or all of which are at right angles to the hinge margin.

teleoconch: the shell of a gastropod, excluding the embryonic whorls (protoconch).

terminal: situated at the end.

toxoglossate: having the radular teeth modified for injecting poison into prey.

trigonal: having the form of a triangle; three-cornered in shape.

tropical: of the warm region between the Tropics of Cancer and Capricorn.

truncate: having the end or apex cut off.

umbilicus: a central cavity in the base of a coiled gastropod shell in which the whorls do not fuse to form a central columella (umbilicate, *adj.*).

varix: a thickened axial ridge reinforcing the outer lip of the aperture in some gastropods, or marking the position of a former outer lip (varices, plural).

ventral: situated near the belly of an animal; of the valve edge opposite the hinge in bivalve; of the apertural side in gastropods.

whorl: one complete turn of a gastropod shell.

BIBLIOGRAPHY

Aartsen, J. J. van, H. P. M. G. Menkhorst, and E. Gittenberger. 1984. The marine Mollusca of the Bay of Algeciras, Spain, with general notes on Mitrella, Marginellidae and Turridae. *Basteria*, suppl. 2, 135 pp.

Abbott, R. T. 1958. The marine mollusks of Grand Cayman Island, British West Indies. *Monographs of the Academy of Natural Sciences of Philadelphia*, no. 11.

Abbott, R. T. 1959. The family Vasidae in the Indo-Pacific. *Indo-Pacific Mollusca* 1(1):15–32.

Abbott, R. T. 1960. The genus Strombus in the Indo-Pacific. *Indo-Pacific Mollusca* 1(2):33–146.

Abbott, R. T. 1961. The genus Lambis in the Indo-Pacific. *Indo-Pacific Mollusca* 1(3):147–174.

Abbott, R. T. 1968. The helmet shells of the world (Cassidae). Part 1. *Indo-Pacific Mollusca* 2(9):7–202.

Abbott, R. T. 1968. *Seashells of North America: A Guide to Field Identification.* New York: Golden Press.

Abbott, R. T. 1972. *Kingdom of the Seashell.* New York: Crown Publishers.

Abbott, R. T. 1974. *American Seashells.* 2nd ed. New York: Van Nostrand Reinhold.

Abbott, R. T. 1989. *Shells.* New York: Portland House.

Abbott, R. T., and S. P. Dance. 1982. *Compendium of Seashells: A Color Guide to More Than 4,200 of the World's Marine Shells.* New York: Dutton.

Adam, W., and W. J. Rees. 1966. A review of the cephalopod family Sepiidae. *The John Murray Expedition 1933–34, Scientific Reports* 11(1):1–165, 46 pls.

Allen, J. A. 1958. On the basic form and adaptations to habitat in the Lucinacea (Eulamellibranchia). *Philosophical Transactions of the Royal Society of London* B. 241:421–484, pl. 18.

Allen, J. A., and R. H. Morgan. 1981. The functional morphology of Atlantic deep water species of the families Cuspidariidae and Poromyidae (Bivalvia): an analysis of the evolution of the septibranch condition. *Philosophical Transactions of the Royal Society of London* B. 294:413–546.

Allen, J. A., and J. F. Turner. 1970. The morphology of *Fimbria fimbriata* (Linné) (Bivalvia: Lucinidae). *Pacific Science* 24:147–154.

Allen, J. A., and J. F. Turner. 1974. On the functional morphology of the family Verticordiidae (Bivalvia) with descriptions of new species from the abyssal Atlantic. *Philosophical Transactions of the Royal Society of London* B. 268:401–536.

Allmon, W. D. 1988. Ecology of Recent turritelline gastropods (Prosobranchia, Turritellidae): current knowledge and paleontological implications. *Palaios* 3:259–284.

Allmon, W. D. 1990. Review of the *Bullia* group (Gastropoda: Nassariidae) with comments on its evolution, biogeography, and phylogeny. *Bulletins of American Paleontology* 99 (335), 179 pp. 15 pls.

Altena, C. O. van Regteren. 1969–1975. The marine Mollusca of Suriname (Dutch Guiana) Holocene and Recent. *Zoologische Verhandelingen*, no. 101 (1969), no. 119 (1971), no. 139 (1975).

Altena, C. O. van Regteren, and E. Gittenberger. 1981. The genus *Babylonia* (Prosobranchia, Buccinidae). *Zoologische Verhandelingen*, no. 188.

Andrews, J. 1977. *Shells and Shores of Texas.* Austin: University of Texas Press.

Aung, M. T. 1948. *Burmese Folk Tales.* Oxford University Press.

Barr, L. and N. Barr. 1983. *Under Alaskan Seas: The Shallow Water Marine Invertebrates.* Anchorage: Alaska Northwest Publishing.

Bayer, F. M. 1971. New and unusual mollusks collected by the R/V John Elliott Pillsbury and R/V Gerda in the tropical Western Atlantic. *Bulletin of Marine Science* 21:111–236.

Behrens, D. W. 1980. The Lamellariidae of the North Eastern Pacific. *Veliger* 22:323–339.

Behrens, D. W. 1980. *Pacific Coast Nudibranchs: A Guide to the Opisthobranchs of the Northeastern Pacific.* Los Osos, California: Sea Challengers.

Bernard, F. R. 1972. The genus *Thyasira* in western Canada (Bivalvia: Lucinacea). *Malacologia* 11:365–389.

Bernard, F. R. 1974. Septibranchs of the Eastern Pacific (Bivalvia Anomalodesmata). *Allan Hancock Monographs in Marine Biology,* no. 8.

Bernard, F. R. 1976. Living Chamidae of the Eastern Pacific (Bivalvia: Heterodonta). *Natural History Museum of Los Angeles County Contributions in Science,* no. 278.

Bernard, F. R. 1979. Identification of the living *Mya* (Bivalvia: Myoidea). *Venus* 38:185–204.

Bernard, F. R. 1983. Catalogue of the living Bivalvia of the Eastern Pacific Ocean: Bering Strait to Cape Horn. *Canadian Special Publication of Fisheries and Aquatic Sciences,* no. 61.

Bernard, P. A. 1984. *Shells of Gabon.* Libreville, Gabon: Author.

Beu, A. G. 1971. Genera of the bivalve family Mesodesmatidae, with comments on some Australasian species. *Journal of the Malacological Society of Australia* 2:113–131.

Beu, A. G. [1981] 1980. Australian gastropods of the family Bursidae. Part 1. The families of Tonnacea, the genera of Bursidae, and revision of species previously assigned to *Tutufa* Jousseaume, 1881. *Records of the Australian Museum* 33:248–324.

Beu, A. G. 1985. A classification and catalogue of living world Ranellidae (=Cymatiidae) and Bursidae. *Conchologists of America Bulletin* 13:55–66.

Beu, A. G. 1988. Taxonomy of gastropods of the families Ranellidae (=Cymatiidae) and Bursidae. Part 5. Early history of the families, with four new genera and recognition of the family Personidae. *Saito Ho-on Kai Special Publication* 2:69–96.

Beu, A. G., and W. O. Cernohorsky. 1986. Taxonomy of gastropods of the families Ranellidae (=Cymatiidae) and Bursidae. Part 1. Adoption of Ranellidae, and review of *Linatella* Gray, 1857. *New Zealand Journal of Zoology* 13:241–266.

Beu, A. G., and E. A. Kay. 1988. Taxonomy of gastropods of the families Ranellidae (=Cymatiidae) and Bursidae. Part IV. The *Cymatium pileare* complex. *Journal of the Royal Society of New Zealand* 18:185–223.

Beu, A. G., and P. A. Maxwell. 1987. A revision of the fossil and living gastropods related to *Plesiotriton* Fischer, 1884 (family Cancellariidae, subfamily Plesiotritoninae n. subfam.). *New Zealand Geological Survey Paleontological Bulletin* 54:1–140.

Beu, A. G., and P. A. Maxwell. 1990. Cenozoic Mollusca of New Zealand. *New Zealand Geological Survey Paleontological Bulletin* 58: 518 pp.

Beu, A. G., and W. F. Ponder. 1979. A revision of the species of *Bolma* Risso, 1826 (Gastropoda: Turbinidae). *Records of the Australian Museum* 32:1–68.

Bieler, R. 1988. Phylogenetic relationships in the gastropod family Architectonicidae, with notes on the family Mathildidae (Allogastropoda). *Malacological Review,* suppl. 4, pp. 205–240.

Bieler, R., and P. M. Mikkelsen. 1988. Anatomy and reproductive biology of two Western Atlantic species of Vitrinellidae, with a case of protandrous hermaphroditism in the Rissoacea. *Nautilus* 102:1–29.

Biggs, H. E. J. 1973. The marine Mollusca of the Trucial Coast, Persian Gulf. *Bulletin of the British Museum (Natural History), Zoology* 24:343–421, 6 pls.

Bosch, D., and E. Bosch. 1982. *Seashells of Oman.* New York: Longman.

Bosch, D., and E. Bosch. 1989. *Seashells of Southern Arabia.* United Arab Emirates: Motivate Publishing.

Boss, K. J. 1966. The subfamily Tellininae in the Western Atlantic: the genus Tellina (part I). *Johnsonia* 4:217–272.

Boss, K. J. 1968. The subfamily Tellininae in the Western Atlantic: the genera Tellina (part II) and Tellidora. *Johnsonia* 4:273–344.

Boss, K. J. 1972. The genus *Semele* in the Western Atlantic. *Johnsonia.* 5:1–32.

Boss, K. J. 1982. Mollusca. Pp. 945–1166 in S. P. Parker (ed.), *Synopsis and Classification of Living Organisms.* Vol. 1. New York: McGraw-Hill.

Boss, K. J., and R. D. Turner. 1980. The giant white clam from the Galapagos Rift, *Calyptogena magnifica* species novum. *Malacologia* 20:161–194.

Bouchet, P., F. Danrigal, and C. Huyghens. 1979. *Sea shells of Western Europe.* Melbourne, Florida: American Malacologists.

Bousfield, E. L. 1960. *Canadian Atlantic Sea Shells.* Ottawa: Department of Northern Affairs and National Resources.

Bratcher, T., and W. O. Cernohorsky. 1987. *Living Terebras of the World.* Melbourne, Florida: American Malacologists.

Brost, F. B., and R. D. Coale. 1971. *A Guide to Shell Collecting in the Kwajalein Atoll.* Rutland, Vermont: Tuttle.

Bullock, R. C. 1974. A contribution to the systematics of some West Indian *Latirus* (Gastropoda: Fasciolariidae). *Nautilus* 88:69–79.

Bullock, R. C. 1988. The genus *Chiton* in the New World (Polyplacophora: Chitonidae). *Veliger* 31:141–191.

Burgess, C. M. 1985. *Cowries of the World.* Cape Town: Seacomber Publications.

Burnay, L. P., and A. A. Monteiro. 1977. *Seashells from Cape Verde Islands.* Lisboa: Authors.

Cate, C. N. 1973. A systematic revision of the Recent cypraeid family Ovulidae. *Veliger,* vol. 15 suppl., 116 pp., 51 pls.

Cate, C. N. 1977. A review of the Eratoidae (Mollusca: Gastropoda). *Veliger* 19:341–366, 15 pls.

Cate, C. N. 1979. A review of the Triviidae (Mollusca: Gastropoda). *San Diego Society of Natural History,* Memoir 10, 126 pp.

Cernohorsky, W. O. 1970. Systematics of the families Mitridae and Volutomitridae (Mollusca: Gastropoda). *Bulletin of the Auckland Institute and Museum,* no. 8.

Cernohorsky, W. O. 1971. *Marine Shells of the Pacific,* revised edition. Sydney: Pacific Publications.

Cernohorsky, W. O. 1972. *Marine shells of the Pacific,* vol. 2. Sydney: Pacific Publications.

Cernohorsky, W. O. 1976. The Mitridae of the World. Part I. The subfamily Mitrinae. *Indo-Pacific Mollusca* 3(17):273–528.

Cernohorsky, W. O. 1978. *Tropical Pacific Marine Shells.* Sydney: Pacific Publications.

Cernohorsky, W. O. 1984. Systematics of the family Nassariidae (Mollusca: Gastropoda). *Bulletin of the Auckland Institute and Museum* no. 14.

Cernohorsky, W. O. 1991. The Mitridae of the World. Part 2. The sub-family Mitrinae concluded and subfamilies Imbricariinae and Cylindromitrinae. *Monographs of Marine Mollusca,* no. 4.

Christenson, A. L. 1985. The identification and study of Indian shell middens in Eastern North America: 1643–1861. *North American Archaeologist* 6:227–243.

Clench, W. J. 1947. The genera Purpura and Thais in the Western Atlantic. *Johnsonia* 2:61–91.

Clench, W. J., and R. D. Turner. 1956. The family Melongenidae in the Western Atlantic. *Johnsonia* 3:161–188.

Clench, W. J., and R. D. Turner. 1960. The genus Calliostoma in the Western Atlantic. *Johnsonia* 4:1–80.

Coan, E. V. 1973. The northwest American Psammobiidae. *Veliger* 16:40–57, 4 pls.

Coan, E. V. 1977. Preliminary review of the northwest American Carditidae. *Veliger* 19:375–386, 4 pls.

Coan, E. V. 1983. The Eastern Pacific Donacidae. *Veliger* 25:273–298, 7 pls.

Coan, E. V. 1984. The Recent Crassatellinae of the Eastern Pacific, with some notes on *Crassinella. Veliger* 26:153–169.

Coan, E. V. 1988. Recent eastern Pacific species of the bivalve genus *Semele. Veliger* 31:1–42.

Coan, E. V. 1990. The Recent eastern Pacific species of the bivalve family Thraciidae. *Veliger* 33:20–55.

Coleman, N. 1975. *What Shell is That?* Sydney: Paul Hamlyn.

Coleman, N. 1976. *Shell Collecting in Australia.* Sydney: Reed.

Coovert, G. A. 1988. A bibliography of Recent Marginellidae. *Marginella Marginalia* 5:1–43.

Coovert, G. A., and H. K. Coovert. 1990. A study of marginellid radulae. Part I: Type 6 radula, *"Prunum/Volvarina"* type. *Marginella Marginalia* 8/9:1–68.

Cosel, R. von. 1989. Three new species of *Solen* (Bivalvia: Solenidae) from the Indian Ocean, with remarks on the Solenidae of Madagascar. *Journal of Conchology* 33:189–208.

Cotton, B. C. 1959–1964. *South Australian Mollusca.* Archaeogastropoda (1959), Pelecypoda (1961), Chitons (1964). Adelaide: Government Printer.

Cowan, I. M. 1974. The West American Hipponicidae and the application of *Malluvium, Antisabia,* and *Hipponix* as generic names. *Veliger* 16:377–380, 4 pls.

Dance, S. P. 1966. *Shell Collecting, An Illustrated History.* London: Faber and Faber.

Dance, S. P. 1969. *Rare Shells.* Berkeley and Los Angeles: University of California Press.

Dance, S. P. 1976. *The Collector's Encyclopedia of Shells.* New York: McGraw-Hill.

Dance, S. P., and W. K. Emerson. 1967. Notes on *Morum dennisoni* (Reeve) and related species (Gastropoda: Tonnacea). *Veliger* 10:91–98, pl. 12.

Deacon, A. B. 1934. *Malekula: A Vanishing People in the New Hebrides.* London: George Routledge and Sons.

Dell, R. K. 1964. Antarctic and subantarctic Mollusca: Amphineura, Scaphopoda and Bivalvia. *Discovery Reports* 33:93–250, pls. 2–7.

Dewdney, S. 1975. *The Sacred Scrolls of the Southern Ojibway.* University of Toronto Press.

Dixon, R. B. 1916. *The Mythology of All Races,* vol. 9: Oceania. Boston: Marshall Jones.

Dorsey, G. A. 1906. *The Pawnee: Mythology* (part I). Washington, D.C.: Carnegie Institution of Washington.

Drivas, J., and M. Jay. 1988. *Coquillages de la Reunion et de l'Ile Maurice.* Paris: Delachaux et Niestle.

Eisenberg, J. M. 1981. *A Collector's Guide to Seashells of the World.* New York: McGraw-Hill.

Emerson, W. K. 1962. A classification of the scaphopod mollusks. *Journal of Paleontology* 36:461–482, pls. 76–80.

Emerson, W. K., and M. K. Jacobson. 1976. *The American Museum of Natural History Guide to Shells: Land, Freshwater, and Marine, from Nova Scotia to Florida.* New York: Knopf.

Fair, R. H. 1976. *The Murex Book: An Illustrated Catalogue of the Recent Muricidae (Muricinae, Muricopsinae, Ocenebrinae).* Published by the author.

Ferreira, A. J. 1985. Chiton (Mollusca: Polyplacophora) fauna of Barbados, West Indies, with the description of a new species. *Bulletin of Marine Science* 36:189–219.

Frazer, J. G. 1925. *The Golden Bough: A Study of Magic and Religion.* London: Macmillan.

Fretter, V. 1984. The functional anatomy of the neritacean limpet *Phenacolepas omanensis* Biggs and some comparison with *Septaria. Journal of Molluscan Studies* 50:8–18.

Fretter, V., and A. Graham. 1962. *British Prosobranch Molluscs.* London: Ray Society.

Fretter, V., A. Graham, and J. H. McLean. 1981. The anatomy of the Galapagos rift limpet, *Neomphalus fretterae. Malacologia* 21:337–361.

Garrard, T. A. 1977. A revision of Australian Architectonicidae (Gastropoda: Mollusca). *Records of the Australian Museum* 31:506–584.

Gerhard, P. 1964. Emperors' dye of the Mixtecs. *Natural History* 73(1): 26–31.

Gibson-Smith, J., and W. Gibson-Smith. 1981. The status of *Pholadomya candida* G. B. Sowerby, I, 1863 [sic]. *Veliger* 23:355–356.

Gofas, S., J. Pinto Afonso, and M. Brandao. 1985. *Conchas e Moluscos de Angola.* Universidade Agostinho Neto.

Gosliner, T. M. 1987. *Nudibranchs of Southern Africa: A Guide to Opisthobranch Molluscs of Southern Africa.* Monterey, California: Sea Challengers.

Gosliner, T. M. 1988. The Philinacea (Mollusca: Gastropoda: Opisthobranchia) of Aldabra Atoll, with descriptions of five new species and a new genus. *Bulletin of the Biological Society of Washington,* no. 8.

Gould, S. J. 1966. Notes on shell morphology and classification of the Siliquariidae (Gastropoda): the protoconch and slit of *Siliquaria squamata* Blainville. *American Museum Novitates,* no. 2263.

Graham, A. 1982. *Tornus subcarinatus* (Prosobranchia, Rissoacea), anatomy and relationships. *Journal of Molluscan Studies* 48:144–147.

Graham, A. 1988. Molluscs: prosobranch and pyramidellid gastropods, 2nd ed. In *Synopses of the British Fauna* (New Series). Linnean Society of London.

Greifeneder, D., R. W. Skinner, M. Widmer, and J. D. Hemmen. 1981. Contributions to the study of Olividae. *Acta Conchyliorum,* no. 1. Club Conchylia, Darmstadt, Germany.

Habe, T. 1968. *Shells of the Western Pacific in Color.* vol. 2, 2nd ed. Osaka: Hoikusha Publishing.

Habe, T. 1977. *Systematics of Mollusca in Japan: Bivalvia and Scaphopoda.* Tokyo: Zukan no Hokuryukan.

Hain, S. 1990. Die beschalten benthischen Mollusken (Gastropoda und Bivalvia) des Weddellmeeres, Antarktis. *Berichte zur Polarforschung* 70:1–181.

Harasewych, M. G. 1983. A review of the Columbariinae (Gastropoda: Turbinellidae) of the Western Atlantic with notes on the anatomy and systematic relationships of the subfamily. *Nemouria*, no. 27.

Harasewych, M. G. 1986. The Columbariinae (Gastropoda: Turbinellidae) of the eastern Indian Ocean. *Journal of the Malacological Society of Australia* 7:155–168.

Harasewych, M. G. 1989. *Shells: Jewels from the Sea.* New York: Rizzoli.

Harasewych, M. G., and R. E. Petit. 1989. The nomenclatural status and phylogenetic affinities of *Syrinx aruanus* Linné 1758 (Prosobranchia: Turbinellidae). *Nautilus* 103:83–84.

Harasewych, M. G., S. A. Pomponi, and T. M. Askew. 1988. Spongivory in pleurotomariid gastropods. *Nautilus* 102:92–98.

Haszprunar, G. 1985. On the anatomy and systematic position of the Mathildidae (Mollusca, Allogastropoda). *Zoologica Scripta* 14:201–213.

Haszprunar, G. 1988. On the origin and evolution of the major gastropod groups, with special reference to the Streptoneura. *Journal of Molluscan Studies* 54:367–441.

Haszprunar, G. 1988. Comparative anatomy of cocculiniform gastropods and its bearing on archaeogastropod systematics. *Malacological Review*, suppl. 4, pp. 64–84.

Herbert, D. G. 1986. A revision of the southern African Scissurellidae (Mollusca: Gastropoda: Prosobranchia). *Annals of the Natal Museum* 27:601–632.

Hickman, C. S., and J. H. McLean. 1990. Systematic revision and supra-generic classification of trochacean gastropods. *Science Series, Natural History Museum of Los Angeles County*, no. 35.

Hinton, A. 1972. *Shells of New Guinea and the Central Indo-Pacific.* Port Moresby: Robert Brown and Associates.

Hoagland, K. E. 1977. Systematic review of fossil and recent *Crepidula* and discussion of evolution of the Calyptraeidae. *Malacologia* 16:353–420.

Hoerle, R. C. 1974. A Recent Caribbean species of the genus *Neritopsis* (Mollusca: Gastropoda). *Tulane Studies in Geology and Paleontology* 11:103–104.

Hoffman, R. 1990. Blue as the sea. *American Scientist* 78:308–309.

Hogendorn, J., and M. Johnson, 1986. *The Shell Money of the Slave Trade.* Cambridge University Press.

Horikoshi, M. 1989. *Seashells of the World: The Shapes and Patterns Designed by Nature, from the Ninomiya Collection.* Chiba, Japan: Natural History Museum and Institute.

Hornell, J. 1914. The sacred chank of India: a monograph of the Indian Conch *(Turbinella pyrum). Madras Fisheries Bulletin*, no. 7.

Houbrick, R. S. 1974. The genus *Cerithium* in the Western Atlantic. *Johnsonia* 5:33–84.

Houbrick, R. S. 1978. The family Cerithiidae in the Indo-Pacific. Part 1: The genera *Rhinoclavis, Pseudovertagus* and *Clavocerithium. Monographs of Marine Mullusca*, no. 1.

Houbrick, R. S. 1979. Classification and systematic relationships of the Abyssochrysidae, a relict family of bathyal snails (Prosobranchia: Gastropoda). *Smithsonian Contributions to Zoology*, no. 290.

Houbrick, R. S. 1980. Observations on the anatomy and life history of *Modulus modulus* (Prosobranchia: Modulidae). *Malacologia* 20:117–142.

Houbrick, R. S. 1981. Anatomy, biology and systematics of *Campanile symbolicum* with reference to adaptive radiation of the Cerithiacea (Gastropoda: Prosobranchia). *Malacologia* 21:263–289.

Houbrick, R. S. 1981. Anatomy of *Diastoma melanioides* (Reeve, 1849) with remarks on the systematic position of the family Diastomatidae (Prosobranchia: Gastropoda). *Proceedings of the Biological Society of Washington* 21:263–289.

Houbrick, R. S. 1984. Revision of the higher taxa in genus *Cerithidea* (Mesogastropoda: Potamidae) based on comparative morphology and biological data. *American Malacological Bulletin* 2:1-20.

Houbrick, R. S. 1985. Genus *Clypeomorus* Jousseaume (Cerithiidae: Prosobranchia). *Smithsonian Contributions to Zoology*, no. 403.

Houbrick, R. S. 1987. Anatomy of *Alaba* and *Litiopa* (Prosobranchia: Litiopidae): systematic implications. *Nautilus* 101:9–18.

Houbrick, R. S. 1987. Anatomy, reproductive biology, and phylogeny of the Planaxidae (Cerithiacea: Prosobranchia). *Smithsonian Contributions to Zoology* no. 445.

Houbrick, R. S. 1988. Cerithioidean Phylogeny. *Malacological Review,* suppl. 4, pp. 88–128.

Howorth, P. C. 1978. *The Abalone Book.* Happy Camp, California: Naturegraph Publishers.

Hughes, R. N. 1986. Anatomy of the foregut of *Morum* Röding, 1798 (Gastropoda: Tonnacea) and the taxonomic misplacement of the genus. *Veliger* 29:91–100.

Hughes, R. N., and W. K. Emerson. 1987. Anatomical and taxonomic characteristics of *Harpa* and *Morum* (Neogastropoda: Harpidae). *Veliger* 29:349–358.

Hughes, R. N., and H. P. Hughes. 1981. Morphological and behavioural aspects of feeding in the Cassidae (Tonnacea, Mesogastropoda). *Malacologia* 20:385–402.

Humfrey, M. 1975. *Seashells of the West Indies.* London: Collins.

Hyatt, H. M. 1970. *Hoodoo, Conjuration, Witchcraft, Rootwork.* Hannibal, Missouri: Western Publishing.

Jacobson, M. K. (ed.) 1974. *How to Study and Collect Shells.* 4th ed. American Malacological Union.

Jacobson, M. K., and W. K. Emerson. 1971. *Shells from Cape Cod to Cape May, with Special Reference to the New York City Area.* New York: Dover.

Jensen, K. R. 1989. A new species of *Cylindrobulla* from Phuket, Thailand, with a discussion of the genus. *Phuket Marine Biological Center Research Bulletin*, no. 52.

Jensen, R. H., and K. B. Clark. 1986. Class Gastropoda. Pp. 397–458, pls. 12–13 *in* Wolfgang Sterrer (ed.), *Marine Fauna and Flora of Bermuda.* New York: Wiley.

Jones, A. M., and J. M. Baxter. 1987. Molluscs: Caudofoveata, Solenogastres, Polyplacophora, and Scaphopoda. In *Synopses of the British Fauna* (New Series). Linnean Society of London.

Jong, K. M. de, and H. E. Coomans. 1988. *Marine Gastropods from Curacao, Aruba and Bonaire.* Leiden: Brill.

Judson, K. B. 1910. *Myths and Legends of the Pacific Northwest.* Chicago: McClurg.

Jung, P. 1974. A revision of the family Seraphsidae (Gastropoda: Strombacea). *Palaeontographica Americana* 8(47):1–72, 16 pls.

Jung, P. 1989. Revision of the Strombina-group (Gastropoda: Columbellidae), fossil and living: distribution, biostratigraphy, systematics. *Schweizerische Paläontologische Abhandlungen* 111:1–298.

Jung, P. and R. T. Abbott. 1967. The genus Terebellum (Gastropoda: Strombidae). *Indo-Pacific Mollusca* 1(7):445–454.

Kaas, P., and R. A. Van Belle. 1980. *Catalogue of Living Chitons.* Rotterdam: Backhuys.

Kaas, P., and R. A. Van Belle. 1985. *Monograph of Living Chitons (Mollusca: Polyplacophora).* Vol. 1. Order Neoloricata; Lepidopleurina. Leiden: Brill.

Kaas, P., and R. A. Van Belle. 1990. *Monograph of Living Chitons (Mollusca: Polyplacophora).* Vol. 4. Suborder Ischnochitonina: Ischnochitonidae: Ischnochitoninae (continued). Leiden: Brill.

Kabat, A. R. 1990. Predatory ecology of naticid gastropods with a review of shell boring predation. *Malacologia* 32:155–193.

Kamma, F. C. 1975. *Religious Texts of the Oral Tradition from Western New-Guinea.* Leiden: Brill.

Kay, E. A. 1968. A review of the bivalved gastropods and a discussion of evolution within the Sacoglossa. *Zoological Society of London, Symposium,* no. 22.

Kay, E. A. 1979. *Hawaiian Marine Shells.* Honolulu: Bishop Museum Press.

Kay, E. A., and M. F. Switzer. 1974. Molluscan distribution patterns in Fanning Island Lagoon and a comparison of the mollusks of the lagoon and the seaward reefs. *Pacific Science* 28:275–295.

Kean, W. L. 1965. Marine mollusks and aboriginal trade in the Southwest. *Plateau* 38:17–31.

Keen, A. M. 1971. *Sea Shells of Tropical West America: Marine Mollusks from Baja California to Peru.* 2nd ed. Stanford University Press.

Keen, A. M. 1980. The pelecypod family Cardiidae: a taxonomic summary. *Tulane Studies in Geology and Paleontology* 16:1–40.

Keen, A. M., and E. Coan. 1974. *Marine Molluscan Genera of Western North America: An Illustrated Key.* 2nd ed. Stanford University Press.

Kilburn, R. N. 1981. Revision of the genus *Ancilla* Lamarck, 1799 (Mollusca: Olividae: Ancillinae). *Annals of the Natal Museum* 24:349–463.

Kilburn, R. N. 1983–1988. Turridae (Mollusca: Gastropoda) of southern Africa and Mozambique. Part 1. Subfamily Turriculinae. Part 2. Subfamily Clavatulinae. Part 3. Subfamily Borsoniinae. Part 4. Subfamilies Drilliinae, Crassispirinae and Strictispirinae. *Annals of the Natal Museum* 25:549–585 (1983); 26:417–470 (1985); 27:633–720 (1986); 29:167–320 (1988).

Kilburn, R. N., and E. Rippey. 1982. *Sea Shells of Southern Africa.* South Africa, Johannesburg: Macmillan.

Kira, T. 1972. *Shells of the Western Pacific in Color.* Vol. 1. [3rd ed.] Osaka: Hoikusha.

Kirtisinghe, P. 1978. *Sea Shells of Sri Lanka.* Rutland, Vermont: Tuttle.

Kool, S. 1987. Significance of radular characters in reconstruction of thaidid phylogeny (Neogastropoda: Muricacea). *Nautilus* 101:117–132.

Kosuge, S., and M. Suzuki. 1985. *Illustrated Catalogue of Latiaxis and Its Related Groups, Family Coralliophilidae.* Institute of Malacology of Tokyo, Special Publ. 1. 83 pp. 50 pls.

Kroeber, A. L., and E. W. Gifford. 1980. *Karok Myths.* Berkeley: University of California Press.

Kuroda, T., T. Habe, and K. Oyama. 1971. *The Sea Shells of Sagami Bay.* Tokyo: Maruzen.

Lalli, C. M., and R. W. Gilmer. 1989. *Pelagic Snails: The Biology of Holoplanktonic Gastropod Mollusks.* Stanford University Press.

Lamprell, K. 1987. *Spondylus,* spiny oyster shells of the world. Leiden: Brill.

Lan, T. C. 1980. *Rare Shells of Taiwan in Color.* Taipei: Author.

Leland, C. G. 1884. *The Algonquin Legends of New England.* Boston: Houghton, Mifflin.

Lewis, H. 1972. Notes on the genus *Distorsio* (Cymatiidae) with descriptions of new species. *Nautilus* 86:27–50.

Liltved, W. R. 1989. *Cowries and their relatives of southern Africa: a study of the southern African cypraeacean and velutinacean gastropod fauna.* Cape Town: Seacomber Publications.

Lindberg, D. R. 1981. *Acmaeidae: Gastropoda, Mollusca.* Pacific Grove, California: Boxwood Press.

Lindberg, D. R. 1986. Name changes in the "Acmaeidae." *Veliger* 29:142–148.

Lindberg, D. R. 1988. The Patellogastropoda. *Malacological Review* suppl. 4, pp. 35–63.

Lindner, G. 1978. *Field Guide to Seashells of the World.* New York: Van Nostrand Reinhold.

Locard, A. 1884. *Histoire des Mollusques dans l'Antiquité.* Paris: J.-B. Baillière.

Long Island Shell Club. 1988. *Seashells of Long Island, New York.*

Lozet, J. B., and J. Dejean-Arrecgros. 1977. *Je Découvre les Coquillages Côtes Européennes et Méditerranéennes.* Paris: André Leson.

Lozet, J. B., and C. Pétron. 1977. *Shells of the Caribbean.* Tahiti: Les éditions du pacifique.

Ludbrook, N. H. 1984. *Quaternary Mollusks of South Australia.* Adelaide: Department of Mines and Energy.

Luque, A. A., J. Templado, and L. P. Burnay. 1988. On the systematic position of the genera *Litiopa* Rang, 1829 and *Alaba* H. and A. Adams, 1853. *Malacological Review,* suppl. 4, pp. 180–193.

Lyons, W. G. 1988. A review of Caribbean Acanthochitonidae (Mollusca: Polyplacophora) with descriptions of six new species of *Acanthochitona* Gray, 1821. *American Malacological Bulletin* 6:79–114.

Lyons, W. G. 1989. Nearshore marine ecology at Hutchinson Island, Florida: 1971–1974. XI. Mollusks. *Flordia Marine Research Publications,* no. 47.

Macpherson, E. 1971. *The Marine Molluscs of Arctic Canada. National Museums of Canada, Publications in Biological Oceanography,* no. 3.

Macpherson, J. H., and C. J. Gabriel. 1962. *Marine Molluscs of Victoria.* Melbourne University Press.

Maes, V. O. 1967. The littoral marine mollusks of Cocos-Keeling Islands (Indian Ocean). *Proceedings of the Academy of Natural Sciences* 119:93–217.

Marcus, E. d. B.-R. 1974. On some Cephalaspidea (Gastropoda: Opisthobranchia) from the western and middle Atlantic warm waters. *Bulletin of Marine Sciences* 24:300–371.

Marincovich, L., Jr. 1973. Intertidal Mollusks of Iquique, Chile. *Natural History Museum of Los Angeles County Science Bulletin,* no. 16.

Marincovich, L., Jr. 1977. Cenozoic Naticidae (Mollusca: Gastropoda) of the Northeastern Pacific. *Bulletins of American Paleontology* 70:169–494.

Marshall, B. A. 1983. A revision of the Recent Triphoridae of Southern Australia. *Records of the Australian Museum,* suppl. 2, 119 pp.

Marshall, B. A. 1983. Recent and Tertiary Seguenziidae (Mollusca: Gastropoda) from the New Zealand region. *New Zealand Journal of Zoology* 10:235–261.

Marshall, B. A. 1988. Skeneidae, Vitrinellidae and Orbitestellidae (Mollusca: Gastropoda) associated with biogenic substrata from bathyal depths off New Zealand and New South Wales. *Journal of Natural History* 22:949–1004.

Marshall, E. 1980. *Pulsellum salishorum* spec. nov., a new scaphopod from the Pacific Northwest. *Veliger* 23:149–152.

Matsukuma, A. 1980. Glycymeridid bivalves from Japan and adjacent areas—III. Alphabetical list of Recent species in the Australasian Indo-Western Pacific waters. *Venus* 39:24–42.

Matsukuma, A. 1989. Taxonomy and geographical distribution of southwestern Japanese species of *Grammatomya, Dysmea* and *Kermadysmea* (Bivalvia: Psammobiidae). *Memoirs of the National Science Museum* (Tokyo), no. 22, 97–118, pls. 1–3.

McLean, J. H. 1967. Western American Scissurellidae. *Veliger* 9:404–409.

McLean, J. H. 1971. A revised classification of the family Turridae, with the proposal of new subfamilies, genera, and subgenera from the Eastern Pacific. *Veliger* 14:114–130, 4 pls.

McLean, J. H. 1978. *Marine shells of Southern California.* Natural History Museum of Los Angeles County, Science Series 24, revised edition.

McLean, J. H. 1981. The Galapagos rift limpet *Neomphalus:* relevance to understanding the evolution of a major Paleozoic-Mesozoic radiation. *Malacologia* 21:291–336.

McLean, J. H. 1984. Systematics of *Fissurella* in the Peruvian and Magellanic faunal provinces (Gastropoda: Prosobranchia). *Contributions in Science, Natural History Museum of Los Angeles County,* no. 354.

McLean, J. H. 1985. The archaeogastropod family Addisoniidae Dall, 1882: life habit and review of species. *Veliger* 28:99–108.

McLean, J. H. 1989. New slit-limpets (Scissurellacea and Fissurellacea) from Hydrothermal Vents. Part 1. Systematic descriptions and comparisons based on shell and radular characters. *Contributions in Science, Natural History Museum of Los Angeles County,* no. 407.

McMillan, N. 1968. *British Shells.* London: Frederick Warne.

Meehan, B. 1982. *Shell Bed to Shell Midden.* Canberra: Australian Institute of Aboriginal Studies.

Merrill, A. S., and R. D. Turner. 1963. Nest building in the bivalve genera *Musculus* and *Lima. Veliger* 6:55–59, pls. 9–11.

Mikkelsen, P. M., and R. Bieler. 1989. Biology and comparative anatomy of *Divariscintilla yoyo* and *D. troglodytes,* two new species of Galeommatidae (Bivalvia) from stomatopod burrows in eastern Florida. *Malacologia* 31:175–195.

Moore, D. R. 1972. *Cochliolepis parasitica,* a nonparasitic marine gastropod, and its place in the Vitrinellidae. *Bulletin of Marine Science* 22:100–112.

Moore, D. R. 1972. Ecological and systematic notes on the Caecidae from St. Croix, U. S. Virgin Islands. *Bulletin of Marine Science* 22:881–899.

Moore, R. C., ed. 1960. *Treatise on Invertebrate Paleontology.* Part I, Mollusca 1. University of Kansas Press.

Moore, R. C., ed. 1969. *Treatise on Invertebrate Paleontology.* Part N, Mollusca 6. Vols. 1, 2. University of Kansas Press.

Morris, P. A. 1966. *A Field Guide to Pacific Coast Shells.* 2nd ed. Boston: Houghton Mifflin.

Morris, P. A. 1973. *A Field Guide to Shells of the Atlantic and Gulf Coasts and West Indies.* 3rd. ed. Boston: Houghton Mifflin.

Morton, B. 1974. Some aspects of the biology and functional morphology of *Cleidothaerus maorianus* Finlay (Bivalvia: Anomalodesmata: Pandoracea). *Proceedings of the Malacological Society of London* 41:201–222.

Morton, B. 1976. The structure, mode of operation and variation in form of the shell of the Laternulidae (Bivalvia: Anomalodesmata: Pandoracea). *Journal of Molluscan Studies* 42:261–278.

Morton, B. 1981. The mode of life and function of the shell buttress in *Cucullaea concamerata* (Martini) (Bivalvia: Arcacea). *Journal of Conchology* 30:295–301, pl. 11.

Morton, B. 1983. Evolution and adaptive radiation in the Gastrochaenacea (Bivalvia). *Journal of Molluscan Studies,* suppl. 12A, pp. 117–121.

Morton, J. E. 1971. *Molluscs,* 4th ed. London: Hutchinson University Library.

Mosquera, E. R. 1983. *Moluscos de la Ria de Vigo: I Gasteropodos.* Author.

Narchi, W. 1975. Functional morphology of a new *Petricola* (Mollusca Bivalvia) from the littoral of Sao Paulo, Brazil. *Proceedings of the Malacological Society of London* 41:451–465.

Nesis, K. N. 1987. *Cephalopods of the World: Squids, Cuttlefishes, Octopuses, and Allies.* Neptune City, New Jersey: T.F.H. Publications.

Nicol, D. 1967. How to distinguish between Limopsis and Glycymeris. *Nautilus* 81:45–46.

Nordsieck, F. 1969. *Die europäischen Meeresmuscheln (Bivalvia).* Stuttgart: Gustav Fischer.

Nordsieck, F. 1972. *Die europäischen Meeresschnecken (Opisthobranchia mit Pyramidellidae; Rissoacea).* Stuttgart: Gustav Fischer.

Nordsieck, F. 1982. *Die europäischen Meeres-Gehäuseschnecken (Prosobranchia).* Stuttgart: Gustav Fischer.

Nordsieck, F., and F. Garcia-Talavera. 1979. *Moluscos Marinos de Canarias y Madera (Gastropoda).* Aula de Cultura de Tenerife.

Oliver, P. G. 1981. The functional morphology and evolution of Recent Limopsidae (Bivalvia, Arcoidea). *Malacologia* 21:61–93.

Olsson, A. A. 1961. *Mollusks of the Tropical Eastern Pacific, Particularly from the Southern Half of the Panama-Pacific Launal Province (Panama to Peru). Panama-Pacific Pelecypoda).* Ithaca: Paleontological Research Institution.

Owen, B., J. H. McLean, and R. J. Meyer. 1971. Hybridization in the Eastern Pacific abalones *(Haliotis). Science Bulletin of the Los Angeles County Museum of Natural History,* no. 9.

Owen, G. 1959. Observations on the Solenacea with reasons for excluding the family Glaucomyidae. *Philosophical Transactions of the Royal Society of London* B. 242:59–97.

Palmer, C. P. 1974. A supraspecific classification of the scaphopod Mollusca. *Veliger* 17:115–123.

Parenzan, P. 1970–1976. *Carta d'identitá delle Conchiglie del Mediterraneo.* Vol. 1, Gasteropodi (1970), Vol. 2, Bivalvi (1974, 1976). Taranto: Bios Taras.

Paul, C. R. C. 1981. The function of the spines in *Murex (Murex) pecten* Lightfoot and related species (Prosobranchia: Muricidae). *Journal of Conchology* 30:285–294, pls. 9–10.

Pechar, P., C. Prior, and B. Parkinson. [1980]. *Mitre Shells from the Pacific and Indian Oceans.* Bathurst, New South Wales, Australia: Robert Brown and Associates.

Petit, R. E., and M. G. Harasewych. 1986. New Philippine Cancellariidae (Gastropoda: Cancellariacea), with notes on the fine structure and function of the nematoglossan radula. *Veliger* 28:436–443.

Petit, R. E., and M. G. Harasewych. 1990. Catalogue of the superfamily Cancellarioidea Forbes and Hanley, 1851 (Gastropoda: Prosobranchia). *Nautilus,* suppl. 1, 69 pp.

Petuch, E. J. 1987. *New Caribbean Molluscan Faunas.* Charlottesville, Virginia: Coastal Education & Research Foundation.

Petuch, E. J., and D. M. Sargent. 1986. *Atlas of the Living Olive Shells of the World.* Charlottesville, Virginia: Coastal Education & Research Foundation.

Pojeta, J., Jr., and N. F. Sohl. 1987. *Ascaulocardium armatum* (Morton, 1833), new genus (Late Cretaceous): the ultimate variation on the bivalve paradigm. *Journal of Paleontology,* 61(6) suppl., 77 pp.

Ponder, W. F. 1980. Cephalic brood pouches in *Planaxis* and *Fossarus* (Fossaridae and Planaxidae, Cerithiacea, Gastropoda). *Journal of the Malacological Society of Australia* 4:257–258.

Ponder, W. F. 1983. Review of the genera of the Barleeidae (Mollusca: Gastropoda: Rissoacea). *Records of the Australian Museum* 35:231–281.

Ponder, W. F. 1983. A revision of the Recent Xenophoridae of the world and of the Australian fossil species (Mollusca: Gastropoda). *The Australian Museum, Memoir* 17. 126 pp.

Ponder, W. F. 1984. A review of the genera of the Iravadiidae (Gastropoda: Rissoacea) with an assessment of the relationships of the family. *Malacologia* 25:21–71.

Ponder, W. F. 1985. A review of the genera of the Rissoidae (Mollusca: Mesogastropoda: Rissoacea). *Records of the Australian Museum,* suppl. 4, 221 pp.

Ponder, W. F. 1985. The anatomy and relationships of *Emblanda emblematica* (Hedley, 1906) (Mollusca: Mesogastropoda: Emblandidae n. fam.). *Records of the Australian Museum* 37:343–351.

Ponder, W. F. 1985. The anatomy and relationships of *Elachisina* Dall (Gastropoda: Rissoacea). *Journal of Molluscan Studies* 51:23–34.

Ponder, W. F. 1987. The anatomy and relationships of the pyramidellacean limpet *Amathina tricarinata* (Mollusca: Gastropoda). *Asian Marine Biology* 4:1–34.

Ponder, W. F. 1988. The truncatelloidean (= rissoacean) radiation—a preliminary phylogeny. *Malacological Review,* suppl. 4, pp. 129–166.

Ponder, W. F. 1990. The anatomy and relationships of the Orbitestellidae (Gastropoda: Heterobranchia). *Journal of Molluscan Studies* 56: 515–532.

Ponder, W. F. 1991. Marine valvatoidean gastropods—implications for early heterobranch phylogeny. *Journal of Molluscan Studies* 57:21–32.

Ponder, W. F., P. H. Coleman, C. M. Yonge, and M. H. Coleman. 1981. The taxonomic position of *Hemidonax* Mörch, 1871 with a review of the genus (Bivalvia: Cardiacea). *Journal of the Malacological Society of Australia* 5:41–64.

Ponder, W. F., and E. H. Vokes. 1988. A revision of the Indo-West Pacific and Recent species of *Murex* s.s. and *Haustellum* (Mollusca: Gastropoda: Muricidae). *Records of the Australian Museum,* suppl. 8. 160 pp.

Ponder, W. F., and A. Warén. 1988. Classification of the Caenogastropoda and Heterostropha—a list of the family-group names and higher taxa. *Malacological Review,* suppl. 4, pp. 288–326.

Ponder, W. F., and E. K. Yoo. 1976. A revision of the Australian and tropical Indo-Pacific Tertiary and Recent species of *Pisanna* (= *Estea*) (Mollusca: Gastropoda: Rissoidae). *Records of the Australian Museum* 30:150–247.

Ponder, W. F., and E. K. Yoo. 1977. A revision of the Australian species of Rissoellidae (Mollusca: Gastropoda). *Records of the Australian Museum* 31:133–185.

Ponder, W. F., and E. K. Yoo. 1978 (1977). A revision of the Eatoniellidae of Australia (Mollusca, Gastropoda, Littorinacea). *Records of the Australian Museum* 31:606–658.

Ponder, W. F., and E. K. Yoo. 1980. A review of the genera of the Cingulopsidae with a revision of the Australian and tropical Indo-Pacific species (Mollusca: Gastropoda: Prosobranchia). *Records of the Australian Museum* 33:1–88.

Powell, A. W. B. 1964. The family Turridae in the Indo-Pacific. Part 1. The subfamily Turrinae. *Indo-Pacific Mollusca* 1(5):227–346.

Powell, A. W. B. 1966. The molluscan families Speightiidae and Turridae. *Bulletin of the Auckland Institute and Museum,* no. 5.

Powell, A. W. B. 1973. The patellid limpets of the world (Patellidae). *Indo-Pacific Mollusca* 3(15):75–206.

Powell, A. W. B. 1979. *New Zealand Mollusca: Marine, Land and Freshwater Shells.* Auckland: Collins.

Quayle, D. B. 1960. *The Intertidal Bivalves of British Columbia.* British Columbia Provincial Museum, Handbook No. 17.

Quinn, J. F., Jr. 1981. A new genus of Turbinellidae (Gastropoda: Prosobranchia), with the description of a new species from the Caribbean Sea. *Nautilus* 95:72–77.

Quinn, J. F., Jr. 1983. A revision of the Seguenziacea Verrill, 1884 (Gastropoda: Prosobranchia). I. Summary and evaluation of the superfamily. *Proceedings of the Biological Society of Washington* 96:727–757.

Quinn, J. F., Jr. 1987. A revision of the Seguenziacea Verrill, 1884 (Gastropoda: Prosobranchia). II. The new genera *Hadroconus, Rotellenzia,* and *Asthelys. Nautilus* 101:59–68.

Quinn, J. F., Jr. 1989. Pleioptygmatidae, a new family of mitriform gastropods (Prosobranchia: Neogastropoda). *Nautilus* 103:13–19.

Radford, E., and M. E. Radford. 1949. *Encyclopedia of Superstitions.* New York: Philosophical Library.

Radwin, G. E., and A. D'Attilio. 1976. *Murex Shells of the World: An Illustrated Guide to the Muricidae.* Stanford University Press.

Rattray, R. S. 1927. *Religion and Art of the Ashanti.* Oxford: Clarendon Press.

Rehder, H. A. 1973. The family Harpidae of the World. *Indo-Pacific Mollusca* 3(16):207–274.

Rehder, H. A. 1980. The marine mollusks of Easter Island (Isla de Pascua) and Sala y Gómez. *Smithsonian Contributions to Zoology,* no. 289.

Rehder, H. A. 1981. *The Audubon Society Field Guide to North American Seashells.* New York: Knopf.

Reid, D. G. 1986. *The Littorinid Molluscs of Mangrove Forests in the Indo-Pacific Region: The Genus Littoraria.* London: British Museum (Natural History).

Reid, D. G. 1989. The comparative morphology, phylogeny and evolution of the gastropod family Littorinidae. *Philosophical Transactions of the Royal Society of London,* series B, 324:1–110, 3 pls.

Reid, R. G. B., and D. G. Brand. 1987. Observations on Australian Solemyidae. *Journal of the Malacological Society of Australia* 8:41–50.

Rice, T. 1973. *Marine Shells of the Pacific Coast.* Tacoma: Erco.

Rice, T. 1991. *A Sheller's Directory of Clubs, Books, Periodicals & Dealers.* 14th ed., 1990–91. Port Gamble, Washington: Author.

Richard, D. 1987. *Shells of Southern Africa.* 2nd ed. Cape Town: Struik.

Rios, E. C. 1985. *Seashells of Brazil.* Rio Grande: Iparanga.

Robertson, R. 1958. The family Phasianellidae in the Western Atlantic. *Johnsonia* 3:245–284.

Robertson, R. 1961. A second western Atlantic Rissoella and a list of the species in the Rissoellidae. *Nautilus* 74:131–136, pl. 9; 75:21–26.

Robertson, R. 1985. Archaeogastropod biology and the systematics of the genus *Tricolia* (Trochacea: Tricoliidae) in the Indo-West-Pacific. *Monographs of Marine Mollusca,* no. 3.

Röckel, D., E. Rolán, and A. Monteiro. 1980. *Cone Shells from Cape Verde Islands: A Difficult Puzzle.* Published by the authors.

Rosenberg, G. 1989. *Phylogeny and Evolution of Terrestriality of the Atlantic Truncatellidae (Prosobranchia: Gastropoda: Mollusca).* Harvard University: Ph.D. dissertation.

Rosenberg, G., and R. Petit. 1987. Ryckholt's *Mélanges Paléontologiques,* 1851–1862, with a new name for *Tudicula* H. & A. Adams, non Ryckholt. *Proceedings of the Academy of Natural Sciences of Philadelphia* 139:53–64.

Rosewater, J. 1961. The family Pinnidae in the Indo-Pacific. *Indo-Pacific Mollusca* 1(4):175–226.

Rosewater, J. 1965. The family Tridacnidae in the Indo-Pacific. *Indo-Pacific Mollusca* 1(6):347–396.

Rosewater, J. 1982. A new species of *Hippopus* (Bivalvia: Tridacnidae). *Nautilus* 96:3–6.

Rosewater, J. 1984. A new species of leptonacean bivalve from off northwestern Peru. (Heterodonta: Veneroida: Lasaeidae). *Veliger* 27:81–89.

Rudman, W. B. 1971. The genus *Bullina* (Opisthobranchia, Gastropoda) in New Zealand. *Journal of the Malacological Society of Australia* 2:195–203.

Runnegar, B. 1979. *Pholadomya candida* Sowerby: the last cadaver unearthed. *Veliger* 22:171–172, 1 pl.

Russell, H. D. 1941. The Recent mollusks of the family Neritidae of the Western Atlantic. *Bulletin of the Museum of Comparative Zoology* 88:347–404, 7 pls.

Safer, J. F., and F. M. Gill. 1982. *Spirals from the Sea: An Anthropological Look at Shells.* New York: Potter.

Salvat, B., and C. Rives. 1975. *Coquillages de Polynésie.* Papeete, Tahiti: Les éditions du pacifique.

Sanders, H. L., and J. A. Allen. 1977. Studies on the deep sea Protobranchia (Bivalvia); the family Tindariidae and the genus *Pseudotindaria.* *Bulletin of Museum of Comparative Zoology* 148:23–59.

Saunders, W. B., and N. H. Landman, eds. 1987. *Nautilus.* The biology and paleobiology of a living fossil. *Topics in Geobiology,* no. 6.

Schiró, G. 1986. Scissurellidae of the Mediterranean Sea. *La Conchiglia* 18(204–205):22–23.

Sharabati, D. 1981. *Saudi Arabian Seashells.* VNU Books International.

Sharabati, D. 1984. *Red Sea Shells.* London: KPI.

Shepard, S. A., and I. M. Thomas. 1989. *Marine Invertebrates of Southern Australia, Part II.* (Mollusca.) Adelaide: South Australian Government.

Short, J. W., and D. G. Potter. 1987. *Shells of Queensland and the Great Barrier Reef: Marine Gastropods.* Bathurst: Robert Brown.

Sigurdsson, J. B., and G. Sundari. 1990. Colour changes in the shell of the tree-climbing bivalve *Enigmonia aenigmatica* (Holten, 1802) (Anomiidae). *Raffles Bulletin of Zoology* 38:213–218.

Sleurs, W. 1985. Marine microgastropods from the Republic of Maldives. 1. Genus Ammonicera Vayssière, 1893, with descriptions of four new species (Prosobranchia: Omalogyridae). *Basteria* 49:19–27.

Smith, B. J. 1976. Revision of the Recent species of the family Clavagellidae (Mollusca, Bivalvia). *Journal of the Malacological Society of Australia* 3:187–209.

Smythe, K. R. 1982. *Seashells of the Arabian Gulf.* London: George Allen & Unwin.

Solem, A. G. 1954. Living species of the pelecypod family Trapeziidae. *Proceedings of the Malacological Society of London* 31:64–84, pls. 5–7.

Soot-Ryen, T. 1955. A report on the family Mytilidae. *Allan Hancock Pacific Expeditions* 20(1):1–175.

Spoel, S. van der. 1967. *Euthecosomata, a Group with Remarkable Developmental Stages (Gastropoda, Pteropoda).* Gorinchem, Netherlands: Noorduijn & Zoon.

Spoel, S. van der. 1976. *Pseudothecosomata, Gymnosomata and Heteropoda (Gastropoda).* Utrecht: Bohn, Scheltema & Holkema.

Springsteen, F. J., and F. M. Leobrera. 1986. *Shells of the Philippines.* Manila: Carfel Shell Museum.

Stanley, S. M. 1977. Coadaptation in the Trigoniidae, a remarkable family of burrowing bivalves. *Palaeontology* 20:869–899.

Stenzel, H. B. 1971. *Treatise on Invertebrate Paleontology.* Part N, Mollusca 6(3). University of Kansas Press.

Takeda, M., and T. Okutani. 1987. *Crustaceans and Mollusks Trawled off Suriname and French Guiana.* Tokyo: Japan Marine Fishery Resource Research Center.

Taylor, J. D. 1990. The anatomy of the foregut and relationships in the Terebridae. *Malacologia* 23:19–34.

Taylor, J. D., N. J. Morris, and C. N. Taylor. 1980. Food specialization and the evolution of predatory prosobranch gastropods. *Palaeontology* 23:375–409.

Tebble, N. 1976. *British Bivalve Seashells,* 2nd ed. Edinburgh: Her Majesty's Stationery Office.

Tenekidis, N. S. 1989. *Conchiglie marine della Grecia.* Athens: Author.

Thomas, D. L., and L. B. Thomas. 1920. *Kentucky Superstitions.* Princeton University Press.

Thomas, M. L. H. 1967. Thracia conradi in Malpeque Bay, Prince Edward Island. *Nautilus* 80:84–87.

Thompson, T. E. 1976. *Biology of the Opisthobranch Molluscs,* vol. 1. London: Ray Society.

Thompson, T. E. 1979. Biology and relationships of the South African sacoglossan mollusc *Volvatella laguncula. Journal of Zoology,* London 189:339–347.

Thompson, T. E. 1988. Molluscs: benthic Opisthobranchs (Mollusca: Gastropoda). *Synopses of the British Fauna (new series),* no. 8 (2nd ed.).

Thorson, G. 1941. Marine Gastropoda Prosobranchiata. *The Zoology of Iceland* 4(60), 150 pp.

Thurston, E. 1912. *Omens and Superstitions of Southern India.* Nast, New York: McBride.

Tornaritis, G. 1987. *Mediterranean Sea Shells Cyprus.* Nicosia: Author.

Tower, D. B. 1945. The use of marine Mollusca and their value in reconstucting prehistoric trade routes in the American Southwest. *Papers of the Excavators' Club* 2(3), 56 pp., 6 pls.

Turgeon, D. D., A. E. Bogan, E. V. Coan, W. K. Emerson, W. G. Lyons, W. L. Pratt, C. F. E. Roper, A. Scheltema, F. G. Thompson and J. D. Williams. 1988. *Common and Scientific Names of Aquatic Invertebrates from the United States and Canada: Mollusks.* American Fisheries Society Special Publication 16.

Turner, H. 1989. *Uncommon and New Mitriform Gastropods from the Indo-Pacific.* Part 1. Birmensdorf: Swiss Federal Research Institute for Forest, Snow and Landscape.

Turner, R. D. 1954–1955. The family Pholadidae in the Western Atlantic and the Eastern Pacific. *Johnsonia* 3:1–160.

Turner, R. D. 1966. *A Survey and Illustrated Catalogue of the Teredinidae.* Cambridge, Massachusetts: Museum of Comparative Zoology.

Vilas, C. N., and N. R. Vilas. 1970. *Florida Marine Shells*. Rutland, Vermont: Tuttle.

Vokes, E. H. 1971. Catalogue of the genus *Murex* Linné (Mollusca: Gastropoda); Muricinae, Ocenebrinae. *Bulletins of American Paleontology* 61(286):1–141 pp.

Vokes, H. E., and E. H. Vokes. 1983. Distribution of shallow-water marine Mollusca, Yucatan Peninsula, Mexico. *Middle American Research Institute,* publ. 54. 183 pp.

Wagner, R. J. L., and R. T. Abbott. 1990. World Size Records 1990. *Standard Catalog of Shells,* suppl. 4, 80 pp.

Waller, T. R. 1972. The Pectinida (Mollusca: Bivalvia) of Eniwetok Atoll, Marshall Islands. *Veliger* 14:221–264, 8 pls.

Waller, T. R. 1978. Morphology, morphoclines and a new classification of the Pteriomorpha (Mollusca: Bivalvia). *Philosophical Transactions of the Royal Society of London* B. 284:345–365.

Waller, T. R. 1980. Scanning electron microscopy of shell and mantle in the order Arcoida (Mollusca: Bivalvia). *Smithsonian Contributions to Zoology,* no. 313.

Waller, T. R. 1984. The ctenolium of scallop shells: functional morphology and evolution of a key family-level character in the Pectinacea (Mollusca: Bivalvia). *Malacologia* 25:203–219.

Waller, T. R. 1986. A new genus and species of scallop (Bivalvia: Pectinidae) from off Somalia, and the definition of a new tribe Decatopectinini. *Nautilus* 100:39–46.

Walls, J. G. [1978]. *Cone Shells: A Synopsis of the Living Conidae.* Neptune City, New Jersey: T.F.H. Publications.

Walls, J. G. 1980. *Conchs, Tibias, and Harps.* Neptune, New Jersey: T.F.H. Publications.

Ward, P. D. 1988. *In Search of Nautilus.* New York: Simon and Schuster.

Warén, A. 1980. Revision of the genera *Thyca, Stilifer, Scalenostoma, Mucronalia* and *Echineulima* (Mollusca, Prosobranchia, Eulimidae). *Zoologica Scripta* 9:187–210.

Warén, A., and P. Bouchet. 1988. A new species of Vanikoridae from the Western Mediterranean, with remarks on the northeast Atlantic species of the family. *Bollettino Malacologico* 24:73–100.

Warén, A., and P. Bouchet. 1989. New gastropods from East Pacific hydrothermal vents. *Zoologica Scripta* 18:67–102.

Warén, A., and P. Bouchet. 1990. Laubierinidae and Pisanianurinae (Ranellidae), two new deep-sea taxa of the Tonnoidea (Gastropoda: Prosobranchia). *Veliger* 33:56–102.

Warmke, G. L., and R. T. Abbott. *Caribbean Seashells.* Narberth, Pennsylvania: Livingston Publishing.

Weaver, C. S., and J. E. duPont. 1970. *Living Volutes: A Monograph of the Recent Volutidae of the World.* Greenville, Delaware: Delaware Museum of Natural History.

Wells, F. E. 1986. A redescription of the sea hare *Aplysia gigantea* Sowerby, 1869. *Journal of the Malacological Society of Australia* 7:173–178.

Wells, F. E., and C. W. Bryce. 1986. *Seashells of Western Australia.* Perth: Western Australian Museum.

Wells, F. E., C. W. Bryce, J. E. Clark, and G. M. Hansen. 1990. *Christmas Shells: The Marine Molluscs of Christmas Island (Indian Ocean).* Christmas Island Natural History Association.

Werner, A. 1925. *The Mythology of All Races,* vol. 7: Armenian and African. Boston: Marshall Jones.

Westervelt, W. D. 1915. *Legends of Old Honolulu.* Boston: George H. Ellis.

Williams, W. 1988. *Florida's Fabulous Seashells.* Tampa: Worldwide Publications.

Wilson, B. R., and K. Gillett. 1971. *Australian Shells.* Tuttle, Rutland, Vermont: Charles E. Tuttle and Company.

Wilson, B. R., and S. E. Stevenson. 1977. Cardiidae (Mollusca, Bivalvia) of Western Australia. *Special Publications of the Western Australian Museum,* no. 9.

Yonge, C. M. 1958. Observations in life on the pulmonate limpet *Trimusculus (Gadinia) reticulatus* (Sowerby). *Proceedings of the Malacological Society of London* 33:31–37.

Yonge, C. M. 1960. Mantle cavity, habits and habitat in the blind limpet, *Lepeta concentrica* Middendorf. *Proceedings of the California Academy of Sciences* 31:103–110.

Yonge, C. M. 1960. Further observations on *Hipponix antiquatus* with notes on north Pacific pulmonate limpets. *Proceedings of the California Academy of Sciences* 31:111–119.

Yonge, C. M. 1971. On functional morphology and adaptive radiation in the bivalve superfamily Saxicavacea *(Hiatella (= Saxicava), Saxicavella, Panomya, Panope, Cyrtodaria). Malacologia* 11:1–44.

Yonge, C. M. 1975. The status of the Plicatulidae and the Dimyidae in relation to the superfamily Pectinacea (Mollusca: Bivalvia). *Journal of Zoology* 176:545–553.

Yonge, C. M. 1977. Form and evolution in the Anomiacea (Mollusca: Bivalvia)—*Pododesmus, Anomia, Patro, Enigmonia* (Anomiidae): *Placunanomia, Placuna* (Placunidae fam. nov.). *Philosophical Transactions of the Royal Society of London* B. 276:453–523.

Yonge, C. M. 1978. On the Dimyidae (Mollusca: Bivalvia) with special reference to *Dimya corrugata* Hedley and *Basilomya goreaui* Bayer. *Journal of Molluscan Studies* 44:357–375.

Yonge, C. M., and B. Morton. 1980. Ligament with lithodesma in the Pandoracea and the Poromyacea with a discussion on evolutionary history in the Anomalodesmata (Mollusca: Bivalvia). *Journal of Zoology (London)* 191:263–292.

Yoo, J. S. 1976. *Korean Shells in Colour.* Seoul: Il Ji Sa.

Young, J. Z. 1960. Observations on *Argonauta* and especially its method of feeding. *Proceedings of the Zoological Society of London* 133:471–479, 2 pls.

Zeigler, R. F., and H. C. Porreca. 1969. *Olive Shells of the World.* Published by the authors.

Zinn, D. J. 1984. *Marine Mollusks of Cape Cod.* Brewster, Massachusetts: Cape Cod Museum of Natural History.

INDEX OF SHELLS